SPACE YEAR 1991

THE COMPLETE RECORD OF THE YEAR'S SPACE EVENTS

Edited by Nigel Macknight

SPACE YEAR 1991

First published in 1990 by Motorbooks International Publishers & Wholesalers, PO Box 2, 729 Prospect Avenue, Osceola, WI 54020 USA.

© Macknight International, 1990

Library of Congress Cataloging-in-Publication Data

ISBN 0-87938-482-4

Printed and bound in Singapore by PH Productions

PERSONNEL

Production

Typographic Source, Stamford, Lincolnshire, England.

Rob Blackman
Andy Winn
Jennifer Harbord
Nick Greenfield
Nigel Parker

Contributors

(Credits appear in parenthesis after each contributor's report)

Nic Booth
Robert Christy
Tim Furniss
Gordon Hooper
Clive Simpson
Reginald Turnill
Mark Ward

Welcome to the inaugural edition of *SPACE YEAR* — an accessible, affordable publication recording and appraising all the major space events which took place over the period 1 July 1989 to 30 June 1990. Generally speaking, we've aimed to chronicle space missions which began, or were continuing, during the relevant twelve-month period — although we have been flexible enough to accommodate the 'grey areas' either side.

For details of missions-in-preparation, look out for upcoming editions. For information on *past* missions — look elsewhere! It is this emphasis on the here-and-now which marks *Space Year* out from comparable publications.

Watch out for *SPACE YEAR 1992* — on sale worldwide November 1991.

Thanks for assistance in preparing Space Year 1991 to all our friends at . . . .

Arianespace, Paris, France
Asiasat, Hong Kong
Ball Aerospace, Stevenage, England
CNES, Paris, France
ESA, Paris, France
General Dynamics, San Diego, California
Grumman, Bethpage, New York
Glavcosmos, Moscow
Hughes, El Segundo
ISAS, Sagamihara-shi, Japan
Jet Propulsion Laboratory, Pasadena, California
Lockheed Missiles & Space, Sunnyvale, California
Marconi, Portsmouth, England
Martin Marietta, Denver, Colorado/Michoud, Louisiana
McDonnell Doughlas, Huntingdon Beach, California
Moron Thiokol, Ogden, Utah
NASA/Ames, Mountain View, California
NASA/Dryden, Edwards, California
NASA/Goddard Space Flight Center, Greenbelt Maryland
NASA/Headquarters, Washington D.C.
NASA/Space Center, Houston, Texas
NASA/Johnson Space Center, Merritt Island, Florida
NASA/Kennedy Space Center, Hampton, Virginia
NASA/Marshall Space Flight Center, Huntsville, Alabama
NASA/Wallops Flight Facility Wallops Island, Virginia
NASDA, Tokyo, Japan
NOAA, Houston, Texas
Novosti Press Agency, London/Moscow
Orbital Sciences, Fairfax, Virginia
Planetary Society, Pasadena, California
Poker Flat Research Range, Fairbanks, Alaska
Rockwell International, Downey/Palmdale, California
Rocketdyne Division/Rockwell, Canoga Park, California
Royal Aerospace Establishment, Farnborough, England
SDIO, Washington D.C.
Space Data, Chandler, Arizona
Space Services, Houston, Texas
Spot Image, Toulouse, France
Swedish Space Corporation, Solna, Sweden
TASS News Agency, London/Moscow
U.S. Air Force, Patrick AFB, Florida/Vandenberg AFB, California/Pentagon, Washington D.C.
U.S. Library of Congress
World Data Centre for Rockets and Satellites Greenbelt, Maryland

also; Lawrence Harris, Graham Smith, George Spiteri and Andrew Wilson.

CONTENTS

REVIEW OF THE YEAR

Surprisingly, the collapse of Communism appears to be forcing bigger changes on Western space policies than on the Soviets. While major revisions of U.S. and European space policies can be expected in the next twelve months, Soviet space programs have emerged from all the political changes as much better focussed. As this edition went to press, pressures were mounting in the U.S. for NASA to be reshaped, because doubts are increasing about the practicability of Space Station *Freedom* and the ability of the Space Shuttle to support it. In Europe, worries about global-warming and pollution disasters seem set to swivel scientists' eyes away from the 'Red Planet', inwards to 'Spaceship Earth'.

A British-built instrument aboard ESA's Earth-resources satellite ERS-1, due for launch early in 1991, should establish whether the Earth really is hotting-up. (And, before panic sets in, it should be noted that, as yet, that is far from being an established fact).

Progress among the setbacks

In both civil and military space, the past year has been marked by startling and unexpected setbacks, which have diverted attention from some very real and worthwhile progress. Technical failures seem to afflict the Soviets, NASA and European space efforts equally — which at least stops one group crowing over the other, as happens all the time in aviation. But the failures add hundreds of millions to current project costs, eating into funds allocated to future missions. Inevitably, one result is that the exciting talk about human bases on the Moon and Mars is increasingly hedged with doubts about the political will to find the money.

Mir becomes a space factory

By mid-June the Soviets' four-year-old Mir space station had grown to 83 metric tonnes, with the addition of the second of the four specialised modules. This was Kristall, described as a "microfactory", which it is hoped will improve Mir's popularity among the Soviet public by enabling the

space station to earn a commercial living.

Kristall, having been first docked to the 'transfer' or axial docking port, was then swung round by robot manipulators to the lateral port opposite Kvant-2, to the great relief of Kaliningrad's Mission Control. It meant that Mir was once again symmetrical, which makes it much easier and more economical to control. Most space-watchers must have found it very disappointing that the media has given so little TV and radio coverage to these very dramatic and difficult operations

After launch, these 19.5-tonne modules automatically search for Mir, then, if all goes well, rendezvous, moor and dock, with the cosmonauts and Mission Control monitoring in case of trouble. But there has been lots of trouble — which has been patiently overcome. First one of Kvant-2's solar panels jammed, and then docking was delayed by a computer fault.

But Kvant-2 was the first right-angled docking to be achieved in space history, either manually or robotically. That is something the U.S. Shuttle has never yet done, but will have to do routinely when it visits Space Station *Freedom* in the late 1990s. In its turn, Kristall failed to dock at the first attempt, but controllers at Kaliningrad, undismayed, reconfigured the systems and success came four days later.

Missions that made history

The two six-month missions performed by Aleksandr Viktorenko and Aleksandr Serebrov (September 1989-February '90) and then by their successors, Anatoly Solovyov and Aleksandr Balandin, were noticed by the Western media only when it was thought the second crew was "stranded" in orbit. We had, however, known within a few days of the launch that the thermal blankets on their Soyuz TM-9 ferry had been partially peeled away at lift-off.

We also knew that if a spacewalk did not cure the problem, a replacement Soyuz could be provided.

During an exciting seven-hour EVA on 17 July, Solovyev and Balandin rolled up and fastened two of the three displaced outer thermal blankets which threatened to obstruct the view of the infrared sensor needed for undocking and re-entry. Because the distance from Kvant-2's airlock to Soyuz TM-9 was 30 meters, they had to make their way between the two without tethers; using mountaineering techniques, attaching and detaching themselves at each step. With their oxygen backpacks almost exhausted they found themselves unable to close Kvant-2's airlock hatch on return, and emergency procedures were needed to re-enter.

It meant another long EVA nine days later, to repair the hatch and recover the two ladders, tools and other equipment which had had to be abandoned during the emergency. These activities led to the launch of the replacement crew, Gennady Manakov and Gennady Strekalov, being postponed until August.

Those two missions have moved space technology forward in ways that will earn a special *niche* in the history books. Difficulties notwithstanding, they have demonstrated the successful use of robotic space station operations, which are much talked about by NASA but have yet to be put into practice.

And the crews have started the first operational space factory, and made the first flights from Kvant's big new docking port on the new 'space motorbike' — the equivalent of NASA's Manned Maneuvering Unit (MMU).

Soviet space critics

The Kristall microfactory, with five furnaces for producing semi-conductors and an installation for processing medical preparations and serum, has long been planned as the answer to the growing criticism of the Soviet space program inside the country. That came to a head in October when Academician Vasily Mishin colorfully condemned it as "very squanderous". He thought that development of Space Shuttle *Buran* was a huge achievement without much practical use, and that the long-duration piloted flights aboard Mir were "dull" and tended to repeat each other.

According to Vladimir Shatalov, head of the Cosmonaut Training Center, Kristall will have an annual production of "hun-

(Left) Symbolizing NASA's urge to soar clear of technical and budgetary setbacks, *Columbia* makes a spritely ascent on 9 January 1990.

(Below) Cynics would say they should have stayed at the breakfast table. The STS-36 astronauts deployed a $500 million spy-satellite, only to learn after landing that it had been blow up by U.S. Space Command because of a major malfunction.

dreds of kilograms" of crystals and other materials which cannot be produced on Earth. They should bring a return of 105 million roubles, compared with Kristall's cost of 80 million. But that can only happen if the Soviets can overcome the problem that has been holding back their space station activities for many years: that is that very little of what is produced on board can be returned because the Soyuz spacecraft have little or no payload capacity left when bringing the cosmonauts back to Earth.

To overcome this problem it has recently been decided that next year the Soviet Shuttle, making its second flight, will dock with Mir. It will have plenty of capacity to bring back a load of processed materials worth their weight in gold many times over — and possibly some cosmonauts as well. Aleksandr Dunayev, head of Glavcosmos, defended the cost of the Shuttle and its Energia launcher against Academician Mishin's attacks on the grounds that they were "quite essential" for defense purposes.

Now they should also be able to bring a commercial return.

NASA Shuttle's achievements

NASA achieved only six of the nine Shuttle missions it had planned in the twelve months from July 1989 — and then were grounded again from mid-May 1990 until September by hydrogen leaks. The grounding, coming on top of the Space Telescope fiasco, has added to U.S. political pressure for NASA to be restructured. But as in the case of the Soviets, the setbacks obscured the fact that three major targets, all years overdue because of delays following the 1986 *Challenger* disaster, *were* achieved.

In October, the crew of *Atlantis* launched the Galileo spacecraft on an eight-year mission of exploration to the asteroids, Jupiter and its moons; in January, the crew of *Discovery* found and returned to Earth the eleven-tonne Long Duration Exposure Facility (LDEF) and its 57 experiments, which had been stranded in orbit for nearly six years; and in April, another *Discovery* crew placed the Hubble Space Telescope in Earth orbit to make a delayed start on its 15-year examination of the Universe.

Discovery and her crew could not be blamed because, once in orbit, it turned out that the mirrors of the main telescope had been inaccurately shaped. One report, which I have been unable to confirm, was that a programer punched a plus instead of a minus sign into a computer as much as ten years ago. A board of investigation was set up in July 1990 to sort out the truth of allegations that pre-launch ground tests were not fully conducted because NASA and the U.S. Air Force were unable to agree about the use of military test facilities.

My own experience, going right back to the creation of NASA, has always been that military obsession with "security", and its frequent use as a weapon to harass NASA, has made genuine cooperation between the two organizations almost impossible.

(Above) A combination of frivolity and wishful-thinking prompted NASA to commission this rendering of LDEF, overgrown with the fruits of the tomato-seed experiment it was carrying.

A Shuttle repair mission should put the Space Telescope in full working order in 1993, but it will add several hundred million dollars to the $1.5 billion already spent on the Hubble program, and the political damage to NASA has been incalculable.

Spy satellite drama

The loss of a $500 million spy-satellite launched by *Atlantis* on the third of the year's secret military missions was another setback that could not be blamed upon the Shuttle — so far as we know. We had to rely upon Soviet reports for the knowledge that the satellite failed to reach the right orbit, and was blown up by U.S. Space Command.

Soviet officials complained that the Pentagon had breached United Nations agreements by not giving proper warnings about the faulty satellite and the possibility that debris might rain down on the USSR.

(Bottom-left) The STS-32 crew should have been in orbit over Christmas and dressed accordingly. Technical problems pushed their flight into the New Year.

(Bottom-right) There was little humor in the delays to mission STS-35. Mike Lounge's expression says it all.

Shuttles grounded by fuel leaks

Leaks from the complex 17-inch disconnect line which feeds liquid hydrogen from the External Tank to the three main Shuttle engines during the first eight minutes of flight were yet another setback. They forced Admiral Richard Truly, NASA's Administrator, to suspend all flights until a solution could be found.

The problem came to light in May just six hours before the launch of *Columbia* with the ASTRO-1 payload aboard. The gas, leaking into *Columbia's* aft fuselage, could have caused an explosion, but was fortunately detected before the crew went aboard. The Orbiter had to be rolled back for repairs, and that mission postponed for some time. Worse still, it was found that *Atlantis*, being prepared on the second launch pad for a military mission, also had hydrogen leaks from the 17-inch disconnect — in different places.

ASTRO-1, an important science mission to study supernovas, white dwarfs and black holes, had been long-awaited. Now, once again, thousands of international scientists and astronomers found their work schedules disrupted.

By now, the wonderful successes of NASA's Voyager 1 and Voyager 2 spacecraft, culminating in the incredibly successful flyby of Neptune in August 1989, were almost forgotten. But some of the same scientists waiting for delayed data from Hipparcos, the Space Telescope and ASTRO-1 have a backlog of work to clear, studying the mountain of stored data from the Voyagers. Nine years after Voyager 2's Saturn flyby, their continued analysis of data from that revealed the existence of an 18th moon, twelve miles in diameter just as we closed for press.

Pad 39A — back in use

THE STS-32 mission saw Pad 39A back in use for the first time since 61-C/*Columbia* blasted-off on 9 January 1986 — just nine days before the *Challenger* disaster (51-L was the first Shuttle launch from Pad 39B). Pad 39A has a long and proud history. It was the starting-point for the first 24 Shuttle missions, and for all but one of the Saturn 5 Apollo missions — including the epoch-making Apollo 11 flight which placed the first human beings — Neil Armstrong and Buzz Aldrin — on the surface of the Moon.

NASA took advantage of the long delay following 51-L/*Challenger* to implement a vast number of improvements to both Shuttle launch pads, starting with 39B. Initially, 39A was deactivated and even some routine maintenance activities were suspended. Consequently, the pad's condition deteriorated slightly. Some of the modifications had been planned long before the *Challenger* accident, while others resulted from the long, hard look NASA took at its operating procedures in the wake of the disaster.

In May 1988, a directive to reactivate 39A was issued, and work began in January '89. All 138 modifications were in place on 39A by the time STS-32 took-off. Practically all of them duplicated improvements made to 39B prior to the launch of STS-26/*Discovery*, the mission which heralded the renewal of Shuttle flight operations in the fall of 1988.

The Pad 39A modifications are estimated to have cost about $50 million. By far the most visible modification is the incorporation of a new weather protection system, designed to shield portions of the Orbiter vehicle which previously were exposed to the onslaught of rain and wind. Without proper protection, the Orbiter's thermal insulation materials — particularly the tiles on the undersurfaces of the spacecraft — are vulnerable to damage from rainstorms, hail and and even windblown debris.

Prior to these modifications, Pad 39A had had a rather rudimentary weather protection system in place for some time. It employed a fabric-type material that was raised and lowered, rather like a sail. After operating with that for a while, NASA realized that something more permanent was required, and design work on a upgraded system began in 1984.

The new-specification weather protection hardware consists of two huge rolling steel doors which are extended between the Orbiter's belly and the External Tank. The doors are supported by frameworks on both the Fixed Service Structure gantry which stands alongside the spacecraft, and the much larger Rotating Service Structure, which swings round to encase the Orbiter during pre-launch preparations.

Besides facilitating a better coverage of the underside of the vehicle, the new system is more durable: it withstands much higher wind-loads than the old 'fabric' system. It is also easier to extend and retract.

Some 'fit-checks' conducted when the STS-32/*Columbia* stack was rolled out to 39A on 28 November confirmed the weather protection system's compatibility with the Shuttle. As had been done on 39B some years earlier, the doors were cycled back and forth several times without incident. In this respect, the weather protection system on 39B had served as the 'pathfinder', some minor interference problems being corrected with surgery to the structure, providing adequate clearance between the vehicle and the unyielding steel doors, and slightly extending some access platforms that were mounted on the doors to ensure that they reached close enough to the vehicle.

The new weather protection doors force some small operational changes to the Shuttle's launch pad procedures. For example, if the Orbiter's wing-mounted elevon control surfaces ever have to be 'exercised' while the spacecraft is ensconsed in the Rotating Service Structure, the doors have to be retracted, because there isn't enough room for the aerosurfaces to be moved freely.

That said, such 'exercising' is carried out but-seldom. The usual time for flexing the Orbiter's aerodynamic control surfaces comes just prior to launch, and by that stage in the countdown the Rotating Service Structure, complete with its weather-doors, has been swung well clear anyway.

The big weather protection doors are designed to withstand windspeeds of up to 83mph when fully deployed and locked in place, but if conditions ever looked like getting that bad, NASA operations directors would already have ordered that the Shuttle be rolled back on its Mobile Launcher Platform to the more protective environment of the Vehicle Assembly Building (VAB).

The doors are designed to take the same loads as the rest of the launch pad system, and — for that matter — all of the systems that are mounted on that structure. If a hurricane reached KSC's doorstep, the doors could be retracted and locked to withstand winds of up to 138mph.

It would take a forecast windspeed in the region of 60-70 knots to force a decision to wheel the Shuttle back to the VAB. Roughly 48 hours of advance-notice is required to get ready to roll back, then it takes about eight hours to get back along the crawler-way and into the VAB.

Among the other modifications made to Pad 39A are: enhanced protection from flames for personnel traversing the Orbiter Access Arm and the rest of the route to the slide-wire escape system 'baskets'; improvements to the humidity and temperature regulation systems in the Payload Changeout Room; and upgrading of the water deluge systems on both the Fixed Service Structure and the Rotating Service Structure to prevent freezing in the feed-pipes.   N.M.

Launchers and spaceports

Now that America's expendable launch vehicles (ELVs) — Titan, Atlas and Delta — are back in use for both military and commercial satellites, U.S. launch-rates are rising again from the low-point of only six in 1986, the year of the *Challenger* accident. By contrast, Soviet launch-rates are dropping from their peak of 101 in 1982. In 1989, U.S. launches had risen to 18, with the Soviet total down to 74. It seems likely that by the mid-90s the two main space powers will level off at 40-50 launches each per year.

The U.S. Air Force is modernising its launch control facilities at Cape Canaveral — which both NASA and the private companies conducting commercial ELV launches are obliged to use — on the basis that there will be over 400 during this coming decade.

Having so many launches from one place, and dependent upon military range safety and other facilities, is becoming increasingly inconvenient. Preparations for civil and scientific launches, as well as for the commercial launches from the Titan, Atlas and Delta pads, have to be stopped for about 48 hours for safety reasons during Space Shuttle countdowns from the NASA pads on nearby Merritt Island; and as several countdowns are often needed before the Shuttle actually lifts-off, the delays quickly mount up.

There are access problems, too, for commercial users needing to pass through military security areas to the launch pads.

Coupled with a growing wish to divorce civil space activities from any sort of military support, there has been increasing interest over the last year in projects for new, independent spaceports which would be truly international. 'Spaceport Florida' is getting a lot of financial support from that State, but would probably still be dependent upon the U.S. Air Force's range facilities. Hawaii is another proposed site, with both polar and equatorial launches possible from one of the islands.

Perhaps the most attractive proposal, however, comes from Australia, where the Cape York Space Agency now has detailed plans for construction of a site on the tip of Queensland. Their plan is to buy Soviet Zenit launchers — comparable with Europe's Ariane in capability, but being offered for sale much more cheaply by Glavcosmos. A team of Japanese companies, as well as a big U.S. consortium, are eager to design and construct the spaceport and U.S. government opposition to the proposal now seems to have been dropped.

Once built, the spaceport would be operated by Australian personnel.

While it is not being emphasised for political reasons, the biggest user would undoubtedly be the Soviet Union, who would find it much more economical to transfer many of their launchers to Cape York from the harsh climate and unfavorable latitude of Tyuratam. Despite opposition from the U.S. on both political and economic grounds, and from Europe — especially France — because it would compete with, and perhaps undercut, the still-growing Ariane launch facility at Kourou in French Guiana, the signs are that Cape York — vigorously supported by the Australian government — will start construction in 1992, aimed at commercial operations commencing in 1997.

Europe in Space

Europe's Ariane launcher is at present maintaining its supremacy, garnering more than 50 percent of the world's commercial launch business. That is in spite of the fact that flight V36 exploded in February — because a bit of cloth, carelessly left behind in the first stage, blocked a water-line to one of the engines. But before that, Arianespace, the European company which operates the Ariane launchers, had had a marvellous run of 17 successful launches, placing 27 satellites into orbit.

A five-month grounding while the cause of the explosion was established was ended by the successful flight of V37 on 25 July 1990, which placed France's TDF-2 television satellite and Germany's DFS Kopernicus-2 communications satellite in orbit. Any unspoken hopes that U.S. competitors would benefit from transferred launch orders to their new commercial ELVs were dashed by the failure of the second Commercial Titan, almost at the same time, to deploy its Intelsat 6 satellite payload correctly. It is now stranded in low-Earth orbit, awaiting possible rescue

(Left) America's Martin Marietta kicked-over the traces of an equally-embarrassing loss (Intelsat 6-F3) sustained just days after the Ariane V36 accident, when it lofted Intelsat 6-F4 into orbit on 23 June.

(Below) An artist's impression of the most critical moment in Japan's historic inaugural mission to the Moon. The Hagoromo sub-satellite, having parted company with its Hiten 'mother-ship', fires its retrorocket to achieve lunar orbit.

during a Shuttle mission in 1992.

Evidence that there has been no loss of confidence in Ariane's overall reliability is that Arianespace has won ten new launch contracts this year — seven of them since the February accident. The backlog of 39 satellites, with a contract value of $2.8 billion means that Arianespace has an almost-full orderbook for four years. Although only five successful launches were achieved in the last twelve months, the company expects to be back to an average of nine per year now that flights have resumed.

Eastern competition

By the mid-1990s, when Arianespace will have worked-off its backlog of orders, Japan expects to be ready with a major bid to take over a big slice of the space business, just as in past decades it moved into automobiles and computer-chips. Japan's Rocket System Corporation is adopting the Arianespace policy in the production of its new H-2 launcher, due to make its first, delayed flight in 1993. The aim is to get prices down by ordering volume production, and to ensure that satellite customers do not have to wait for a launcher to be built.

The threatened Japanese takeover — they have recently demonstrated an interplanetary capability by placing a scientific satellite in lunar orbit — may well reverse the international slowdown in space developments of the past few years because of big business's short-term commercial approach. China, also clamoring for commercial orders, has now proved its ability to match Ariane 4's lifting capability with the first successful launch of a Long March 2E in mid-July. Its cargo included Pakistan's first home-built satellite.

The world's major aerospace companies are all eager to share in government-provided money — up to $40 billion per year — for development and construction of military, meteorological and remote-sensing satellites, and, most of all, for the development of the U.S./International Space Station *Freedom*. But they have been less enthusiastic about investing their own money to support long-term ventures, like the development of new materials and medicine-processing in microgravity.

Smaller countries, formerly with only a small stake in space — like Italy and Spain — are now seizing the opportunity by making long-term investments to match what is already being done by France and West Germany, and to overtake less enthusiastic countries like Great Britain.

Israel's second westward launch (against Earth's rotation) in March was an interesting demonstration of that country's growing technical capability, but is not posing any immediate commercial threat. Among developing countries, South Korea plans to launch its first indigenous sounding rocket next year, and its first experimental satellite in 1996, probably on its own launcher and from its own coastal launch site over the Sea of Japan.

Cheaper space flight
— still elusive

The search for cheaper ways of using space, either by means of cheaper launchers or smaller satellites, is now concentrated on smaller satellites. The long-awaited launch of the Pegasus booster, dropped from a modified B-52 bomber commanded by ex-astronaut Gordon Fullerton in April, successfully fired two small satellites into accurate orbits. The advantage of this system is that almost any big jet can be converted into a Pegasus carrier, and it can obviously take-off from any large airport.

Arianespace was quick to make a deal with the team which developed Pegasus, enabling it to market the system in Europe. But first indications are that, although the system will be useful for military space activities — one of the experimental satellites on the first mission was for the U.S. Navy — its costs are unlikely to be much, if any, cheaper than conventional expendable launchers. Arianespace tried a different approach in January this year when flight V35 — carrying the SPOT-2 remote-sensing satellite — used its spare payload capacity to carry six 'microsats' ranging in weight from 10 to 48 kilograms.

The two largest, Uosats 3 and 4, were built by England's University of Surrey on a budget of only £700,000.

Space spinoffs

Spinoff developments from space activities continue to percolate right through our lives, little noticed or acknowledged by ordinary people — particularly those given to condemning space expenditure as wasteful. A recent example came in June

(Bottom-left) **Pegasus and its Boeing NB-52 carrier-plane during a 'captive' test flight.**

(Below) **'Fergie' was a distinguished visitor to NASA's Johnson Space Center, Houston in November.**

1990, when a British Airways Boeing 747 took-off from London/Heathrow *en route* to Bombay. Its new ASDAR (Aircraft to Satellite Data Relay) equipment automatically collects atmospheric data and transmits it to geosynchronous meteorological satellites, which relay the information to ground-stations in Europe, the U.S. and Japan.

When this experimental system gains widespread acceptance, airline pilots will have up-to-the-minute information on air temperatures, wind speeds and direction, and — most important of all — air turbulence: vital safety information when they make decisions about take-off, landing and routing.

NASA's annual *Spinoff* book continues

to detail the astonishing range of benefits flowing from space research. Most touching among them are the aids for handicapped children, such as the adaptation of the cooling system on the Moonwalking suits. Water-cooled garments worn by children born without sweat-glands stop them getting overheated and enable them to live near-normal lives.

A critical year ahead

The whole structure of NASA is now under review, with the setting up, at the request of Vice President Dan Quayle, of yet another investigative panel. "How can NASA become a more robust organization?" he wants to know. There are strong pressures growing to split it up, and hand over at least some of its responsibilities to a young, fresh organization. One influential U.S. space-watcher, just back from touring Soviet facilities — including Baikonur — where he learned that scientists there have been given the go-ahead for a Mir-2 space station in 1995, told me gloomily: "NASA is still designing a space station they can't build and the astronauts can't maintain on-orbit. Back to the Moon and on to Mars? Ridiculous with NASA!"

That pessimistic view is not shared by President Bush and Dan Quayle, who continues to express support for both NASA and the $30 billion Space Station *Freedom*, with launch of its first element due in 1995 and completion in 1999. And NASA's own head, Richard Truly, has been wanting such an inquiry for some time because he thinks it will strengthen, not weaken NASA. In July however it was true that *Freedom* was overweight — 625,000 pounds compared with a ceiling of 512,000 pounds — and underpowered, needing 56kW just to operate it compared with the planned 45kW.

But every big project, says NASA reassuringly, is overweight and underpowered at this stage in its development!

Problems like that are understood by NASA's international partners on *Freedom* — the European Space Agency, Canada and Japan — who between them are spending $7 billion on their contributions to the Station. But they continue to complain bitterly that it is very difficult to work with NASA, because once again this year, while NASA says it must spend $2.5 billion in 1991 to keep *Freedom* on target, Congress proposes to cut that by $200 million or more.

While Shuttle *Endeavour* is nearing completion ahead of schedule for its first flight in early-1992, NASA's hopes of rebuilding Shuttle mission rates to 12-14 per year — essential to support *Freedom* and fulfil other mission requirements — are a long way from fulfilment. The Director of Kennedy Space Center has just gone on record as saying that another Orbiter will be needed after *Endeavour,* but prospects of persuading Congress to fund that as well look bleak.

The U.S. government's attitude to all these questions will affect the 13 European ministers' decisions in mid-1991 when they must decide whether to authorise ESA to go ahead with Hermes, the spaceplane that will give Europe independence in manned

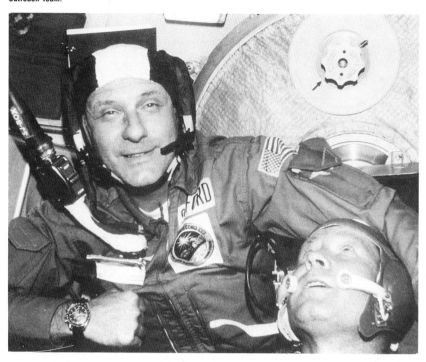

(Below) **Veteran astronaut Tom Stafford, seen (left) with Alexei Leonov during the joint U.S./Soviet ASTP mission in 1975, is now heading a Moon-Mars Outreach Team.**

spaceflight — or whether to cancel it. Politics, not technical capability, will decide the issue, and the conclusion is impossible to forecast.

Mars by 2019?

Such decisions, of course, will also affect the continuing arguments about long-term targets in space exploration.

President Bush set a target in July 1989 for a permanent lunar base to be established, followed by the landing of astronauts on Mars by 2019 — 50 years after Apollo 11 made the first Moon landing. The plan then was to use *Freedom* as a "stepping-stone", or launch pad, first to the Moon and then to Mars. But industrialists expecting to use the station for microgravity-processing are strongly opposed to such a plan; using *Freedom* as a 'way-station', they say, would cause far too much disturbance to make microgravity work practical or profitable.

Now it is being suggested that it would be much cheaper and quicker to go direct to the Moon and Mars, bypassing *Freedom* altogether. General Tom Stafford, a veteran astronaut who made four spaceflights, has recently been appointed to head a Moon-Mars Outreach Team to look for new ideas.

Collaboration caution

The Soviet Union has offered many times to collaborate with the U.S. on a manned Mars expedition — President Gorbachev proposed it to President Reagan in 1986.

Superpower collaboration would spread the cost — estimated by some at $400 billion — and perhaps bring forward the first mission by 10-12 years. The Soviets are also eager to make commercial use of the Energia rocket, which in addition to launching the Shuttle Orbiter, is capable of placing up to 150 tonnes in low-Earth orbit. One Energia flight could do the job of five U.S. Shuttle missions when it comes to orbiting elements of Space Station *Freedom* in 1995-99. But the U.S. government, and for that matter NASA's top brass, are very reluctant to allow their projects to become dependent upon the Soviets — even though it would save billions of dollars which they will probably have to spend on an unmanned Shuttle-C (Cargo) launcher to do the job Energia can do already.

The U.S. government worries first about giving the Soviets access to their technology, and then about what would happen if relations with the Soviets suffer the sort of setbacks that occurred in China.

Cautiously, U.S. and Soviet working groups are feeling their way towards more space collaboration by discussing the possibility of giving a Soviet cosmonaut a flight on the U.S. Shuttle in return for a flight by a NASA astronaut on a Soyuz mission to Mir. This would probably take place around 1995 — which would be 20 years after the famous Apollo-Soyuz Test Project (ASTP) mission, when Apollo and Soyuz spacecraft docked in orbit for the first, and only, emotional Soviet-American handshake in space.

Short-term prospects

If *Freedom* and Hermes are given the go-ahead, it seems inevitable that their cost will be balanced by the cancelling of some cherished scientific projects in the next twelve months. That process has already started in the U.S. with the cancellation of $12.1 million for one of the most exciting of all space projects — the Search for Extraterrestrial Intelligence (SETI). The one hope of avoiding such cuts is that it could be decided to save jobs and pre-serve advanced-technology work by trans-ferring slices of the now-overloaded defense budgets to space projects.

That could especially apply to the $18 billion being spent in 1990 on military space activities in the United States.

R.T.

(Below) **Celebrations of the 20th anniversary of the first manned Moon landing provided much-needed visibility for plans for future manned exploration. Here, Dan Quayle, George Bush and Apollo 11 astronauts Neil Armstrong, Buzz Aldrin and Michael Collins share a lighter moment at the National Air and Space Museum in Washington D.C.**

The Top Ten?

Everybody who joins the illustrious ranks of the spacefarers possesses special qualities and qualifications. That said, the Editor — throwing caution to the wind — volunteers his personal 'gallery' of the year's top achievers.

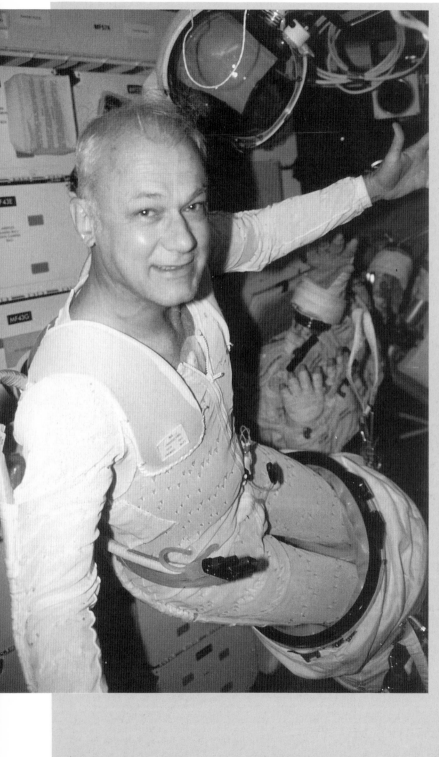

1: Bruce McCandless

After serving 23 years as an astronaut, Bruce made his second space flight in 1989 — demonstrating the patience and dedication required to stay the course. He almost got the chance to put several years of mission-specific EVA training into practice when one of the Hubble Space Telescope's solar-cell arrays was slow to deploy — a situation to which he applied the right blend of aplomb and humor.

2: Pierre Thuot

Pierre was one of several 'rookies' who were busily working their way through the mandatory one-year training and evaluation phase at the time of the *Challenger* disaster, and went on to make their first space flights this year. The self-assured naval aviator made a highly-creditable first performance on the military STS-28/*Columbia* mission.

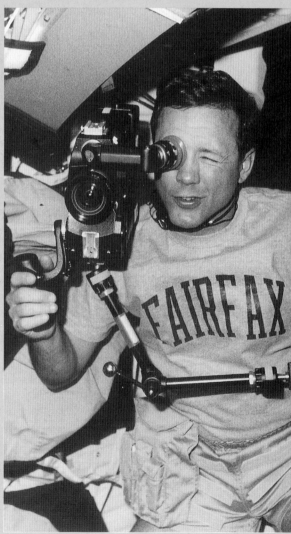

3: Don Williams

We proffer a hearty *Bon Voyage!* to the likeable man from Indiana who commanded the tricky Galileo deployment mission with such apparent ease last fall. Don Williams has departed NASA for pastures new, but his achievements won't be forgotten.

5: Jim Wetherbee

Jim's exploits as drummer in the all-astronaut rock band *Max Q* earned him more publicity than his 'day job' — until this year. Now that he's broken into the Gold Pin league, watch him take some of the most prestigeous flight assignments this decade and NASA has to offer.

4: Aleksandr Serebrov

If ever a man paid his dues, it was Aleksandr Serebrov! Overcoming what must have been a very frustrating series of setbacks, he scored a great personal triumph by taking the new Ikar-YMK 'space bicycle' on its first flight outside the Mir space station.

6: Dan Brandenstein

Dan's post as Chief of the Astronaut Office was ably filled by Mike Coats in the training period for STS-32/*Columbia*, allowing him to concentrate on what was probably the most demanding U.S. mission of the year. His unflustered handling of the LDEF retrieval — and the first night landing of the post-*Challenger* era, at an all-time record weight for an incoming Shuttle — marks him out as a man who leads from the front.

7: Kathy Sullivan

Kathy was disappointed when the opportunity to photograph the Hubble Space Telescope's moment of departure evaded her. She had the best excuse in the world, however — she was occupying *Discovery's* airlock in preparation for a critical spacewalk. Next time....

8: Brewster Shaw

Brewster's sometimes prickly manner can unsettle the unwary, but on STS-28 he demonstrated why his status as a top-flight Commander is unassailable.

10: Bonnie Dunbar

No-one could fault Bonnie's performance during the LDEF retrival. The consequences of a misjudgment during proximity operations with the twelve-ton LDEF free-flyer do not bear thinking about.

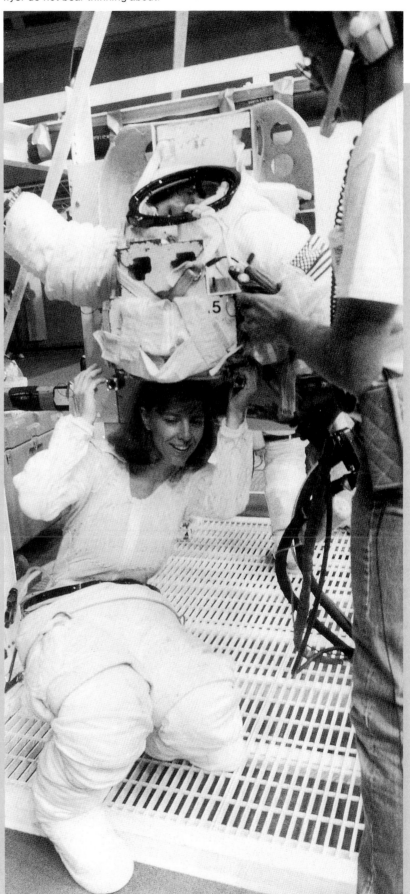

9: Franklin Chang-Diaz

A low-profile approach belies Franklin's unswerving ability to get the job done. If an EVA comes his way soon, he'll have achieved it all.

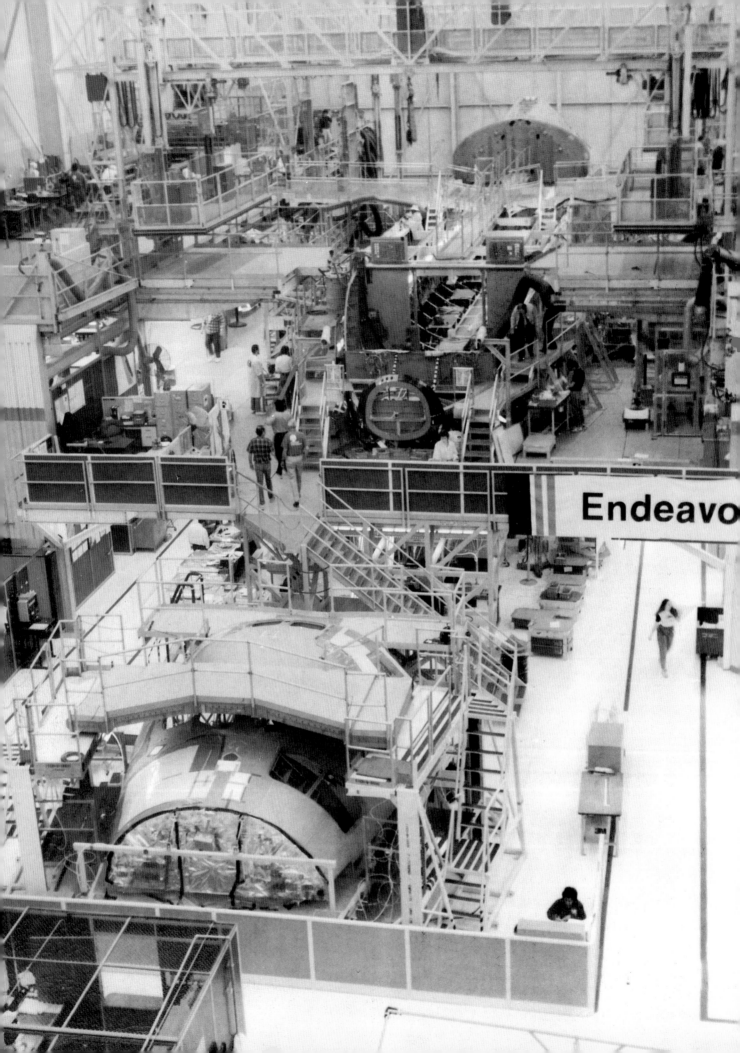

THE MAKING OF ENDEAVOUR

Throughout the timeframe encompassed by this inaugural edition of *Space Year*, a new Shuttle Orbiter was taking shape on NASA's behalf. Known to the personnel producing her simply as OV-105 (Orbiter Vehicle 105), but now bearing the word *Endeavour* on her starboard wing, this new spacecraft carries with it a substantial proportion of the hopes of America's manned space program. When completed, OV-105 will join her sister-ships, *Columbia* (OV-102), *Discovery* (OV-103) and *Atlantis* (OV-104), to restore NASA's Shuttle fleet to the number of vehicles originally contracted for in 1972 and operated with many successes from April 1981 to January '86, when Orbiter *Challenger* (OV-099) was so violently and publicly destroyed.

The history of OV-105 can be traced to a $400-million contract awarded to Rockwell by NASA's Johnson Space Center in April 1983. It called for the fabrication of a batch of major spare parts known as 'structural spares' that could be called on should significant damage be sustained by an operational Orbiter.

Specifically, these items were: an aft-fuselage section; a crew compartment; a Forward Reaction Control System (FRCS) module; upper and lower forward-fuselage sections (the crew compartment is located between these two elements), the latter to include the nose landing-gear doors); a pair of payload bay doors; a vertical stabilizer unit, including the rudder/speed-brake assemblies; an aft body-flap; and a pair of the rear-fuselage-mounted Orbital Maneuvering System (OMS) pods.

Such a comprehensive selection almost transcended the traditional notion of 'spares', and effectively comprised an entire Orbiter vehicle in broken-down form, less the myriad smaller items required to fully outfit the craft, including computers, fuel cells, and wiring looms.

At the time of the *Challenger* accident in January 1986, the structural spares construction program was still in progress. It was not in fact completed until the latter part of 1987, by which time events had overtaken the original intention of merely building up a spare-parts inventory, and directed the emphasis toward assembling a brand new Orbiter vehicle.

Eighteen months after the *Challenger* disaster, on 31 July 1987, NASA — having at last won-through a barrage of political/budgetary wranglings — awarded Rockwell International a contract to employ the 'structural spares' as the basis for the construction and outfitting of a *Challenger*-replacement Orbiter vehicle.

Rear Admiral Dick Truly, NASA Associate Administrator for Spaceflight (and himself a former Shuttle astronaut), said of the contract award; "The completion of these negotiations and the commencement of full production of this new Orbiter mark a major milestone in our return to safe, reliable and effective spaceflight.

(Far-left) A birds-eye view of activities under way in Building 150 — the Orbiter assembly facility at Rockwell International's Palmdale, California plant. *Endeavour's* upper-forward fuselage can be seen in the foreground, the lower-forward fuselage is visible at center, and in the far background is the aft-fuselage.

(Below) OV-105's mid-fuselage section being positioned on jack-stands in Station 2 on the Orbiter 'production line'.

(Right) **Endeavour's vertical stabilizer, with rudder/speedbrakes already attached, is suspended above a portable work-station.**

(Below) **The starboard wing is moved into position for mating with the mid-fuselage.**

"Those government and contractor people who oversee and construct this spacecraft are setting out on a task which is of the utmost importance to America's future in space."

The cost-plus-award/incentive-fee contract between NASA and Rockwell became effective on 1 August 1987, and had a target price of $1.3 billion. Its terms demanded that Rockwell fabricate, assemble, test, check-out and deliver the new Orbiter vehicle within 45 months.

Rockwell determined that management and some fabrication would take place at its Downey headquarters facilities near Los Angeles, and that assembly and checkout of the new craft would take place at Palmdale, some 40 miles northeast of the city, not far from Edwards Air Force Base.

Additionally, 40 to 50 percent of the fabrication and testing, as well as support services, were assigned to more than 100 subcontractor companies, spreading the workload — and those NASA dollars — right across America.

Other elements required to replace hardware lost in the *Challenger* disaster included three Space Shuttle Main Engines (SSMEs), and miscellaneous crew equipment and support services. Funding for these items was provided by Congress at President Reagan's request in 1987, and were acquired through separate contracts with other companies.

Rockwell itself has fabricated many of the key structural elements of the new Orbiter, but original suppliers are furnishing the other items of hardware required to complete it. These include the general-purpose computers, the inertial measurement units, the environmental-control/life-support system, fuel cells and so forth.

It is worth mentioning at this juncture that all the specification upgrades and modifications incorporated into the other three Orbiter vehicles following the *Challenger* disaster are automatically going into the construction of OV-105.

In addition, two other major modifications yet to be fitted to *Discovery, Atlantis and Columbia* — namely upgraded computers and a drag-chute system — will be fitted to OV-105 before delivery to NASA (dates have yet to be set for the installation of these new features into the three operational Orbiters). The drag-chute will be installed immediately under the trailing edge of the vertical stabilizer, for deployment just after main landing-gear touchdown, reducing braking loads.

The mid-fuselage section was already in storage at Palmdale at the time of the *Challenger* accident, so once the contract to create OV-105 was awarded, this was removed from its crate and set up in a workstation ready to accept the other major

(Left) Workers install thermal-protection materials on the OMS pods, which were then returned to the St. Louis, Missouri facility of contractor McDonnell Douglas for fitment of internal hardware.

(Bottom-left) Close-up view of the lower-forward fuselage shortly prior to mating with the mid-fuselage.

(Bottom-right) Lower-forward and mid-fuselage elements, joined as one.

(Below) A Rockwell worker inspects *Endeavour's* airlock, which will accomodate Shuttle spacewalkers sometime after February 1992.

(Right) **Endeavour's** aft-fuselage section, with ports for the three SSMEs (main engines), which will be installed at Kennedy Space Center on delivery.

(Below) The aft-fuselage, now attached to the mid-fuselage, awaits the addition of thermal-protection materials.

structural elements.

OV-105's vertical stablilizer, built by Fairchild of Farmingdale, Long Island, was set up in a work-station at Palmdale in November 1987.

The craft's wings and elevons were transported from the makers, Grumman Corporation of Bethpage, New York, to join the assembly program. They came via the Panama Canal to Long Beach, California, and from there were trucked to Palmdale, arriving in February 1988. In May, they were mated to the mid-fuselage section, thereby forming a structural 'backbone' for the rest of the construction operation.

In February '88, the two OMS pods had been shipped from McDonnell Douglas's St Louis, Missouri facility to Palmdale. They were not ready for mating with the primary structure, as they still required the installation of many items of internal hardware. However, that internal installation work could not be accomplished immediately, due to the time-lag inherent in building such high-technology hardware, so Rockwell 'stole a march' on the schedule by taking the pods in-house and fitting as much of the external thermal-protection materials as possible during the period that the pods would otherwise have been lying idle at St Louis.

When this work was completed — on 31 January 1989 — the two OMS pods were duly shipped back to St Louis to enable McDonnell Douglas to install all the necessary internal hardware.

In August '88, the lower-forward fuselage had gone up for mating with the mid-fuselage, having been trucked over the relatively short distance from Rockwell's Downey facility to Palmdale.

Another key milestone was passed when the upper-forward fuselage section was transported the short distance from Rockwell's Downey facility to Palmdale on 8 September '89.

The four segments which constitute the payload bay doors arrived at Palmdale from the manufacturer — Rockwell's North American Aircraft subsidiary in Tulsa, Oklahoma — on consecutive days; 25, 26, 27 and 28 October 1989. Thermal protection system (TPS) materials were then attached to their external surfaces, and torque-tubes and latches were installed, pending integration with the Orbiter in August '90.

The aft-fuselage assembly made the trip up to Palmdale on 15 December, and was mated on the 18th, and on 23 February 1990, the crew compartment followed. It was mated with the primary structure on 9 March, while the upper-forward fuselage section was mated on 4 May.

On 19 October, the final major element, the Forward Reaction Control System (FRCS) unit, was to be moved from Downey to Palmdale and prepared to integration.

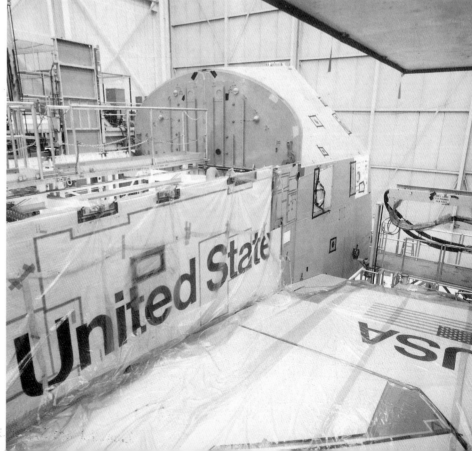

(Right) Endeavour's pressurized crew compartment is hoisted for positioning in the lower-forward fuselage, visible just behind it. The upper-fuselage (foreground) will then be installed over it.

(Below) A Rockwell worker inspects a windshield interface on the crew compartment prior to installation of the gold Mylar insulative blanketing material.

(Above) Blanket-type thermal-protection material is cut to the correct shape.

(Left) Workers gently guide the crew compartment into position in the lower-forward fuselage.

9105202

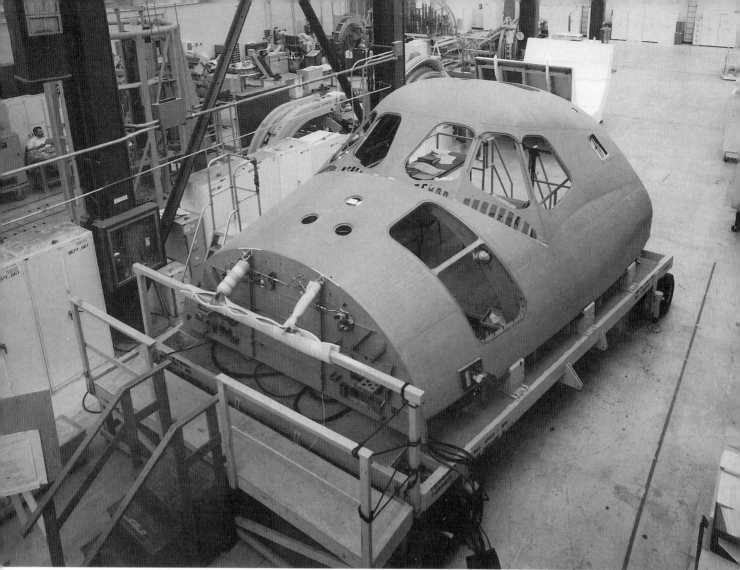

After that, a vast amount of wiring and sub-systems installation must take place in all corners of the craft's structure, although one should not undervalue the tremendous strides that have already been made in this direction.

NASA's final acceptance test is still scheduled for 8 February 1991; all the individual subsystems will be completed, checked-out and tested, then the entire vehicle will be 'integrated' and checked-out and tested as a whole.

The formal rollout ceremony remains slated for April. Rollout of OV-105 promises to be a grand occasion, and is currently scheduled for April 1991. The $1.3-billion contract specifies that the Orbiter will be delivered to NASA will all systems installed, with the exception of the two rear-fuselage mounted OMS pods and the three main engines, which will be fitted at the Cape.

We won't be treated to the spectacle of OV-105 being transported overland from Palmdale to Edwards Air Force Base as the other Orbiters were. Edwards, of course, is the starting-point for the long coast-to-coast flight down to Kennedy Space Center, atop NASA's Boeing 747 Shuttle Carrier Aircraft (SCA).

Instead of making the traditional snail's-pace 38-mile overland trek, OV-105 will be flown directly out of Palmdale and on to the Cape. This alternative arrangement has been made possible by the decision

(Top-left) **Close-up view of** _Endeavour's_ **upper-forward fuselage section in Building 290 at Downey shortly prior to its transfer to Palmdale.**

(Left) **General view of** _Endeavour_ **as she takes shape. Ducts provide air-conditioning for certain humidity- and temperature-critical areas.**

(Above) **The upper-forward fuselage is placed over the crew compartment.**

(Right) **The aft body-flap and elevons in Building 150.**

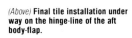

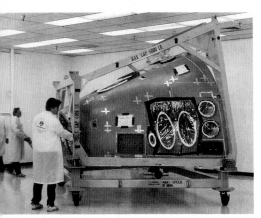

(Above) **Final tile installation under way on the hinge-line of the aft body-flap.**

(Top-right) **Installing the last few tiles under the mid-fuselage in Building 150 at Palmdale.**

(Right) **Technicians move** *Endeavour's* **Forward RCS module from Building 290 to the 659 Precision Clean Room at Downey.**

(Below) **After attention in Building 659, the FRCS module will be slotted into** *Endeavour's* **forward fuselage.**

(Far-right: top) **A Rockwell technician attends a wiring-loom in the aft-fuselage area, just behind SSME (main engine) Position 2.**

(Far-right: bottom) ***Endeavour's* flightdeck prior to installation of seats and the various instrument panels.**

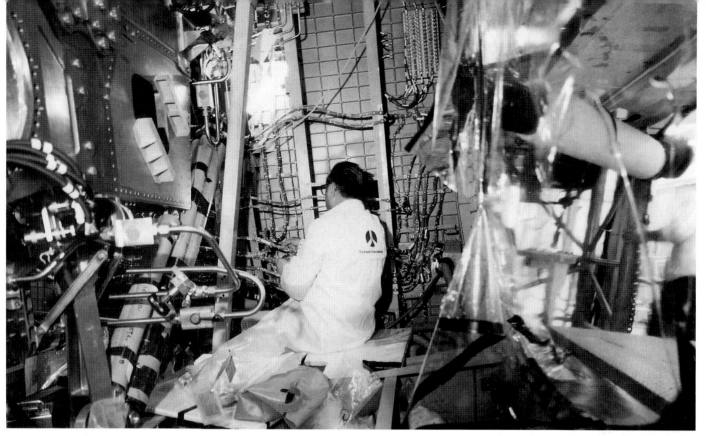

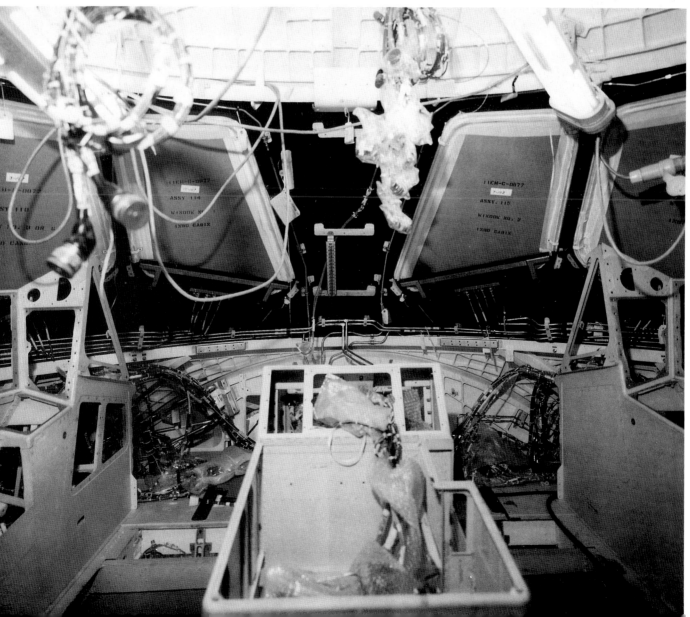

(Below) **Although it was a comparatively simple task, application of these words to the starboard wing was a major psychological boost for the entire NASA/contractor team.**

Naming the new Shuttle

FOR A long time, the new Orbiter was known somewhat impersonally as simply OV-105. Then it was officially named *Endeavour* after the first vessel commanded by Captain James Cook, the legendary British explorer, navigator and astronomer.

The name was finally chosen by President Bush on 10 May 1989, and resulted from a nationwide Orbiter-naming competition involving over 71,000 students in elementary and secondary schools across the USA.

But there's more to the story of how OV-105 became *Endeavour* than one might first imagine...

House Joint Resolution 559, introduced 10 March 1986 by Congressman Tom Lewis (Republican-Florida), called for the name of the *Challenger*-replacement Orbiter to be selected from suggestions submitted by students. Entries in this competition had to be supported by classroom projects, which were completed during the fall '88 semester.

All entries had to be submitted by 31 December last year, and there were over 6,100 entries in all. The judging criteria were; 80 percent for the quality and creativity of the educational project to support and justify each name submitted, and 20 percent for the name's pronounceability for transmission and its ability to convey the American pioneering spirit.

The name had to be that of a seafaring vessel used in research or exploration.

A total of 41 names were submitted, and these were reviewed by panels selected by the state education agencies in each of the 50 American states, the District of Columbia, four U.S. Territories, the Bureau of Indian Affairs, and schools administered by the U.S. Department of Defense and the U.S. Department of State.

A shortlist was drawn up, and these were the 29 finalists:—

Adventure	Horizon
Blake	Investigator
Calypso	Meteor
Deepstar	Nautilus
Desire	North Star
Dove	Pathfinder
Eagle	Phoenix
Endeavor	Polar Star
Endeavour	Resolution
Endurance	Rising Star
Godspeed	Royal Tern
Griffin	Trieste
Gulf Stream	Victoria
H.M.S. Chatham	Victory
Hokule'a	

Some of these names had been borne by spacecraft before. *Eagle*, for example, was the name of the Apollo 11 Lunar Module, while *Pathfinder* was the name given to the four-fifths-scale Orbiter mockup built for NASA's Marshall Space Flight Center in Huntsville, Alabama, and now displayed on a plinth outside the adjacent Alabama Space and Rocket Center.

Phoenix was an early suggestion for *Apollo* 7's callsign; the first American manned spaceflight following the *Apollo* 1 pad fire disaster in which three astronauts perished.

It is interesting to note that the names *Challenger 2*, *Spirit of America*, *Challenger 7*, *Liberty*, *Independence* and *Constitution* — all of which had been put forward for previous Shuttle Orbiters and had figured high on many people's 'probable' list for OV-105 — did not make the shortlist.

The national winner in Division 1 of the Orbiter-naming competition (kindergarten through grade 6) were the fifth-graders of Senatobia Middle School, Senatobia, Mississippi. The team created a space camp simulation, where they taught lower elementary students facts about space exploration by means of nine types of 'hands-on' activities, ranging from packaging payload experiments and wireless communication, to working a Shuttle-type robotic manipulator arm and trying on a team-made spacesuit.

In the Division 2 category (grades 7 through 12), the winning team was from the Tallulah Falls School, Inc., Tallulah Falls, Georgia. The nine-member team was composed of math students in grades 8-12, and the team project was two-fold. They developed an innovative math magazine called *Math Exploration with James Cook*, written on three education levels, and they created a play entitled *Where on Earth?...*, comparing Cook's 18th-century sea exploration to the Orbiter *Endeavour's* 20th-century space exploration.

Both winning teams proposed the name *Endeavour*.

In August 1768, on *HMS Endeavour's* maiden voyage, Captain Cook observed and recorded the transit of the planet Venus. In the view of the winning students, Cook's navigations, explorations and discoveries eventually led Man to the possibilities of space exploration.

"In selecting the name *Endeavour*, the students and the President have identified a name that symbolizes perfectly NASA's goals of space exploration and discovery", said Dale Myers, NASA's Acting Administrator. "The nation can rest assured that we will use this ship with the same commitment that Captain Cook used his in the pursuit of new knowledge to benefit all Mankind".

The two winning teams were recognized in a Rose Garden ceremony at the White House on 16 May, together with the five recently-returned STS-30/*Atlantis* astronauts.

(Bottom) One sight we shall never see again. *Endeavour* will be the first new Orbiter *not* to make the 38-mile overland trek from Palmdale to Edwards Air Force Base for the delivery flight to Kennedy Space Center. This is *Enterprise*, back in 1977.

(Below) NASA Acting Administrator Dale Myers, who spoke at the *Endeavour* naming ceremony.

to remove from storage an Orbiter Lifting Facility (OLF) previously held in storage at nearby Vandenberg Air Force Base. Erection of the OLF, which was originally to have supported Shuttle missions out of Vandenberg before that plan was postponed indefinitely, is scheduled for completion in April '91. In fact, the OLF may even be ready a couple of months earlier.

At the Cape, the completed OV-105 will undergo an overall test, integration and cycling period, before being rolled-out to the launch pad for a Wet Countdown Demonstration Test (WCDT) and a Flight Readiness Firing (FRF) prior to its first flight in February 1992.

NASA will then have a craft capable of creating her own legend, just as her illustrious sister-ships have done.

N.M.

ENDEAVOUR HIGHLIGHTS:

EVENT	MONTH
Authority to proceed	August 1987
Set up mid-fuselage in work station, Palmdale	October 1987
Set up vertical stabilizer in work station, Palmdale	November 1987
Receive wings/elevons at Palmdale from Grumman, Bethpage, New York	February 1988
Receive Orbital Maneuvering System (OMS) pods at Palmdale from McDonnell Douglas Astronautics Company, St. Louis, Missouri	February 1988
Ship lower-forward fuselage to Palmdale from Downey	May 1988
Mate wings to mid-fuselage, Palmdale	August 1988
Ship right-hand and left-hand OMS pods to MDAC from Palmdale for systems installation	January 1989
Ship upper-forward fuselage to Palmdale from Downey	September 1989
Complete wiring checkout on mid-fuselage	October 1989
Ship payload bay doors to Palmdale from Rockwell's North American Aircraft facility in Tulsa, Oklahoma	October 1989
Complete wiring checkout on crew module	November 1989
Ship aft-fuselage to Palmdale from Downey	December 1989
Mate aft-fuselage, Palmdale	January 1990
Ship crew module to Palmdale from Downey	February 1990
Mate crew module, Palmdale	March 1990
Mate upper-forward fuselage, Palmdale	March 1990
Begin power-on systems testing	July 1990
Ship Forward Reaction Control System (FRCS) module to Palmdale from Downey	July 1990
Complete mating of all major structural components, except OMS pods	October 1990
Complete final acceptance test, Palmdale	February 1991
Vehicle rollout from Palmdale for delivery to Kennedy Space Center (KSC), Florida	April 1990
Deliver OMS pods to KSC from Palmdale	September 1991
First space flight (STS-52)	February 1992

AMERICAN
MANNED
MISSIONS

DEPARTMENT OF DEFENSE

STS-28 COLUMBIA

After over three years confined to the ground, Shuttle Orbiter *Columbia* returned to full flight status to the great relief of everybody connected with her. She blasted-off from Kennedy Space Center, Florida on Tuesday 8 August, carrying a top-secret military spy satellite rumored to be an upgraded version of the KH-11. *Columbia* had had 258 modifications incorporated into since her last space mission, 61-C, which ended just ten days before the *Challenger* disaster. Her return to flight status meant that NASA at last had all three surviving Orbiter vehicles on active duty; sufficient to fulfil all its commitments until the *Challenger*-replacement Orbiter, *Endeavour,* enters service in 1992.

(Above) **The Crawler-Transporter withdraws, having deposited the STS-28 stack and its Mobile Launcher Platform on Pad 39B.**

(Top-right) **Moral support from the STS-28 crew's wives, on the astronauts' arrival in Florida. Left to right; Susan Adamson, Kathleen Ann Shaw, Lynne Brown, Lois Richards and Patti Leestma.**

(Right) **Lighthearted crew portrait.**

LAUNCH

On board for the 30th Shuttle mission — designated STS-28 — were three-spaceflight veteran Brewster Shaw (Commander), first-time spacefarer Dick Richards (Pilot), and Mission Specialists Dave Leestma, Jim Adamson and Mark Brown. Leestma flew on the 41-G/*Challenger* mission in October '84, but Adamson and Brown were 'space rookies'.

Lift-off was delayed beyond the 07:57 opening of the launch window by the presence of haze and fog in the vicinity of the Shuttle Landing Facility (SLF) at KSC. The SLF must be clear of impediments to visibility during launch, because it would be used in the event of a major problem developing during the initial stages of ascent, under a contingency known as the RTLS (Return to Launch Site) abort.

In the event, visibility had improved to six miles at launch, *Columbia* finally getting away at 8:37 am local time (13:37 pm GMT). Other weather flight rules were well within limits. At the Transatlantic Abort Landing (TAL) sites, Ben Guerir was *"No-go"* due to crosswinds, but Moron was *"Go"* throughout, and Zaragoza was *"Go"* after a rain-shower cell moved out by launch time.

Ascent was into a 180 x 191-statute-mile orbit inclined at 57 degrees relative to the equator. Shuttle oriented itself for the high-inclination trajectory by performing a 140-degree roll to the right under automatic guidance some ten seconds after lift-off. *Columbia* headed along a northeasterly track which roughly paralleled the eastern seaboard of the United States. The spacecraft passed within 50 miles of Cape Hatteras, North Carolina.

The three SSME main engines were shut down, as usual, some eight minutes after lift-off, when *Columbia* was abeam Atlantic City, New Jersey.

Details of STS-28's countdown activities were kept secret, so the precise launch time could not be forecast. Observers were kept 'in the dark' until T minus 9 minutes, when the customary public affairs commentary commenced. Intercom exchanges between *Columbia's* flight crew and ground controllers were broadcast

until the moment of orbital insertion. Commander Brewster Shaw could be heard making the familiar *"Roll program"* call ten seconds after lift-off, then at T + one minute, 17 seconds, the CAPCOM in the Mission Control Center at Houston radioed, *"Columbia, go at throttle-up."*

Some three minutes into the flight, the CAPCOM informed *Columbia's* crew that they had acheived sufficient altitude and energy to reach emergency landing facilities at Zaragoza, Spain on two engines if a TAL abort became necessary.

ON-ORBIT

By its fifth circuit of the Earth, *Columbia* had reached a 184 x 191-statue-mile orbit. The ten-ton USA-38 tactical/strategic reconnaissance satellite was deployed at 8:06 pm GMT, about seven-and-a-half hours after *Columbia's* lift-off. Unlike the Lacrosse spy-sat that was deployed during the previous all-military Shuttle mission, STS-27/*Atlantis* in December '88, this latest satellite was not lifted from the payload bay by the Orbiter's mechanical arm prior to release, but was sprung free in the manner perfected during numerous previous deployments.

The Canadian-built arm apparently was not installed for mission STS-28.

From the high-inclination, 91-minute-period orbit, the satellite's high-resolution imaging systems are able to scan most of the Soviet land mass, as well as the Middle East. The spy-sat is also likely to be monitoring Soviet missile and space-rocket launches, and maintaining all-weather surveillance of military movements within the Soviet Union and the nations of the Warsaw Pact, but it can also be moved at short notice to view trouble-spots elsewhere; Beirut, for example.

A secondary payload carried by *Columbia* — said by many to have been a satellite, though it was not actually released from the cargo hold during this mission — weighed just 275 pounds and was developed jointly by NASA's Goddard Space Flight Center in Greenbelt, Maryland, and the NASA/Caltech Jet Propulsion Laboratory (JPL) in Pasadena, California.

(Above) **Ground support convoy personnel swarm around** *Columbia* **right after wheelstop. Defueling and toxicity testing, and other immediate post-flight procedures were all in progress at the time this photo was taken (from a U.S. Army helicopter).**

(Right) **The STS-28 astronauts walk out to the 'Astrovan'** *en-route* **to the launch pad. Commander Brewster Shaw leads Pilot Dick Richards and Mission Specialists Dave Leestma, Jim Adamson and Mark Brown.**

(Bottom) **Airborne for the first time in 3½ years, _Columbia_ leaps away from the water-deluge system, clearly seen in operation here.**

(Below) **_Columbia_ pictured during the long process of modification for reflight. Denuded of her OMS pods, Forward RCS module, main engines and many other systems, she is being wheeled into the Orbiter Maintenance and Refurbishment Facility (OMRF).**

It is thought to have been an experiment package related to the Strategic Defense Initiative (SDI) program.

Among the middeck experiments being carried aboard _Columbia_ on this mission was a human skull, dubbed the 'Phantom Head', heavily instrumented to measure radiation dosages in high-inclination orbits. The fact that this bizarre cargo was carried on STS-28 only came to public attention six months later, when full details of the manifest for the STS-31/_Discovery_ Hubble Space Telescope deployment mission — on which the skull was slated to make its third space flight — were released.

Details of the 'Phantom Head' appear elsewhere in this report.

While _Columbia_ was aloft, KSC had thunderstorms just about every afternoon, while White Sands had several thunderstorms — and even Edwards had thunderstorms on three afternoons. Both lakebeds received some rain, but too little to change their status from "Green". With DoD facilities placed at its disposal, STS-28 had the most ambitious weather support on-orbit since the Shuttle program began. In summary, it was also regarded as one of the easier missions with regard to forecasting and staying within flight-rules constraints.

RE-ENTRY & LANDING

Its five-day mission completed, _Columbia_ returned to Earth at 06:38 am local time (13:38 pm GMT) on Sunday 13 August. The landing — on lakebed Runway 17 at Edwards — was an excellent one, aided by ideal weather. Post-flight inspection revealed that between 60 and 100 of _Columbia_'s thermal-protection tiles had sustained sufficient (though minor) damage to warrant replacement, and three tiles were found to be missing altogether.

It was determined that _Columbia_'s Forward RCS unit should be replaced prior to the spacecraft's next mission, STS-32.

N.M.

FOR THE RECORD
- 126th manned spaceflight.
- 60th U.S. manned spaceflight.
- 29th Shuttle space mission.
- 8th mission by Orbiter _Columbia_.
- Brewster Shaw became 37th person, and 19th American, to make three spaceflights.
- Leestma became 97th person, and 58th American, to make two spaceflights.
- Adamson, Brown and Richards became joint 216th people, and joint 127th Americans, in space.

(Right) **A KSC tile technician pampers Columbia in the OMRF.**

(Below) **Deep within the aft compartment, a technician attends to pipework associated with the main engines.**

(Bottom-left) **Before the OMRF was completed, Columbia occupied a corner of the Vehicle Assembly Building (VAB).**

(Bottom-right) **Tile work continued in the Orbiter Processing Facility (OPF). In the background, an SSME main engine.**

Columbia back into space

COLUMBIA WAS the third and final Orbiter to return to flight status following the near-three-year grounding of the Shuttle fleet after the Challenger disaster. After spending a great deal of time getting low-key attention in the Orbiter Maintenance and Refurbishment Facility (OMRF) at KSC, Columbia was finally moved into the Orbiter Processing Facility (OPF) in June 1988 to join the launch flow in-earnest.

With the pressure well and truly on to get Discovery and Atlantis into space before the end of the year, Columbia's managers found their craft taking third place in the line. No time was wasted getting Columbia into the OPF once the opportunity arose. Within hours of Discovery vacating OPF Bay 1 to enter the VAB, Columbia was wheeled in to take her place. In the OMRF, and then in the OPF, the main task was to implement the so-called 'return-to-flight' modifications that were an upshot of the Presidential Commission investigation into the Challenger accident.

A vast number of modifications were made, too numerous to detail here. The most important modifications are, however, worth recounting. A reinforced carbon-carbon (RCC) 'chin' was fitted between the existing RCC nosecap and the forward edge of the nose landing-gear well; the new telescopic-pole crew escape system was installed; modified versions of the massive '17-inch disconnect' valves set into the Orbiter's belly — through which thousands of gallons of liquid nitrogen and liquid oxygen flow on their way from the External Tank to the three main engines during ascent — were fitted; improvements were made to the wiring system and the power-distribution system; and the thermal protection system was upgraded, with many previously tiled areas being stripped and covered with the newer-specification FRSI, FRCI and AFRSI 'blanketing' materials.

Columbia, being the first of NASA's Orbiter fleet to be outfitted for spaceflight, way back in the late-1970s, had gradually become somewhat outdated specification-wise. Independent of the 'return-to-flight' modification work, that situation was substantially remedied.

STATISTICAL ANALYSIS: STS-28/ COLUMBIA

Crew:
Brewster Shaw (Commander)
Dick Richards (Pilot)
Dave Leestma (MS1)
Jim Adamson (MS2)
Mark Brown (MS3)

Orbiter: *Columbia* (OV-102)
(Prior missions — 7; STS-1, STS-2, STS-3, STS-4, STS-5, STS-9/Spacelab 1, 61-C)

External Tank: ET-31
(Splashdown zone: Latitude 38.64 degrees south/Longitude 149.65 degrees west — Pacific Ocean, 145 miles south of Tahiti)

SSME Position 1: Engine 2019
(Prior total firing time: 6,559 seconds: prior missions — 4; STS-9/*Columbia*, 51-J/*Atlantis*, 61-B/*Atlantis*, STS-26/*Discovery*)

SSME Position 2: Engine 2022
(Prior total firing time: 1,827 seconds: prior missions — 2; STS-26/*Discovery*, STS-29/*Discovery*)

SSME Position 3: Engine 2028
(Prior total firing time 1,828 seconds: prior missions — 2; STS-26/*Discovery*, STS-29/*Discovery*)

Forward RCS: FRC-2
(Prior missions — 7; STS-1/*Columbia*, STS-2/*Columbia*, STS-3/*Columbia*, STS-4/*Columbia*, STS-5/*Columbia*, STS-9/*Columbia*, 61-C/*Columbia*)

Port OMS: LP-03
(Prior missions — 7; 41-C/*Challenger*, 41-D/*Discovery*, 51-A/*Discovery*, 51-C/*Discovery*, 51-D/*Discovery*, 51-J/*Atlantis*, 61-B/*Atlantis*)

Starboard OMS: RP-04
(Prior missions — 3; 51-B/*Challenger*, 51-F/*Challenger*, 61-C/*Columbia*)

Mobile Launcher Platform: MLP-2
(Pad 39B)

SRBs: Flight Set 5

SRB case use history:

Element	Left Booster	Right Booster
F. Dome	ETM-1	51-A, 61-C, QM-6
Cyl.	DM-9	GTM-3, STS-3, 41-G, 61-B, DM-8
C.F. Cyl.	DM-9	New
Cyl.	41-B, 51-I, DM-9	41-G, 61-B
C.F. Cyl.	QM-6	New
Cyl.	41-C, 51-J, DM-9	DM-5, 41-B, 51-I, DM-8
C.F. Cyl.	New	DM-8
ET Attach	41-G, 61-B, QM-6	51-A, 61-C, QM-7
Stiffener	DM-3, QM-3, STS-5, 51-G	GTM-3, STS-9, 51-F
Stiffener	DM-3, QM-3, STS-5, 51-G	STS-2, 41-C
Aft Dome	DM-8	61-A, QM-6

Launch:
13:37 GMT/08 August 1989
Kennedy Space Center, Florida

Landing:
14:38 GMT/13 August 1989
Edwards Air Force Base, California

Orbits: 80.5

Distance: 1,835,600 nautical miles

Mission Elapsed Time:
5 days, 1 hour, 0 minutes, 53 seconds
(121 hours, 0 mins, 53 secs)

Weights:
Launch/classified
Landing/classified

Cargo bay payloads: Classified

Middeck payloads: 'Phantom Head' (remainder classified)

Orbital inclination: 57.0 degrees

Major orbital maneuvers:

Date	Time (GMT)	Perigee (miles)	Apogee (miles)	Period (mins)
8 Aug	13:17	180	191	90.5
	18:58	184	191	90.5
	no further maneuvers			

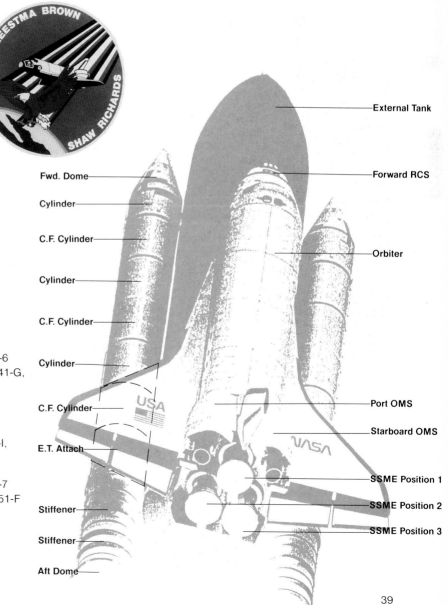

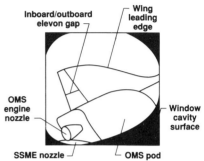

Inboard/outboard elevon gap — Wing leading edge

OMS engine nozzle

SSME nozzle — OMS pod

Window cavity surface

Columbia's infrared 'eye'

SINCE THE 61-C mission back in January 1986, *Columbia* has carried a host of sensors to quantify conditions an Orbiter encounters in flight, thereby assisting those whose job it is to design the next generation of reusable spaceplanes. Atop *Columbia*'s tailfin has been a particularly intriguing sensor package called SILTS — an acronym for Shuttle Leeside Temperature Sensing experiment.

To learn more about it, we spoke with David Throckmorton, Assistant Head of the Aerothermodynamics Branch of NASA's Langley Research Center in Hampton, Virginia. NASA/Langley is the lead center for SILTS-related activities. Throckmorton and co-investigator Vince Zoby are the SILTS program's leading figures.

So just what does SILTS do? Well, imagine if an expert on aerothermodynamics could somehow stand on top of the Shuttle Orbiter's tailfin during re-entry, viewing the play of heating effects across the upper (leeside) surfaces of the vehicle as it comes down. The measurements he or she took from such a vantage point could provide detailed temperature-profile 'maps' of immense benefit to the designers of future winged re-entry vehicles.

SILTS — which has a longer life-expectancy than an aerothermodynamisist when subjected to white-hot temperatures! — is helping to unlock the secrets of aerothermal effects in hypersonic flight. Despite exhaustive computer-simulation exercises, there were large uncertainties in the Shuttle designers' understanding of the heating processes which would take place over the Orbiter surfaces during re-entry. After all, such flight conditions could not be duplicated in windtunnels and test chambers here on Earth, and advanced computational techniques capable of creating such an environment artificially were simply not available in those days.

As a result of their uncertainties, the Shuttle's designers added more thermal protection material than was probably required. With human lives at stake, it was only proper to err on the side of safety. There is a significant penalty, however, because carrying additional thermal protection means having less weightlifting capacity left for payloads.

Larger reusable spacecraft of the future might potentially incur an even greater penalty, because they will carry a correspondingly greater weight of thermal protection materials. Therefore, although it was too late to do anything about the existing Shuttle design, NASA determined that the next-generation shuttlecraft which might ultimately replace the current craft would benefit from an improved understanding of the dynamics of re-entry vehicle hypersonic heating profiles.

An opportunity to make such an advance in knowledge came with the original idea for the SILTS concept by Langley's James Dunavant about 15 years ago. The fruit of Dunavant's inspired thinking is only too plain to see today: the top section of *Columbia*'s vertical tail has been replaced with a 20-inch-diameter Rockwell International-built pod housing an infrared camera and associated control equipment. The camera's field-of-view is 40 degrees which, by way of comparison, equates the SILTS infrared 'eye' with a camera of the type you may have at home, but fitted with a wide-angle lens.

SILTS' camera can rotate to look through either of two 2½-inch-diameter infrared-transparent 'windows' set into the dome-shaped forward end of the pod; one forward-facing, the other oblique. One window looks straight down toward the fuselage and the leading edges of the Orbiter's wings at the point where they meet the fuselage. The base of the tailfin is also visible through this window.

The other window, being set at an angle to the Orbiter fuselage centerline, permits most of the port wing and the port Orbital Maneuvering System (OMS) pod to be viewed.

A constant supply of nitrogen gas at room-temperature flows across the windows during re-entry to provide an insulative cushion from the onslaught of extreme temperatures caused by the friction between the Orbiter and the surrounding atmosphere. If this was not done, the sensitive infrared 'eye' would only see the windows themselves, rather than what lies beyond them.

On Shuttle missions 61-C, STS-28 and STS-32, the only operational uses of the system thus far, SILTS came into action at an altitude of 400,000 feet, when *Columbia* (travelling at 16,700 mph) issued an automatic computer command to eject thermal-protection plugs off the two tail-mounted window ports. At that point, the infrared camera started operating, alternately viewing the port wing and then the fuselage every eleven seconds until the Orbiter had dropped to a height of about 80,000 feet and slowed to a speed of about 1,500 mph.

In a 20-minutes period of operation, over 110 pairs of infrared images can be captured and stored on the on-board OEX (Orbiter Experiment) tape-recorder for subsequent processing and analysis. A malfunction during the 61-C maiden outing caused some major data-interpretation headaches for NASA/Langley personnel assigned to the SILTS program, but these were overcome for STS-28.

The system was due to be used again on mission STS-35/*Columbia* in mid-1990.

SILTS EXPERIMENT COMPONENTS

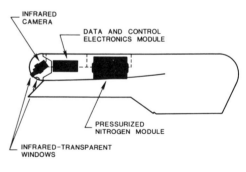

INFRARED CAMERA

DATA AND CONTROL ELECTRONICS MODULE

PRESSURIZED NITROGEN MODULE

INFRARED-TRANSPARENT WINDOWS

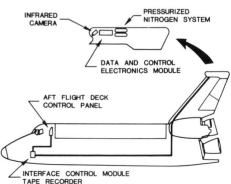

INFRARED CAMERA

PRESSURIZED NITROGEN SYSTEM

DATA AND CONTROL ELECTRONICS MODULE

AFT FLIGHT DECK CONTROL PANEL

INTERFACE CONTROL MODULE TAPE RECORDER

Human skull flown on Shuttle

MEDICAL RESEARCH took an interesting turn when a human skull was flown aboard STS-28/*Columbia*. It took about six months for this information to reach the general public, as the skull was flown on two secret Department of Defense missions (it also flew on STS-36/*Atlantis*) before its carriage on the civilian STS-31/*Discovery* Hubble Space Telescope deployment mission in 1990 lifted the veil of secrecy.

That veil — for reasons best known to the DoD — extended to on-board medical activities,even though these did not in themselves pose any 'national security' risk. Known as the 'Phantom Head', the 11-pound human skull is the primary element of a Detailed Supplementary Objective designated DSO 469 and entitled Inflight Radiation Dose Distribution. DSOs take many different forms and are an integral part of secondary pay-load activities on Shuttle missions. This particular experiment is a joint NASA/DoD investigation to study the penetration of radiation into the cranial cavity. Data will be vital to planners of Space Station *Freedom* orbital operations, which will subject astronauts to extended radiation exposure.

The skull belonged to a person who donated their body to medical science, but had no knowledge that it might be flown into orbit. Based on its small size, the skull is probably that of a female. The 'Phantom Head' is a commercially-available model used in clinical and research settings. It is covered and filled with a plastic material specially formulated to be radio-equivalent to human skin and tissue. The 'Phantom Head' measures about six inches deep, by eight inches deep, by ten inches high and was for its space flights sliced into ten layers mounted on a plastic base. The layers are marked from zero to nine, beginning at the top of the head.

For ease of stowage aboard the Shuttle, only the top nine layers are flown.

Hundreds of thermoluminescent dosimeters are located throughout the head. Plastic nuclear track detectors are placed between each of the skull's layers. The dosimeters and detectors measure heavy-ion primary radiation and secondary radiation fragments, thus recording radiation exposures at both skin and depth levels.

Other flight equipment employed in the DSO 469 experiment includes a passive photon spectrometer, an electronic radiation counter, polyethylene spheres (known as 'Bonner Spheres') for measuring neutron fluctuations, and activation foils. Ground support equipment includes a thermo-luminescent dosimeter reader, a plastic nuclear track detector measurement instrument, an IBM-compatible personal computer and low-level counting room and radioactivity measuring instrumentation.

The 'Phantom Head' is stowed in a mid-deck locker aboard the Shuttle during ascent and re-entry. Once in orbit, astronauts mount the head on the Orbiter's starboard wall at the foot of an astronaut's sleeping bag using Velcro patches. The head is stored in a fire-retardant Nomex pouch while in the mid-deck locker and remains in the pouch when mounted. All three space flights have carried the head into orbits characterized by a higher-than-usual radiation environment. STS-28 launched to a 57-degree inclination; STS-36 went to 62 degrees; and STS-31, although it only launched to the Shuttle's 'standard' 28.5-degree-inclination orbit, climbed to a record altitude (for the Shuttle) of 330 nautical miles.

After each flight, the skull is immediately flown from the Edwards, California landing site back to Johnson Space Center in Texas for detailed analysis at NASA's Medical Sciences Division there.

Alderson Research Laboratories of Stanford, Connecticut began manufacturing 'phantom' models in the 1950s. In 1989, it sold various elements of the business, including the manufacturing of the skull-based research articles, to Phantom Laboratory of Salem, New York. The U.S. Air Force has loaned this particular model to NASA.

Future plans include flying the torso of a human cadaver aboard the Shuttle, to verify laboratory predictions as to internal-organ radiation dosage. The torso would presumably be stapped into a refrigerated cell within the payload bay.

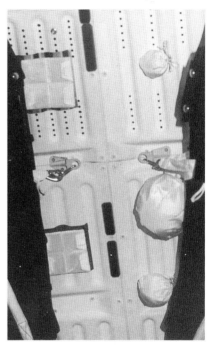

Various views of the 'Phantom Head', including stowed in its Nomex pouch for flight (below). **The 'Bonner Spheres'** (above) **measure neutron fluctuations and are also stowed in Nomex pouches for flight.**

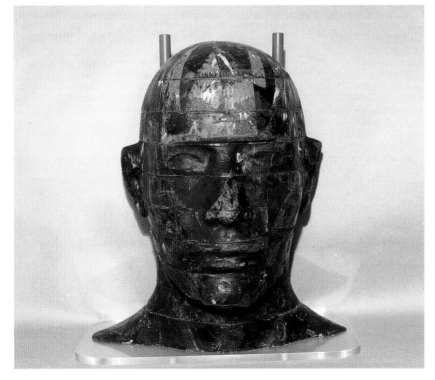

STS-34 ATLANTIS

A second planetary spacecraft was deployed by NASA's Space Shuttle on Wednesday 18 October. The Galileo Jupiter-explorer was set free from the payload bay of Orbiter *Atlantis* just over six hours after blast-off from Kennedy Space Center's Pad 39B. Lift-off time was 12.54pm EDT. We discussed the mission with Commander Don Williams and Mission Specialist Shannon Lucid soon after the flight ended. Both were making their second space flights. The other crew members were Pilot Mike McCulley, and Mission Specialists Franklin Chang-Diaz and Ellen Baker. Chang Diaz was making his second space flight, McCulley and Baker (*nee* Shulman) their first.

LAUNCH

There was a countdown scrub on the opening of the launch 'window' on 12 October, caused by a faulty main engine controller. The clock stayed put at the built-in hold at T minus 19 hours for five days while the controller was changed-out. Weather problems intervened on 17 October, prompting another scrub at T minus five minutes. At that point, the clock was recycled to T minus 11 hours, and the countdown resumed at 8:36 that evening.

Don Williams described the thunder-storm that had built up nearby, and then drifted over the Shuttle Landing Facility. "I could barely see the fringes of that from where we sat on the launch pad. The weather was beautiful on the launch pad itself." Over the intercom, Williams and his crew were kept informed as the situation developed: "There was a rather small window that day — 17 or 18 minutes — so anything that cut into that was clearly going to have an impact." Mike Coats, at that time Acting Chief of the Astronaut Office, flew one of the Shuttle Training Aircraft (STAs) on a weather-appraisal sortie, while another astronaut — Ken Reightler, located in the Launch Control Center at the Cape — made decisions based on data he was receiving, not only from Coats in the STA, but also from various remote sensors, including a relatively new system that's in place around the Kennedy Space Center: one which detects electrical potential, thereby aiding assessments as to the probability of a lightning strike in any particular area.

"That's very, very important, of course, when you're flying an electrical flying machine," Don Williams told me afterwards, matter-of-factly.

Don went on to recall his impressions of the launch itself: "This was my first flight in the launch/entry escape suit that we're now wearing — the pressure suits. The G-loads, to me, appear to be a little higher than I remember them the last time, and I think that's probably because of the addit-ional weight that you're carrying around

in these suits: harnesses, parachutes, breathing apparatus and all sorts of things — survival gear — that goes with the suit.

"Other than that, the first stage on the solid rocket motors was pretty much as I remember it."

Williams and his crew had to deal with three minor malfunctions during the ascent. An APU (Auxiliary Power Unit) controller shifted to the high-speed range which required them to take some action on board; then the main controller in a flash-evaporator — part of the cooling system — malfunctioned, causing them to switch to some secondary and backup controllers which are not as efficient, resulting in an increase in cabin temper-ature; and a 'multiplexer/demultiplexer' in the aft of the Orbiter failed just before the OMS burn that put them into the correct orbit.

The 'multiplexer/demultiplexer' that fail-ed was FA-1 (for Flight Aft Number 1), and although we risk getting into a complicated description, the subject is worthy of a little amplification. MDMs, as they're called, are flying-control communications devices. They do two things. Working in one direction, they take the analog signals from various sensors (in the case of FA1, sensors located in the aft part of the Orbiter) and convert them to digital signals which can be understood by the digital computers that fly the vehicle and monitor the systems.

Operating in the opposite direction, they take the digital commands from the computers, translate them into analog signals, and send them out to the controls and effectors, such as the hydraulic systems, actuators for the aerosurfaces and engine bells, and various valves and control systems in the RCS and the OMS and elsewhere.

ON-ORBIT

Deployment of the Galileo spacecraft, which represents the fruits of a $1.3 billion, 13-year program, had — as one might expect — been the subject of intensive pre-mission training for the two astronauts (Shannon Lucid and Ellen

(Top) **Pictured from the Shuttle Training Aircraft (STA) flown by Mike Coats, the STS-34/*Atlantis* stack pours on the coals.**

(Above) **Backdropped against the blackness of space, the Galileo/IUS combination drifts serenely clear.**

(Below:) **Don Williams leads his crew from the Operations and Checkout Building for the Terminal Countdown Demonstration Test (TCDT), the traditional 'dress rehearsal' for launch day.**

Baker) charged with setting it safely on its way. I asked Shannon to outline this aspect of the mission: "Ellen and I did the typical thing that we do for an IUS flight, and that is spend a lot of time in the Single Systems Trainers going through the various IUS procedures and learning to deal with all the malfunctions that they've dreamt up and could happen.

"Then we spent some time in the SMS *(Shuttle Mission Simulator — Ed.)* doing IUS deploy scenarios with the entire crew, and we also had three Joint Integrated Sims, which tied together the people at JPL, the people out at Sunnyvale who run the IUS, and the people here at JSC."

The primary malfunction scenarios the crew trained for pre-mission included those which involved the failure of the tilt-table in the Shuttle's payload bay to raise the 19-ton Galileo/IUS stack into the proper position for deployment. In that event,

Modifications made to Atlantis since her last flight

SINCE *ATLANTIS'S* last flight, STS-30 in May — the Magellan Venus radar-mapper deployment mission — a total of 34 modifications had been made to her. One of the most significant modifications was the installation of an 'RTG purge' system. It came into use prior to Galileo's deployment, and is worthy of a more detailed description.

Galileo, of course, is equipped with two General Electric-built radioisotope thermoelectric generators (RTGs): nuclear power sources fuelled by plutonium-dioxide, which decays to produce heat, which is in turn converted to electricity to service onboard systems. Galileo has RTGs because solar-cell arrays, which supply electrical power on most spacecraft types, would be useless once the craft got as far as distant Jupiter, where the Sun is just a tiny speck.

While Galileo was in the Orbiter's payload bay, being powered by the Shuttle's own electrical system, the RTG case temperature was maintained (at a level conductive to the wellbeing of payload instrumentation located nearby) by means of an alcohol-water coolant mixture circulated through them by a system fitted to *Atlantis* during the post-Magellan mission turnaround period.

The RTG purging operation consisted of some valve movements which cleared the water-alcohol coolant from the supply lines and ejected excess fluid from an opening in the Orbiter's fuselage side. The purpose was two-fold; firstly, to ensure that there would not be a release of fluid sufficient to exert a force on the IUS and cause it to wobble; and, secondly, to ensure that errant droplets of water-alcohol didn't contaminate Galileo's delicate scientific instruments.

Of the other modifications implemented to *Atlantis* since the STS-30 mission, the so-called 'flutter buffet' is notable. It features special instrumentation on the vertical tail and on the left and right outboard elevons; ten accelerometers were installed on the vertical tail and one on each of the elevons. These instruments are designed to measure in-flight loads on the Orbiter's structure.

Franklin Chang-Diaz and Ellen Baker would have performed a spacewalk to effect the manual raising of the tilt-table: they were trained in the specific EVA procedures prior to flight.

A malfunction scenario the crew had paid particular attention to in their pre-mission training was one involving the communications links with Galileo; specifically a device called the PI (Payload Interrogator), a deployable antenna on the Orbiter which is used when the IUS is passing data to and fro through the Shuttle system prior to deployment. As things turned out, they were glad they did, because the PI didn't lock up in its extended position for a while. Shannon Lucid: "When I'd asked our main trainer, pre-flight, what he thought was the most likely thing to go wrong if anything did happen, that was what he predicted. He told us just to hold tight — not to dash off and do anything — because there's a history of the PI not locking-up, but then it would lock up after a period of time.

"Of course, that's just what it did."

Prior to deployment, if anything had gone seriously wrong, the STS-34 crew could have brought the Galileo/IUS combo back to Earth. Once it left *Atlantis's* cargo bay, however, there was nothing they could have done to retrieve it, so it was imperative that pre-deployment checkouts were totally thorough.

Final Checks

Leading the deployment effort were Shannon Lucid and Ellen Baker, and their initial activities were focussed on the various control panels and displays located on the aft flightdeck, adjacent to the windows which overlook the payload bay. After extracting the appropriate checklists, Shannon and Ellen spent their time carefully checking the configuration of the switches and sending a couple of test commands to the two-stage IUS, then watching on the closed-circuit TV system monitor as the upper stage's aft nozzle moved in response.

Then they configured the switches to send further commands, this time to verify telemetry links, before taking a break for lunch.

About an hour prior to deployment, a final round of checks were initiated and Lucid commanded the IUS tilt-table to elevate to 29 degrees, while Ellen Baker

(Below:) **The spent External Tank tumbles toward the Earth's atmosphere less than ten minutes into flight.**

monitored the data-flow from her position on the starboard side of the aft flightdeck area. Ground controllers, after confirming the integrity of telemetry links, then issued a *"Go"* for deploy. At this point, umbilicals connecting the IUS/Galileo stack to *Atlantis* were released and the tilt-table was raised to 58 degrees.

One significant difference between this and previous IUS deployments was the 'RTG purge' operation conducted when the payload stack had been raised into the release position (this is detailed in a separate panel, which also outlines the modifications made to Orbiter *Atlantis* to support this and future planetary spacecraft deployments). "With all that taken care of, we just had to wait for the deploy time, and then we deployed it," said Shannon.

Deployment took place on the ascending node of *Atlantis's* sixth orbit. Shannon described at length the complex inter-relationship between *Atlantis's* launch window constraints at KSC and the Galileo launch window constraints up in low-Earth orbit, then hinted intriguingly that — had the deployment been delayed for any reason — there was considerably more leeway built into that particular window than mission planners were prepared to officially state...

I pressed Shannon as to how far past the formal close of the deployment window they might have ventured. She laughed, "Well, I'm not just real sure! I never could pin anybody down. I know, on one simulation, they were willing to go out 20 minutes after the deploy window. They just wanted to get it going."

As the Galileo/IUS combination drifted serenely clear, Commander Don Williams

(Bottom:) **The Galileo/IUS combination, tilted in its cradle, moments before departure from** *Atlantis's* **payload bay.**

(Below:) **The Southern Lights, or** *Aurora Australis,* **photographed by an STS-34 crewmember.**

slowly backed *Atlantis* away with the RCS thrusters, then he and Pilot Mike McCulley worked together to undertake the OMS burn that put a safe distance between the two spacecraft prior to ignition of the IUS's first-stage motor. The IUS burn was triggered by an automatic timer, set into action at the moment of departure from the tilt-table.

During our interview, Shannon Lucid enthused about her role in the next phase of Jovian exploration. "I was just thoroughly happy to be involved with Galileo, and with all the Galileo folks. That's really

a neat project. Some of those people have been working on it for their entire working career. One thing that struck me, when we were raising the Galileo/IUS stack up to 29 degrees: I looked out the window, and they had the words 'Galileo' and 'NASA' inscribed right there at the interface between them. 'Galileo' was in script letters and 'NASA' was in block letters.

"The thought that I had, right at that moment seeing that, was: when you see script letters, it sort of reminds you of romance of adventure, and the block letters remind you of pure practicality. So

I thought, this is just a perfect example of a marriage of romance and adventure and practicality — the romance and adventure of going out to Jupiter, and the practicality of NASA putting it together and getting it to this point."

Don Williams was also well pleased with the Galileo deployment. "I couldn't be happier with the way it went, particularly the performance of Shannon and Ellen. Mike kept us pointed in the right direction, Franklin handled the cameras, and I kinda kept things going together.

"As the spacecraft left the payload bay, I think I also perhaps breathed a sigh of relief, but I also marvelled at the fact that this piece of complex machinery — that was invented and designed by Mankind — was going to travel to another world over the course of the next few years, and here it was leaving the cargo bay of Shuttle *Atlantis*.

"Then there was also the size of the entire stack with the Inertial Upper Stage on the back. It was huge."

Secondary payloads

Throughout the remainder of the mission, the flight crew members engaged in their respective responsibilities to the various secondary payloads. Franklin Chang-Diaz, who — as MS2, or 'Flight Engineer', had sat in the center seat for ascent and entry to assist Williams and McCulley, particularly in the event of malfunctions — now took the leading role in wielding the IMAX motion-picture camera. Needless to say, the highlight of the footage he captured promised to be that which shows Galileo's deployment.

Franklin and Ellen Baker were encumbents of the EV1 and EV2 assignments respectively, trained pre-mission to under-take a contingency EVA in the event of a payload bay door malfunction or an IUS tilt-table failure. Flight rules state that the person assigned to the prime role for an IUS deploy — in this case Shannon Lucid — should remain inside the craft, so it logically fell to Ellen and Franklin to train for spacewalks.

Shannon's secondary payload responsibilities were the Polymer Morphology (PM) experiment, developed by the 3M Corporation, and an ice-crystal experi-

Briefly: Don Williams

Born: Lafayette, Indiana, on 13 February 1942.
Physical description: Brown hair; brown eyes; height 5 feet, 11 inches; weight 155 pounds
Education: Graduated from Otterbein High School, Otterbein, Indiana in 1960; received a of science degree in Mechanical Engineering from Purdue University in 1964.
Family: Married to the former Linda Jo Grubaugh of Sturgis, Michigan. Has two children; Jonathan Edward (born 17 September 1974), and Barbara Jane (born 10 July 1976).
Recreational interests: Enjoys all sports activities. His interests also include running, wood-working and photography.
Organizations: Member of the Society of Experimental Test Pilots.
Special Honors: Awarded 31 Air Medals, two Navy Commendation Medals with Combat V, two Navy Unit Commendations, a Meritorious Unit Commendation, the National Defense Medal, an Armed Forces Expeditionary Medal, the NASA Space Flight Medal, the Vietnam Service Medal (with 4 stars), a Vietnamese Gallantry Cross (with gold star), and the Vietnam Campaign Medal.
Experience: Received his commission through the NROTC program at Purdue University. Completed flight training at Pensacola, Florida; Meridian, Mississippi; and Kingsville, Texas, receiving his wings in May 1966.

After A-4 Skyhawk training, Williams undertook two Vietnam deployments aboard the *USS Enterprise* with Attack Squadron 113. He served as a flight instructor in Attack Squadron 125 at Naval Air Station Lemoore, California for two years and transitioned to A-7 Corsair 2 aircraft. He undertook two additional Vietnam deployments aboard *Enterprise* with CVW-14 staff and Attack Squadron 97, completing a total of 330 combat missions.

In 1973, Williams attended the Armed Forces Staff College. He graduated from the U.S. Naval Test Pilot School at Patuxent River, Maryland in June 1974, and was assigned to the Naval Air Test Center's Carrier Suitability Branch of Flight Test Division there. From August 1976 to June 1977, following reorganization of the Naval Air Test Center, he was head of Carrier Systems Branch, Strike Aircraft Test Directorate. He reported next for A-7 refresher training and was assigned to Attack Squadron 94 when selected by NASA.

Williams has logged over 5,000 hours flying time, which includes over 4,500 hours in jets and 745 carrier landings.
NASA Experience: Williams was selected as an astronaut candidate by NASA in January 1978. In August 1979, he completed the mandatory one-year training and evaluation period, making him eligible for assignment as a pilot on future Space Shuttle flight

crews. Since then he has had various support assignments, including working at the Shuttle Avionics Integration (SAIL) as a test pilot, and at the Kennedy Space Center participating in Orbiter test, checkout, launch and landing operations. From September 1982 through July 1983, he was assigned as the Deputy Manager, Operations Integration for the Shuttle program office at Johnson Space Center, Houston, Texas.

Williams' first space flight took place in April 1985, when he flew as Pilot on the 51-D/*Discovery* mission. The 51-D crew deployed the Anik-C comsat for Telesat of Canada, and the Syncom 4-F3 comsat for the U.S. Navy. A malfunction in Syncom resulted in the first unscheduled spacewalk of the Shuttle program, when Jeff Hoffman and the late David Griggs — ably assisted by RMS arm operator Rhea Sheddon — attempted to activate the satellite.

After 168 hours and 109 orbits of the Earth, *Discovery* landed at Kennedy Space Center on 19 April 1985.

Don Williams resigned from NASA and the Navy on 26 February 1990. On 1 March, he joined the Science Applications International Corporation of Houston as a senior systems engineer. Commenting on this career-change, Williams said: "I reached my goal as a pilot, which was to command a mission. Now it's time to go on to other challenges."

Briefly: Shannon Lucid

Born: 14 January 1943, in Shanghai, China, but considers Bethany, Oklahoma to be her home-town.
Physical description: Brown hair; blue eyes; height 5 feet 9 inches; weight 150 pounds.
Education: Graduated from Bethany High School, Bethany, Oklahoma in 1960. Received a bachelor of science degree in Chemistry from the University of Oklahoma in 1963, and master of science and doctor of

philosophy degrees in Biochemistry from the University of Oklahoma in 1970 and 1973 respectively.
Family: Married to Michael F. Lucid of Indianapolis, Indiana. Has three children; Kawai Dawn (born 19 September 1968), Shandara Michelle (born 13 January 1970), and Michael Kermit (born 22 August 1975).
Recreational interests: Enjoys flying, camping hiking and reading.
Experience: Dr. Lucid's experience includes a variety of academic assignments, such as teaching assistant at the University of Oklahoma's Department of Chemistry from 1963-64; senior laboratory technican at the Oklahoma Medical Research Foundation from 1964-66; chemist at Kerr-McGee, Oklahoma City, Oklahoma from 1966-68; graduate assistant at the University of Oklahoma Heath Science Center's Department of Biochemistry and Molecular biology from 1969-73; and research associate with the Oklahoma Medical Research Foundation in Oklahoma City from 1974 until her selection to NASA's astronaut candidate training program.

Dr. Lucid is qualified as a commercial, instrument and multi-engine pilot.
NASA experience: Dr. Lucid was selected as an astronaut candidate by NASA in January 1978. In August 1979, she completed a one-year training and evaluation period, making her eligible for assignment as a Mission Specialist on future Space Shuttle flight crews. Some of her technical assignments have included; the Shuttle Avionics Integration Laboratory (SAIL), the Flight Software Laboratory in Downey, California, working with the rendezvous and proximity operations group; and Astronaut Office interface at Kennedy Space Center, Florida, participating in payload testing, Shuttle testing, and launch countdowns.

Dr. Lucid flew as a Mission Specialist on the seven-day 51-G/*Discovery* flight, which launched from KSC on 17 June 1985. The 51-G crew, which included Frenchman Patrick Baudry and Prince Salman Al-Saud of Saudi Arabia, launched three comsats — Morelos-A, Arabsat-1B and Telstar-3D — and deployed and later retrieved the Spartan-1 free-flyer, which performed 17 hours of X-ray astronomy while separated from the Shuttle.

Discovery landed at Edwards Air Force Base, California on 24 June 1985.

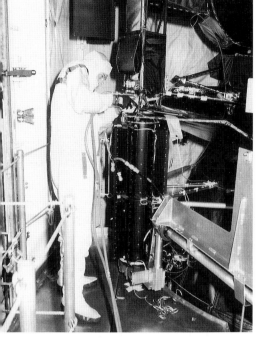

(Below:) **Galileo's RTG nuclear powerplants were the cause of much controversy.**

ment proposed by a young student named Tracy Peters, formerly of Ygnacio High School, Concord, California. We'll look at each of them in turn, briefly — the latter, through the words of Commander Don Williams, who was Shannon's backup on this experiment.

Designed to explore the effects of microgravity on polymeric materials as they are processed in space, 3M's Polymer Morphology payload was operated via a small, NASA-supplied laptop computer that served as an input and output device for the experiment's main computer. Polyethelyne, nylon-6 and various polymer blends were the materials selected for processing on this, the first space flight opportunity for the PM apparatus.

Young Tracy Peters' student experiment was directed at a fascinating realm of research: one based on the fact that liquid water has been discovered at

FOR THE RECORD

- 128th manned spaceflight.
- 61th U.S. manned spaceflight.
- 30th Space Shuttle mission.
- 5th mission by Orbiter _Atlantis_.
- Galileo became the second planetary spacecraft to be deployed by a manned spacecraft.
- Chang-Diaz, Lucid and Williams became joint 99th persons, and joint 59th Americans, to make two space flights.
- Baker and McCulley became joint 219th persons, and joint 130th Americans, in space.

temperatures far below water's freezing point. In the event, the experiment posed a few problems, as Don explained: "The ice-crystal experiment turned out to be a little more complex than we originally thought, when it didn't work initially and we had to troubleshoot it with some procedures from the ground and then really start it over and bypass some of the automatic controls that had been built into it."

Another significant secondary experiment being carried on STS-34 was the Shuttle Solar Backscatter Ultraviolet Instrument, or SSBUV, developed by NASA's Goddard Space Flight Center in Greenbelt, Maryland and housed in two 'Getaway Special' canisters in _Atlantis's_ payload bay. SSBUV — which was another of Franklin Chang-Diaz's responsibilities, though Don Williams backed him up — was designed to calibrate similar ozone-measuring instruments currently in orbit aboard the National Oceanic and Atmospheric Administration's NOAA-9 and NOAA-11 Tiros-series geosynchronous satellites.

Global concern over the depletion of the ozone-layer has sparked increased emphasis on developing and improving ozone-measurement methods and instruments. The SSBUV measures the amount and height distribution of ozone in the upper-atmosphere. Some 17 times a day, _Atlantis_ and the two Tiros satellites passed over the same point on the Earth within a one-hour 'window'. Data from identical instruments aboard both spacecraft was gathered at those times for calibration.

Because ozone absorbs in the ultraviolet, an ozone measurement can be derived from the ratio of backscatter radiation at different wavelengths, providing an index of the vertical distribution of ozone in the Earth's atmosphere.

Ellen Baker had two secondary payloads to take care of during STS-34. One was dedicated to studies of growth hormone concentrations and distribution in plants (in this case, corn seeds which were kept in total darkness throughout the mission), the other to lightning studies. The latter is known as the Mesoscale Lightning Experiment (MLE), and it builds on data gathered in recent years by NASA, using not only the Space Shuttle, but also high-flying Lockheed U-2 airplanes, to observe lightning characteristics above convective storms.

RE-ENTRY & LANDING

Atlantis's re-entry sequence differed from that planned, due to the fact that it was two Earth revolutions (about three hours) early to avoid forecast weather constraints at the Edwards, California landing site. As a result, the Orbiter flew a different entry

Meteorological matters

WEATHER WAS an important factor in the STS-34 mission, both at launch and landing. The original forecast for the 17 October launch attempt was for generally good weather. In the event, however, there were rain-showers within 20 miles of the launch site — which was a violation of flight rules. During the course of the morning, the forecast was amended to thunder-storms within 20 miles, resulting in a scrub.

NOAA's Steve Sokol, a key figure in the weather team for Shuttle missions, described what led to the decision to scrub that day: "Radar video and aircraft reports gradually increased rain-shower tops to 25,000 (feet), with increasing radar intensities. Therefore, I introduced thunderstorms within 20 miles, which caused the scrub — especially when actual thunder and lightning was reported eight miles west at 17:12 Zulu _(GMT)_: the launch was scheduled for 16:57.

"Anyway, we were near the end of the launch window."

On the following day, things looked more promising: the original forecast was for generally good weather. Later, however, thunderstorms were predicted within 20 miles — a _"No-go"_ violation. Fortunately, on this occasion things went the other way, and NOAA personnel were able to update the forecast, removing the likelihood of thunderstorms.

Steve Sokol: "The rain-showers moved north of the Cape and were disipating due to a strong inversion. Therefore, I updated the forecast to take out the thunderstorms." For the uninitiated, an 'inversion' is when there are warmer temperatures aloft that tend to cap-out the developing storm. They put a lid on it, so to speak.

STS-34's TAL sites were changed several times — between Zaragoza, Moron and Ben Guerir — before officials decided on one at the last minute. Only one TAL needs to be clear of weather violations for lift-off to be approved. Sokol: "They were all marginal that day. Zaragoza had carried rain-showers and thunderstorms as close as 18 miles northwest on the radar. The aircraft reported it wasn't really a significant rain shower, however."

Ben Guerir was initially selected as the prime TAL site. Increasing cloud-cover had been noted on satellite images of the area, and aircraft despatched confirmed the presence of some rain-showers, but then they cleared. Later, though, personnel at Ben Guerir reported rain-showers (based on an aircraft report), and Zaragoza was selected as the prime TAL site five minutes before launch.

Then there was a further switch! Aircraft reported new showers and Zaragoza's status was amended to _"No-go,"_ so Ben Guerir — where things had miraculously improved — was reselected as the prime TAL site during flight, after _Atlantis_ had been actually launched.

Moron was generally _"No-go"_ throughout; occasionally due to forecast rain-showers (which didn't materialize), but they had some haze in the area, too. Visibility was 4½ miles, against the manatory five miles. Edwards had an extremely rare fog on the morning _Atlantis_ was due to return — two orbits early, to beat forecast crosswinds. The visibility varied from one-sixteenth of a mile to seven miles in a very short timeframe just prior to the deorbit burn; within ten minutes. It only reached the required fives miles within the final ten minutes before deorbit burn.

United States

(Top) Seen from orbit, Lake Mead behind Hoover Dam — visible as a white speck at left. The Colorado River flows in from right-center, into Lake Mead and out of frame at bottom left center.

(Above) Triumphant STS-34 crewmembers pose with NASA officials after the landing at Edwards. Left to right; Don Puddy, chief of flight crew operations, Mike McCulley, Don Williams, Ellen Baker, Franklin Chang-Diaz, Shannon Lucid, Bill Lenoir, Acting Associate Administrator for Space Flight, and Dick Truly, NASA Administrator.

"It was a beautiful day coming across the California coast. We were in a little bit of a left bank, and then rolled the wings level just as we crossed the coastline. I looked up the San Joaquin Valley, where I used to fly as a Navy pilot, and could see all the way from Los Angeles to San Francisco as we descened through 105,000 feet or so there." Here, Don's referring to his days at Naval Air Station Lemoore, 30 miles south of Fresno, where he started out flying A-4 Skyhawks, then graduated to A-7 Corsair 2s — though most of his operational flying was done from aircraft-carriers.

"When we went subsonic I took control of the spacecraft to see what it was going to fly like, since I had never flown it before. I was pleased to learn that it felt exactly like the Shuttle Training Aircraft, perhaps even a little crisper than the STA. It was very responsive — it did exactly what I wanted it to when I moved the hand controller or the rudder pedals.

"The thing that impressed me that I perhaps wasn't quite ready for, and I probably should have been had I thought about it, is when you're flying the Shuttle Training Aircraft or the simulator — but in particular the Shuttle Training Aircraft — obviously, you have to run the engines on that airplane and there's a great deal of aerodynamic noise and engine noise. The Orbiter is very quiet: in fact, it has almost no sound at all. As we flew around the Heading Alignment Circle subsonic, and down the outer glideslope, and then through the pre-flare and the final flare maneuver to the touchdown, it was almost like it was a simulator with the sound system turned off.

"It felt the same, it looked the same, but it sounded different."

Veteran flyer Williams was generally very pleased with his touchdown, though during our lengthy discussion he offered, "I initially thought we were a little fast". He wasn't, however, because the targeted-for airspeed was 195 knots, and that's exactly what he achieved.

Nosewheel test

A tiny idiosyncrasy made its presence felt as the main gears contacted the dry-lakebed surface. "As we touched down" Don says, "Franklin called that we did not have the 'weight-on-wheels' signal, which changes the flight control gains from the flight to the rollout gains, and that effects the pitch-down. But within a couple of seconds, I think the struts compressed and made the switches, and Franklin made the call that we did have the 'weight-on-wheels' signal."

As *Atlantis* derotated, Mike McCulley called out the airspeeds, then with the nose-gear firmly in contact with the runway, Don performed a pre-planned nosewheel

profile, and had to make up nearly 500 nautical miles of crossrange, as opposed to making up about 25 had it flown a nominal entry profile.

When a Shuttle Orbiter re-enters, it performs a series of 'roll-reversals' under computer guidance, slipping back and forth across the mean ground-track line in order to use up its downrange energy and target for the landing site. Don Williams: "Because we came in earlier, the roll-reversals were at different places. In this particular case, this meant a great deal of time in a left bank — practically from entry interface on down to Mach 13½.

"What's up Doc?"

MEDICAL consultations between astronauts in space and NASA physicians on earth were renewed on the STS-34/*Atlantis* flight, and were to be a feature of all future Shuttle missions. The intention is to help improve the understanding, and provide timely treatment of, initial space motion-sickness symptoms.

A private medical communication (PMC) is now scheduled between Shuttle crew members and Flight Surgeons in the Mission Control Center at Houston during pre-sleep periods on the first two days of each flight: astronauts usually overcome any symptoms of space-sickness after the first couple of days.

Additionally, consultations may be requested by either the crew or the Flight Surgeons.

Discussing the renewal of PMCs, Dr Jeff Davis, chief of the Johnson Space Center's Medical Operations Branch, said: "While symptoms vary from one person to another, most cases are mild and constitute little more than an inconvenience to the crew member. Given the variation in symptoms and available treatments, we felt it would be useful to plan routine consultations for the first two days of each mission."

NASA said the consultations will be confidential because of the physician-patient relationship and privacy laws. If a crew health problems affects a mission adversely, the Flight Surgeon will prepare a statement for public release which addresses the nature, gravity and prognosis of the situation. Information beyond that required to understand the impact on the mission will not be released.

Astronauts with a professional background in medicine have flown on many Shuttle missions. On STS-34, for example, there was Ellen Baker. In addition to her responsibilities toward the Galileo deployment, Ellen — as with other medical doctors who fly on Shuttle missions — took the lead role on the so-called DSOs, or Detailed Supplementary Objectives: the medical tests that are conducted on Shuttle travellers to gather data on all aspects of human physiology in weightlessness (muscle responses, blood pressure, cardiovascular functioning, etc).

Interestingly, Ellen started her career with NASA not as an astronaut, but as a medical officer: back in 1981. In that capacity, she manned the Surgeon's console in Mission Control during several Shuttle flights, before being selected as a spacefarer herself as part of the agency's Group 10 intake.

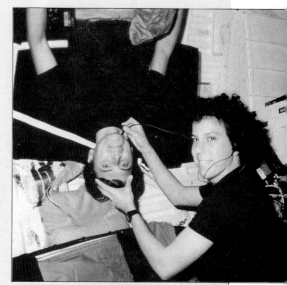

(Above.) **Mission Specialist Ellen Baker, a medical doctor, monitors the blood flow of fellow MS Franklin Chang-Diaz.**

steering test; veering off to the left at about 140 knots, then holding a parallel course to the runway centerline, about 40 feet away from it, steering back to the runway centerline at about 100 knots or so, then establishing *Atlantis* back on the centerline before starting braking.

Don again: "We didn't start braking until about 80 knots or so, I guess, which is perhaps a little slow, and so the rollout ended up being a little longer than it would have had we tried to stop it on a short runway. But it was 10,000-and-some number of feet, which is a reasonable amount, I think. The runway is almost an unlimited length. I wasn't too worried about that."

This exercise was a test of the most recent set of changes made to the functioning of the Shuttle's nosewheel steering system; part of an ongoing improvement effort. In between the Commander's input and the actual deflection of the nosewheels lies a great deal of electronic interplay. The intention of this latest series of tests was to verify that, if the Commander needs to make a nosewheel steering input at a rather high speed because of a control problem — a crosswind, a below-pressure tyre, or even a blown-out tyre — that the Orbiter would still be controllable at those kinds of speeds.

Accelerometers measured the nosewheel steering system's response during STS-34's runway rollout, and engineering teams subsequently analysed the resulting data to see how these latest modifications worked 'under pressure'.

Don's overall impression of STS-34 indicated that the Shuttle program, now well-established in its post-recovery phase, was set in high-competence mode: "The spacecraft performed just magnificently. We had very few systems problems. It was a very clean spacecraft, both inside and outside, and that's a real tribute to the teams down in Florida who prepare these vehicles for launch, and also to the folks who can actually build a machine as complex as this and have it operate in such an outstanding manner, with very few anomalies."

Shannon Lucid, too, was delighted with the outcome of STS-34 — and also a little relieved: "Ellen and I were just so happy to see Galileo go out of the payload bay. We both made the comment that happiness was an empty payload bay at that point! It just gives you a really good feeling when you work toward a goal and then see it accomplished in such a great manner."

N.M.

Stop that Shuttle!

THE OCTOBER launch of *Atlantis* and her nuclear-powered payload, Galileo, encountered the strongest opposition to any Space Shuttle mission yet, and although Galileo made it safely into space, protest groups said they'll continue to fight against NASA's plans to launch other nuclear-powered spacecraft.

The source of the controversy lay within Galileo's two plutonium-fueled electric generators, called RTGs (Radioisotope Thermoelectric Generators). Opponents to the launch of STS-34/*Atlantis* claimed a *Challenger*-type accident involving Galileo could spread radioactive contamination across Florida, resulting in thousands of cancer-related deaths. They also worried about the potential danger of accidental re-entry as Galileo swings by Earth twice more on its way to Jupiter along the Delta-VEEGA trajectory (see *Planetary Missions*).

The protesters, made up of enviromentalists, anti-nuclear groups, peace activists, scientists and movie stars, fought to get the Galileo mission postponed until safer power systems could be developed. They backed their demands with court actions, media blitzes and attempts to physically block the launch.

Federal court Judge Gasch refused the groups' bid for an injunction to stop the mission, agreeing with NASA lawyers that the Agency had followed all the proper steps and complied with environment regulations. Judge Gasch went on to say that, "There is no evidence that anyone has ever been injured by plutonium leaking from a satellite."

A subsequent appeal was also rejected, clearing the way for the launch of *Atlantis.*

Throughout the altercation, NASA and the U.S. Department of Energy (which was responsible for delivering the nuclear power system to the Cape) had stood by the safety record of the RTGs, citing their safe use on 22 missions over 28 years. NASA admits to three accidents involving RTGs, but claims that in each case the generators performed as designed and no injuries resulted.

The first such accident occured in 1964, when a U.S. Navy weather satellite (Transit 5BN) failed to achieve polar orbit and burned-up over the Indian Ocean. At the time, RTG design criteria called for the unit, to disperse its fuel in the event of accidental re-entry, which it did. Scientists from the Atomic Energy Commission measured radioactivity in air and soil samples and estimated that 17,000 curies of radioactive material were released as the satellite burned up at an altitude of 75 miles.

Since 1964, RTGs have been designed to contain all of their plutonium-238 fuel. The effectiveness of this approach was tested in two subsequent accidents, one involving a mission abort (Nimbus B1 in 1968), the other involving an Earth re-entry (Apollo 13 in 1970). On both occasions, the RTGs performed according to design requirements and released no plutonium.

The Soviet Union has been less successful with its nuclear-powered spacecraft, experiencing two accidents involving RTGs and at least three incidents involving space nuclear-reactors. The RTG accidents occured on failed lunar missions which burned up in the atmosphere and released radioactivity over the Earth. Soviet incidents of accidental re-entry of nuclear reactors involved Cosmos-series Radar Ocean Reconnaissance Satellites (referred to as RORSATS by Western analysts).

The most damaging of these accidents occured in 1978, when Cosmos 954 failed to boost into its planned *"nuclear-safe"* storage orbit. Parts of the craft survived re-entry and spread nuclear material over 40,000 square kilometers of Canada's Northwest Territories. No injuries were reported in this remote region of the country, and since the clean-up operation was completed by the governments of Canada and the United States, no detectable contamination has been found.

NASA officials point to the successful use of RTGs on the Apollo Moon missions, Viking Mars Landers, and on the Pioneer and Voyager spacecraft, as proof of the system's safety, reliability and value in powering craft dedicated to the exploration of space. RTGs are now used only on deep-space missions (200 million miles beyond Earth) or planetary science platforms (ALSEPs on the Moon; Vikings on Mars). In addition, NASA claims no other power source offers the low weight, long life and high reliability that these missions demand.

Anti-nuclear activists are not impressed. Some claim NASA is conspiring with the nuclear power industry and the Departments of Defense and Energy to promote the use of nuclear power in space. At a pre-launch press conference staged at Kennedy Space Center, this allegation was launched by Bruce Gagnon, leader of the Florida protest group that tried to stop Galileo. "It's no coincidence that General Electric, the manufacturer of the generators on Galileo, is also the largest recipient of 'Star Wars' research and development dollars in the nation. We believe that Galileo is an icebreaker, that it's part of a national program to get the American public and government used to the idea of putting nuclear power in space.

"We think that the arms race is now moving towards space with first-strike weapons technologies, and we believe that this otherwise innocuous interplanetary space probe — one that we would not normally protest against — is being used by these forces to get people used to the idea of seeing space militarized."

Mr. Gagnon became a peace activist while serving in the U.S. Air Force and now coordinates the activities of the Florida Coalition for Peace and Justice (FCPJ), a state-wide coalition of 75 different peace groups and church communities in over 40 Florida cities. The FCPJ organized protests involving a few dozen disgruntled Florida residents and anti-nuclear activists from a far away as Canada, Italy and Japan. Protesters staged publicity campaigns, picketed the Kennedy Space Center and vowed to physically block the launch if court actions failed.

The legal battle against Galileo was waged by two Washington-based environmental groups; the Christic Institute (a public interest group funded by religious organizations) and the Foundation on Economic Trends (best known for its litigation over the Three Mile Island nuclear accident).

Even Hollywood got into the protest act, with several movie stars including Dennis Weaver, Morgan Fairchild and Lindsay Wagner, voicing their opposition to the launch. At a Hollywood press conference, Wagner — the former *Bionic Woman* — summed-up the group's stand. "We feel as a public, we have not been treated fairly by NASA... We were never asked if we wanted this *(Galileo's nuclear power system)* as part of the bargain."

Within the scientific community, few experts protested against Galileo's launch, but those who *did* raised serious questions over the practice of launching nuclear payloads near population centers. Richard Cuddihy, an expert on radiation-poisoning and member of a federal panel that reviews space launches involving nuclear power, stated his opposition to the mission in a 5 September memo. "Launching from Florida puts a large number of people at risk. A safer way to launch these types of missions would be from unmanned rockets at remote locations," he said.

Despite the forceful opposition mounted by a variety of groups, Galileo earned the legal, scientific and governmental support to embark on its historic mission. The final go-ahead from a Washington District Court, issued just two days before the originally-planned October 12 launch date, cleared the way for NASA and pushed protesters to their threatened last resort; that of physical intervention against launch procedures.

Security around the Kennedy Space Center was beefed-up with extra patrols, high-tech surveillance systems, low-flying helicopters, night-vision equipment, swat teams, and — as one security offical put it — *"Mama Nature"* (an apparent reference to the Cape's many-thousand resident alligators, mosquitos, snakes and other wildlife). A total of nine protesters were arrested for trespassing in the days leading up to launch. There were some tense moments on Monday 16 October, when the protest vessel *MS Green Peace* penetrated KSC's 27-mile exclusion zone, but tension eased when the ship radioed that it was merely *en route* to Key West.

By launch day, KSC security officials reported no further incidents, and after a one-day weather delay, *Atlantis* went safely into orbit for a successful deploy of Galileo.

Protesters vowed to continue their fight against nuclear-powered space missions, despite NASA's respectable RTG-powered mission record. Their attention was then centered on the next big interplanetary goal; the launch of the solar polar probe Ulysses in October 1990. Beyond that, they plan on targeting NASA's next-generation nuclear-powered spacecraft: the SP-100s. As Gagnon put it, "We're going to stay on this for some time."

M.W.

STATISTICAL ANALYSIS: STS-34/ ATLANTIS

Crew:
Don Williams (Commander)
Mike McCulley (Pilot)
Shannon Lucid (MS1)
Franklin Chang-Diaz (MS2/EV1)
Ellen Baker (MS3/EV2)

Orbiter: *Atlantis* (OV-104)
(Prior missions — 4; 51-J, 61-B, STS-27, STS-30)

External Tank: ET-27
(Splashdown zone: Latitude 3.41 degrees north/Longitude 147.60 degrees west — Pacific Ocean,138 miles southeast of Hawaii)

SSME Position 1: Engine 2027
(Prior total firing time: 1,806 seconds: prior missions — 2; STS-27/*Atlantis*, STS-30/*Atlantis*)

SSME Position 2: Engine 2030
(Prior total firing time: 1,857 seconds: prior missions — 2; STS-27/*Atlantis*, STS-30/*Atlantis*)

SSME Position 3: Engine 2029
(Prior total firing time: 1,809 seconds: prior missions — 2; STS-27/*Atlantis*, STS-30/*Atlantis*)

Forward RCS: FRC-4
(Prior missions — 4; 51-J/*Atlantis*, 61-B/*Atlantis*, STS-27/*Atlantis*, STS-30/*Atlantis*)

Port OMS: LP-01
(Prior missions — 10; STS-6/*Challenger*, STS-7/*Challenger*, STS-8/*Challenger*, 41-B/*Challenger*, 51-B/*Challenger*, 51-F/*Challenger*, 61-A/*Challenger*, STS-27/*Atlantis*, STS-30/*Atlantis*)

Starboard OMS: RP-03
(Prior missions — 9; 41-D/*Discovery*, 51-A/*Discovery*, 51-C/*Discovery*, 51-D/*Discovery*, 51-G/*Discovery*, 51-I/*Discovery*, 61-A/*Challenger*, STS-26/*Discovery*, STS-29/*Discovery*)

Mobile Launcher Platform: MLP-1
(Pad 39B)

SRBs: Flight Set 6

SRB case use history:

Element	Left Booster	Right Booster
F. Dome	QM-7	41-D, 61-A
Cyl.	DM-2, STS-5, 51-A, 61-C, QM-6	DM-4, STS-2, STS-9, 51-I
C.F. Cyl.	QM-6	New
Cyl.	41-B, 51-I, QM-7	51-A, 61-C
C.F. Cyl.	DM-9	QM-7
Cyl.	New	51-A 61-C
C.F. Cyl.	QM-7	New
E.T. Attach	51-J, PVM-1	New
Stiffener	QM-7	61-A, STS-26
Stiffener	61-A, QM-7	61-A, STS-26
Aft Dome	QM-7	DM-3, QM-3, STS-9, 51-I, PVM-1

Launch:
16:53:40 GMT/18 October 1989
Kennedy Space Center, Florida

Landing:
16:34:00 GMT/23 October 1989
Edwards Air Force Base, California

Orbits: 79

Distance:
1,800,000 nautical miles

Mission Elapsed Time:
4 days, 23 hours, 41 minutes, 0 seconds
(119 hrs, 41 mins, 0 secs)

Weight:
Lift-off/4,523,810 pounds
Landing/195,283 pounds

Cargo bay payloads:
Galileo spacecraft to Jupiter
Shuttle Solar Backscatter Ultraviolet (SSBUV)

Middeck payloads:
Growth Hormone Concentration & Distribution in Plants (GHCD)
Mesoscale Lightning Experiment (MLR)
Polymer Morphology (PM)
Sensor Technology Experiment (STEX)

Orbital inclination: 34.3 degrees

Major orbital maneuvers:

Date	Time (GMT)	Perigee (miles)	Apogee (miles)	Period (mins)
18 Oct	17:36	183	189	90.4
19 Oct	02:24	186	206	90.7

no further maneuvers

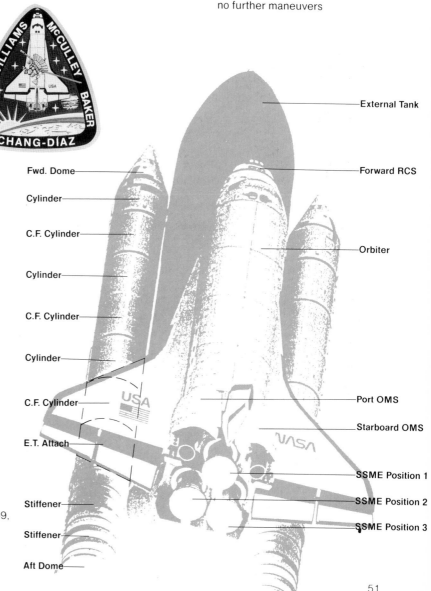

Fwd. Dome
Cylinder
C.F. Cylinder
Cylinder
C.F. Cylinder
Cylinder
C.F. Cylinder
E.T. Attach
Stiffener
Stiffener
Aft Dome

External Tank
Forward RCS
Orbiter
Port OMS
Starboard OMS
SSME Position 1
SSME Position 2
SSME Position 3

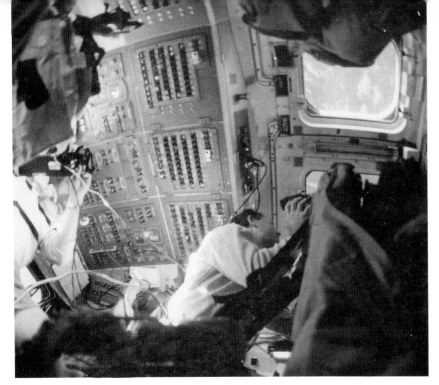

(Left) Intense mid-deck activity is evident in this view from *Discovery*'s 'staircase'. Physicians Story Musgrave *(left)* and Manley Carter are doubling as photographers.

(Below) Carter savors his first taste of space.

DEPARTMENT OF DEFENSE

STS-33 DISCOVERY

At 07:24 Eastern Standard Time on Wednesday 22 November, Shuttle mission STS-33/*Discovery* lifted-off from Kennedy Space Center's Pad 39B to commence what was intended to be four days of activities (it turned out to be five) on behalf of the U.S. Department of Defense. This was the first night-time launch in the renewed flight program: the last time a Shuttle lifted-off in darkness was at the start of mission 61-C/*Columbia* in January 1986, shortly before the *Challenger* disaster. It was indicative of NASA management's steady regaining of confidence in the reusable spacecraft's capabilities.

ployment of its primary payload, details of which have been kept secret. It is known to have been a 5,985-pound military signal-intelligence (SIGINT) satellite mounted atop a Boeing-built IUS upper stage. The SIGINT is capable of eavesdropping on voice, telemetry, and other transmissions from Soviet and Chinese military and diplomatic sources. It is under the control of the National Security Agency, having been set free from *Discovery*'s payload bay on the seventh orbit.

An identical satellite was launched on the first Department of Defense Shuttle mission, 51-C/*Discovery*, in January 1985.

U.S. Air Force Colonel Fred Gregory served as STS-33 Commander. His Pilot was USAF Colonel John Blaha. Both were making their second space flights: Blaha replaced David Griggs, who was killed in the crash of a vintage airplane he was flying on 17 June. Mission Specialists on STS-33 were U.S. Navy Captain Manley Carter, and civilians Story Musgrave and Kathy Thornton. Musgrave served as MS2, or 'Flight Engineer'. Carter and Thornton were 'space rookies', Musgrave a veteran of two previous missions.

Manley Carter and Story Musgrave are physicians. This indicated that on-board experimentation subsequent to the SIGINT's deployment had a particular bias toward studies of human physiology in weightlessness. Notably, Kathy Thornton is a nuclear physicist by profession, confirming rumors that experimentation related to the SDI 'Star Wars' research program was being undertaken.

Due to the military nature of the activities conducted aloft, we were unable to conduct our usual post-mission

LAUNCH

STS-33's launch window was 70 minutes long, and the countdown proceeded with only the most minor of glitches: a 90-second hold at T-5 minutes, while a manual pressure adjustment was made to the aft-fuselage purge circuits. The launch and RTLS weather were excellent, with the only concern being crosswinds in excess of ten knots for the night RTLS at KSC. TAL weather was acceptable, even though it looked out-of-limits earlier in the day.

Discovery was lofted into a 110 x 280-nautical-mile orbit inclined at 28.45 degrees. The altitudes reached during this mission were far higher than average for the Shuttle.

ON-ORBIT

Three firings of the Orbital Maneuvering System (OMS) engines positioned *Discovery* in the correct orbit for de-

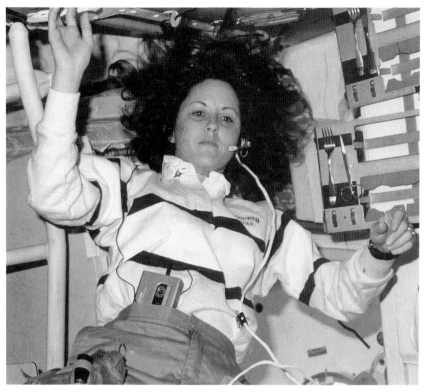

interviews with members of the flight crew. There had been renewed debate as to whether such all-enveloping security restrictions are necessary for military Shuttle missions, particularly in view of recent developments within the Eastern Bloc, which had in turn taken place against the background of a general relaxation in East-West tensions.

NASA officials *were* permitted to reveal some details of the STS-33 flight crew's training activities prior to the mission, though none of these pertained to the SIGINT deployment. During the month prior to launch, Fred Gregory and John Blaha completed their approach and landing training requirements by flying numerous simulated Orbiter landings in the Shuttle Training Aircraft (STA), a heavily-modified Grumman Gulfstream 2 executive jet which mimics the spacecraft's low lift-over-drag descent profile and handling characteristics.

STA flights took place from the Shuttle Landing Facility (SLF) at Kennedy Space Center, at White Sands Space Harbor, New Mexico and at Edwards AFB, California.

During the final two weeks prior to flight, Gregory and Blaha piloted an Air National Guard Boeing KC-135 airplane to enhance their proficiency in handling larger flying machines (the Shuttle Orbiter weighs 100 tons). Normally NASA's NKC-135 'Vomit Comet' is employed for this purpose, but the aircraft was undergoing maintenance at its Ellington Field, Houston base at the time the STS-33 crew would have required it.

RE-ENTRY & LANDING

While *Discovery* was in space, the only weather concerns were tropical storms at the emergency landing site at Guam, and rain-showers, low cloud-ceilings and crosswinds at Ben Guerir. Mission controllers were briefed accordingly by NOAA personnel.

The mission was planned to land on Sunday 26th, but the winds at Edwards were gusting to 35 knots at payload bay door closing time and forecast to be out-of-limits at deorbit time and at touchdown time. Consequently, the decision was made to wave-off until Monday. Even then, allowance had to be made for the prevailing wind conditions. Thirty-five minutes after the deorbit burn was completed, a decision was taken to target for hard-surface Runway 04, not dry lakebed Runway 17 as originally planned. Due to the high orbital altitude *Discovery* maintained during this mission, it took about 20 minutes longer to re-enter the Earth's atmosphere following the deorbit burn.

N.M.

(Below) **From this angle, late-afternoon lighting effects make STS-33's landing look like it took place at night.**

A primer on emergency landing options

EMERGENCY landing sites are identified across the globe and are available to the Shuttle during climbout from Kennedy Space Center (KSC). These are all existing airports characterized by 15,000-foot-plus runways with wide shoulders and located in favorable geographical positions, but in some cases they have been furnished with upgraded facilities to support an incoming Orbiter.

As the *Challenger* accident so vividly demonstrated, nothing can be done to help the crew during the first two minutes of flight, when the twin solid rocket boosters (SRBs) are firing. The range of contingencies come into effect after the SRBs have expended their supplies of propellant, and begin with the Return To Launch Site (RTLS) option. This contingency envisions a computer-controlled 'turnover' maneuver under the power of the remaining SSMEs, premature jettisoning of the giant External Tank, and a gliding approach to the Shuttle Landing Facility (SLF) at KSC.

If one of the three SSME main engines fails soon after the RTLS threshold has been passed, the Shuttle can reach one of the four Transatlantic Abort Landing (TAL) sites; Ben Guerir in Morocco, Banjul in The Gambia, and Zarogoza and Moron (pronounce it *Morone*) in Spain.

In addition to the TAL sites, there are a number of designated Downrange Abort Sites. One is Hoedspruit Air Base in South Africa, another is Roberts Field in Liberia, another is Kinshasa N'Djili in Zaire. If the Shuttle has reached a higher point in its ascent at the moment of an SSME failure, a Downrange Abort Site is available as far afield as RAAF Amberley in Australia.

Assuming an even higher altitude has been reached at the time trouble strikes, the next available emergency landing option is an Abort Once Around (AOA). This would result in a landing at either White Sands Space Harbor, New Mexico, or the prime landing site at Edwards Air Force Base, California.

Not all of the emergency landing sites are in line for a given Shuttle ascent, but there are always enough of them available close to the line of travel, and with suitable weather conditions prevailing, to allow the Orbiter to coast in to a landing. The abort-landing procedure works on a 'pass-one-go-on-to-the-next' basis. The Downrange Abort Sites, for example, lie in what might term 'a thin gray area' of options and are only available for a few short seconds during the ascent, between the TAL and AOA options.

Once the ascending Shuttle has passed the AOA threshold, the final option available is Abort To Orbit (ATO), where the vehicle 'claws' its way to a lower-than-usual orbit. In some respects, ATO isn't an abort in the true sense of the word, in that the Shuttle is able to continue its mission, albeit with some restrictions to payload activities.

ATO is currently the only Shuttle abort option to have been employed in flight. During ascent of the 51-/*Challenger*/Spacelab 2 stack on 29 July 1985, one SSME had to be shut down as a precautionary measure following a sensor failure. A 173-nautical-mile orbit was established, and the mission ran to its intended duration of nearly eight days. The astronomers on board would have preferred the planned 200-nautical-mile orbit to ensure optimum viewing conditions, of course, but at least they were able to undertake their mission.

It is worth relating that the sites mentioned above are but a small fraction of the total options available once the Shuttle is established in orbit. There are about 40 designated emergency landing sites scattered across the globe, all capable of mounting the minimum crew rescue and fire-suppression effort. NASA accepts that, since all but a few of these sites are equipped with the special facilities demanded by the Orbiter in its landing mode, some damage might by sustained to spacecraft systems. For example, the avionics might become overheated for want of proper cooling.

That would be a small price to pay to get the Orbiter and her crew safely back to Earth in the type of dire situation that would warrant an emergency landing.

(Above) **Story Musgrave was making his third space voyage.**

FOR THE RECORD
- 132nd manned spaceflight.
- 64th U.S. manned spaceflight.
- 33rd Shuttle space mission.
- 6th mission by Orbiter *Atlantis*.
- Hilmers and Mullane became joint 41st persons, and joint 22nd Americans, to make three space flights.
- Creighton became 106th person, and 65th American, to make two space flights.
- Casper and Thuot became joint 227th persons, and joint 137th Americans, in space.

STATISTICAL ANALYSIS: STS-33/ DISCOVERY

Crew:
Fred Gregory (Commander)
John Blaha (Pilot)
Manley Carter (MS1/EV1)
Story Musgrave (MS2)
Kathryn Thornton (MS3/EV2)

Orbiter: *Discovery* (OV-103)
(Prior missions — 8; 41-D, 51-A, 51-C, 51-D, 51-G, 51-I, STS-26, STS-29)

External Tank: ET-38
(Splashdown zone: Latitude 28.56 degrees south/Longitude 86.42 degrees east — Indian Ocean, 1,140 miles southeast of the Cocos slands)

SSME Position 1: Engine 2011
(Prior total firing time: 4,767 seconds: prior missions — 3; STS-9/*Columbia,* 51-J/*Atlantis,* 61-B/*Atlantis*)

SSME Position 2: Engine 2031
(Prior total firing time: 1,630 seconds: prior missions — 1; STS-29/*Discovery*)

SSME Position 3: Engine 2107
(Prior total firing time: 1,528 seconds: prior missions — nil)

Forward RCS: FRC-3
(Prior missions — 8; 41-D/*Discovery,* 51-A/*Discovery,* 51-C/*Discovery,* 51-D/*Discovery,* 51-G/*Discovery,* 51-I/*Discovery,* STS-26/*Discovery,* STS-29/*Discovery*)

Port OMS: LP-04
(Prior missions — 5; 51-G/*Discovery,* 51-I/*Discovery,* 61-C/Columbia, STS-26/*Discovery,* STS-29/*Discovery*)

Starboard OMS: RP-01
(Prior missions — 10; STS-6/*Challenger,* STS-7/*Challenger,* STS-8/*Challenger,* 41-B/*Challenger,* 41-C/*Challenger,* 41-G/*Challenger,* 51-J/*Atlantis,* 61-B/*Atlantis,* STS-27/*Atlantis,* STS-30/*Atlantis*)

Mobile Launcher Platform: MLP-2
(Pad 39B)

SRBs: Flight Set 7

SRB case use history:

Element	Left Booster	Right Booster
F. Dome	61-C, PVM-1	STS-26
Cyl.	DM-3, QM-3, STS-5, 41-D, 61-A	DM-4, STS-5, 51-J, QM-7
C.F. Cyl.	New	QM-7
Cyl.	51-A, 61-C	51-F
C.F. Cyl.	New	New
Cyl.	51-F	61-B
C.F. Cyl.	New	New
ET Attach	STS-26	STS-26
Stiffener	New	51-I, TEM-1
Stiffener	STS-26	51-I, TEM-1
Aft Dome	STS-26	STS-2, 41-B, DM-7

Launch:
00:23:30 am GMT/23 November 1989
Kennedy Space Center, Florida

Landing:
00:31:32 am GMT/28 November 1989
Edwards Air Force Base, California

Orbits: 78

Distance:
1,808,246 nautical miles

Mission Elapsed Time:
5 days, 0 hours, 7 minutes, 32 seconds
(125 hrs, 7 mins, 32 secs)

Weights:
Take-off/Classified
Landing/Classified

Cargo bay payloads: Classified

Middle deck payloads: Classified

Orbital inclination: 28.5 degrees

Major orbital maneuvers:

Date	Time (GMT)	Perigee (miles)	Apogee (miles)	Period (minutes)
23 Nov	01:00	126	131	88.4
	04:50	129	333	91.8
	06:23	129	345	92.0
	09:54	147	347	92.3
	no further maneuvers			

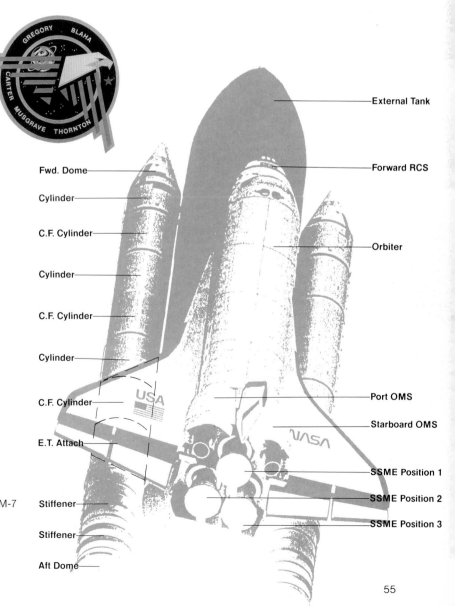

Fwd. Dome
Cylinder
C.F. Cylinder
Cylinder
C.F. Cylinder
Cylinder
C.F. Cylinder
E.T. Attach
Stiffener
Stiffener
Aft Dome

External Tank
Forward RCS
Orbiter
Port OMS
Starboard OMS
SSME Position 1
SSME Position 2
SSME Position 3

STS-32 COLUMBIA

NASA successfully staged one of the most ambitious Shuttle missions ever with flight STS-32/*Columbia,* which set off from Kennedy Space Center's newly refurbished Pad 39A on Tuesday 9 January to deploy the Syncom 4-F5 communications satellite for the U.S. Navy and to retrieve the LDEF free-flyer deployed in low-Earth by the Shuttle *Challenger* during the 41-C mission in April 1984. A NASA/Langley payload, LDEF — the Long Duration Exposure Facility — was designed to test the responses of a wide variety of materials to a prolonged period in the harsh space environment. The hiatus in Shuttle flight operations following the *Challenger* accident extended that prolonged period way beyond the planned term: almost to six years...

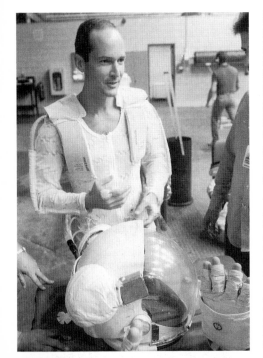

(Top) **Pre-flight: David Low prepares to don an EMU spacesuit for a training session in the WET-F neutral-buoyancy facility at Houston.**

(Above) **Dan's delight! Throughout 17 January, STS-32 Commander Dan Brandenstein was not allowed to forget his 47th birthday. Well, could *you* forget an inflatable birthday cake?**

LAUNCH

STS-32 Commander was Dan Brandenstein, his position as Chief of the Astronaut Office having been temporarily assigned to Mike Coats. Brandenstein flew as pilot on mission STS-8/*Challenger* in August 1983 and Commander of mission 51-G/*Discovery* in June 1985. The experience gained on the first of these flights, in particular, will have proved invaluable to him on STS-32, because STS-8 ended with the first-ever nocturnal landing of the American manned space program, and STS-32's LDEF rendezvous commitment demanded another night-time landing.

It was the such landing of the post-*Challenger* era, and only the third in the entire history of the Shuttle program. Coming so soon after the STS-33/*Discovery* mission's first post-*Challenger* nocturnal lift-off last November, STS-32's night-time landing could be seen as further evidence of NASA's steady regaining of confidence in the reusable spacecraft's capabilities.

Dan Brandenstein's Pilot was Jim Wetherbee, making his first space flight. We interviewed him, and Mission Specialist Bonnie Dunbar, in the course of preparing this report. Two other Mission Specialists participated in STS-32: 'space rookies' Marsha Ivins and David Low. Dunbar, making her second space flight, and Low were assigned the contingency EVA roles: if the Syncom satellite had failed to unlatch automatically prior to deployment, they could have performed a spacewalk to manually unlatch it.

Similarly, if LDEF had failed to latch down into the payload bay following retrieval, Dunbar and Low could have accomplished this manually. They had also trained for the traditional EVA contingencies; failure of the payload bay doors to open, and so forth.

Jim Wetherbee characterizes the STS-32 pre-flight training regime: "Essentially, we had three missions to train for; the Syncom deploy, the rendezvous on the LDEF satellite, and then of course all the experiments that we had on board".

Wetherbee wasn't the only crew member, postflight, to describe this as, "a kind of mini-Spacelab mission".

Wetherbee told the author that he put in about 1,500 hours of simulator time prior to STS-32, working all the malfunction scenarios, as well as routine flight procedures, "In the event, there were very few problems, so I didn't have to exercise much of what I'd learned over the previous year," he mused.

Bonnie Dunbar put in her fair share of simulator time, on top of the 'basic syllabus' all the Mission Specialists undertake. Her primary assignment was as lead astronaut on the LDEF retrieval, so a lot of the emphasis in Bonnie's pre-flight training schedule was placed on RMS arm operations. She reckons she'd put in at least 100 hours of 'flight-specific' RMS training by the time STS-32 blasted off.

Three different facilities were employed in this, each contributing some unique dimension to the training. "There's no way of really modelling the arm in a three-dimensional environment, because the real arm can't even carry its own weight in zero-G. You have to make some compromises," Bonnie told us.

Among the training aids are large balloons sized and shaped to mimic particular payloads. Although they're not high-fidelity representations, they give the astronaut a feeling for size and depth-perception. The latter cannot be adequately modelled in any of the highly-computerized 'scene-generated' simulators. Another thing that's difficult to mimic is the dynamics of the mechanical arm: in particular it's tendency to have some degree of residual motion on stopping.

The arm is fabricated from graphite-epoxy materials and there's a degree of flexibility in it. "We're not talking about something extreme, but it's something that you need to know about," Dunbar told us.

Several technical problems at the pad prior to Christmas had delayed the launch into the New Year, then a countdown attempt on 8 January resulted in a scrub when poor weather conditions developed at the Cape. In our discussions, Jim Wetherbee noted the uncommon calm that day at Pad 39A which, hitherto, had been swarming with personnel implementing finishing touches to a major pad upgrade program.

"When we were driving out there, my first thought was that there weren't a whole lot of people around the launch pad, as there had been when we'd been there on previous occasions *(for countdown simulations and so on — Ed.)*. It was kind of exciting to see that we were really going to get down to do it. We went through the initial countdown, and I could see out my window that it was starting to clear up, so I was convinced that we were going. But of course the weather was coming from the other side of the vehicle, over on Dan's side.

"He could see that it wasn't all that great over where the runway is *(the Shuttle Landing Facility, used for an emergency landing in the event of an aborted ascent)*, and they made the right decision to turn around and try it again the next day. It's a little bit disappointing when you find out you're not going to go, but that passes within a couple of minutes. It gave us an extra day to relax and do a little bit of running."

At the opening of the launch 'window' the weather had been observed "*Go*", but the forecast was "*No-go*": both have to be "*Go*" for the countdown to continue. Sure enough, the weather closed in on the Shuttle Landing Facility (SLF), and remained out-of-limits for the remainder of the 'window'.

On the following day, 9 January, it was a different matter, although an area of low cloud less than 1,000 feet above ground level was observed by the STA over the launch pad and moving inland. This observation temporarily caused the forecast to be "*No-Go*", but at the L minus nine-minute hold, the forecast was updated to "*Go*" and launch took place at 7:35am local time, right on the opening of the launch window. "The thing that pleasantly surprised me," Jim confided, "was that I wasn't thinking of anything except the systems — watching them all to make sure that everything was working correctly as we went on uphill. During the launch, everything was exactly the way I was told it was going to be. The ascent felt the same as what I expected. I saw the same things that everybody told me I was going to see — except for one thing. Just after MECO, when we were up on-orbit and I saw the Moon come up for the first time, it really impressed me.

"I looked at it for about two seconds and it was two seconds I'll never forget as long as I live. The two things that impressed me were how bright it was and how clear it was. It was perfectly in focus and clear

because we didn't have to look through the atmosphere. I have never seen a sight that was that clear. It looked kinda close to me. The Earth, on the other hand, looked kinda far."

Jim was clearly relishing his first experience of space travel; "The thing that impressed me about the Earth was the curvature of the horizon. I thought, when I saw pictures from Earth orbit, that it was a fisheye lens that people were using to make the Earth look so curved — but 200 miles is a long way and I was really surprised at how curved the horizon was. The Earth to me looked pretty small and we looked pretty high."

An S-band communications system failure and some 'sooting' of *Columbia*'s

LDEF post-flight

STS-32 WAS a unique mission for payload operations, as specialists had to perform not only 'up-processing' (i.e. preflight operations to prepare the Syncom payload for integration into the Orbiter), but also 'down-processing' for 57 experiments that had been exposed to the harsh space environment for more than five years aboard the Long Duration Exposure Facility (LDEF).

In supporting the return of LDEF, the KSC payload team, working closely with Langley Research Center, planned a post-flight flow that accentuated the preservation of the scientific data. In addition, special research teams from Langley, which sponsored the project, were at KSC when LDEF returned.

LDEF remained in *Columbia's* payload bay during routine post-flight servicing at Edwards Air Force Base, California and during the ferry-flight back to KSC.

To assist in maintaining experiment integrity, an air-conditioned purge system was hooked up to the Orbiter during its stay at Edwards and the overnight stops. This system kept conditioned air circulating through the payload bay.

Once *Columbia* was in the Orbiter Processing Facility (OPF), LDEF was removed from the cargo bay, placed in a payload canister and transported to the Operations and Checkout Building (O&C). There, LDEF was loaded from the canister to the LATS (LDEF Assembly and Transportation System). This special 'cradle' is 55 feet long, 17 feet wide, and 21 feet high. LATS also was used during the pre-launch processing of LDEF.

LDEF occupied the O&C for several days. Then, supported by the LATS, it was transferred to the Spacecraft Assembly and En-

capsulation Facility, where the experiments were taken off the frame and turned over to researchers.

At KSC, LDEF was turned over to Langley personnel for off-line facility and experiment operations. Before any experimental activities or operations began, there was an initial inspection of LDEF and its experiments to check the general condition of the spacecraft and to look for any unexpected changes.

Once the initial inspection was completed, all of the Principal Investigators (PIs) and the Special Investigation Groups (SIGs) conducted detailed visual inspections of the entire LDEF and all of the visible experiment hardware.

Experiment trays were then removed from the LDEF and taken on ground support equipment transporters to an experiment operations area. After batteries were removed from once-active experiments, the trays went to a work-bench zone where the PIs performed closer inspections and took basic measurements. After the PIs had completed their procedures, the experiment hardware was properly configured, packaged and shipped to the PIs' laboratories.

An accessible LDEF database is being developed to document all of the information resulting from the LDEF mission. It is anticipated that this unique body of data on space experiments and the effects of long-term exposure in space of typical spacecraft hardware will become a valued resource to future spacecraft designers. Structures like LDEF provide a relatively inexpensive way to conduct experiments and may be reusable. Requirements for the use of the LDEF or similar facilities for follow-on flights will be evaluated at a later date.

windscreens were the only anomalous features of ascent.

FOR THE RECORD
- 130th manned spaceflight.
- 63rd U.S. manned spaceflight.
- 32nd Shuttle space mission.
- 9th mission by Orbiter *Columbia*.
- Brandenstein became 40th person, and 21st American, to make three space flights.
- Dunbar became 104th person, and 64th American, to make two space flights.
- Ivins, Low and Wetherbee became joint 223rd persons, and joint 134th Americans, in space.

More mobility!

A THIRD Mobile Launcher Platform (MLP-3) modified from Apollo/Skylab (Saturn booster) to Space Shuttle specifications saw its first use on STS-32. The platform served as the starting point for the historic Apollo 11 mission, all three manned Skylab missions, and the U.S. element of the ASTP joint mission with the Soviet Union in 1975.

Modification of Saturn-specification platforms to Shuttle standard is a complex affair involving a great many internal and external alterations. The primary external modifications are removal of the 115-meter-tall service tower structure, and replacement of the single exhaust opening required for the Saturn 1B and Saturn 5 vehicles with three exhaust openings corresponding to the Shuttle's cluster of three aft-mounted main engines and two solid rocket boosters.

ON-ORBIT

Some 25 hours into the mission, on Day 2, the first major milestone was passed with the deployment of Syncom 4-F5: the last in a series of five U.S. Navy comsats built by the Hughes company. Measuring 15 feet long and 13 feet in diameter, it is designed to provide worldwide, high-priority communications between aircraft, ships, submarines and land-based stations for the U.S. military services and the Presidential Command Network.

During the 'Frisbee-fashion' deployment, Jim Wetherbee took charge of *Columbia's* systems while Commander Brandenstein coordinated overall crew activities. David Low and Bonnie were responsible for the employment itself, in prime and backup roles respectively: the former attended to the appropriate panel in the aft flightdeck area overlooking the payload bay, while the latter occupied the Commander's seat, working the CRT/computer interface. Marsha Ivins engaged in photo-documenting what was happening.

After the comsat had drifted clear of *Columbia*, Brandenstein and Wetherbee performed a separation-burn maneuver to increase the clearance between the two spacecraft prior the the automatic firing of the Syncom's first stage solid-rocket perigee kick motor (PKM) which, along with several liquid-rocket apogee motor firings, boosted the satellite to the correct geosynchronous orbit.

The undoubted highlight of STS-32 was the retrieval of LDEF: the first large spacecraft designed specifically for such an operation. The long delay in mounting a mission to recover it meant that STS-32 took on the mood of a 'rescue flight' because of the twelve-sided, twelve-ton free-flyer was within weeks of descending too low for capturing.

Initially, the rendezvous process was done totally by computer, with three of the astronauts making literally hundreds of data inputs, and a large team on the ground contributing. During the middle phase of the rendezvous, to borrow a phrase from Jim, "We started to phase in the big computer — Dan's brain — that we had programmed over the previous year".

Wetherbee was making a lighthearted reference to the introduction of manual flying procedures, though still computer-aided: Brandenstein was looking at a computer CRT screen and flying the craft with RCS burns. When *Columbia* was in close to the LDEF, the phase known as 'proximity operations' began, and that was totally manually controlled by Brandenstein, who had by this time vacated his position in the Commander's seat on the left side of the flightdeck and was now peering through *Columbia's* overhead windows.

He was getting range and range-rate data from the Orbiter's radar system, and from Bonnie Dunbar's calls, based on triangulation with on-board cameras.

Columbia had passed below the satellite, looped around in front of it, and then been positioned above it, facing payload baydown. As *Columbia* closed in from above, Brandenstein made a yaw maneuver to align the grapple fixture on the satellite with the Orbiter's mechanical arm. He was controlling the spacecraft in such a way that it had virtually no closure-rate with LDEF in the terminal phase of capture, as Jim Wetherbee explained: "You don't want to close too fast with something that big and massive. With the risks involved, you want to keep the closure very controlled and very slow and Dan was able to do that.

Briefly: Jim Wetherbee

Born: 27 November 1952, in Flushing, New York.

Physical description: Brown hair; grey eyes; height, 6 feet 4 inches; weight, 190 pounds.

Education: Graduated from Holy Family Diocesan High School, South Huntington, New York in 1970; received a bachelor of science degree in Aerospace Engineering from the University of Notre Dame in 1974.

Family: Married to the former Robin DeVore Platt of Jacksonville, Florida. Has one child; Kelly DeVore (born 28 March 1986).

Recreational interests: Enjoys tennis, skiing, softball, racquetball, basketball, running and music (plays drums in the all-astronaut band, *Max Q*).

Organizations: Member of the Society of Experimental Test Pilots.

Honors: Awarded the Navy Achievement Medal, and two Meritorious Unit Commendations.

Experience: Wetherbee received his commission in the U.S. Navy in 1975 and was designated an aviator in December 1976. After training in the A-7E Corsair 2 aircraft, he was assigned to Attack Squadron 72 (VA-72) from August 1977 to November 1980 aboard the *USS John F. Kennedy*, and logged 125 night carrier landings. He was then selected to attend the U.S. Naval Test Pilot School at Patuxent River, Maryland.

Following training in 1981, he was assigned to the Systems Engineering Test Directorate, where he was a project officer and test pilot for the weapons delivery system and avionics integration for the F/A-18 aircraft. He was subsequently assigned to Strike Fighter Squadron 132 (VFA-132) for operational flying in the F/A-18 from January 1981 until his selection for the astronaut candidate program.

He has logged over 2,400 hours flying time and 345 carrier landings in 20 different aircraft types.

NASA experience: Wetherbee was selected as an astronaut candidate by NASA in May 1984. In June 1985 he completed the mandatory one-year training and evaluation period, qualifying him for assignment as a pilot on future Space Shuttle flights crews.

STS-32/*Columbia* was his first space mission.

"He took his time about it and I was impressed with how well he did it."

By this time, Bonnie Dunbar had switched to the 'fine' (vernier) control mode of the RMS arm, preparing for the final drive in to the grapple fixture on LDEF — a translation of about 25 inches. "This is the kind of operation where you try to not work in parallel. In simulation, we found that's the best way of doing it, because there's some interactions you can't control: if you've got the arm going the same time the Orbiter is, it's a lot less controllable.

"Dan would drive in the Orbiter so that the target was in the end-effector (the 'hand' of the arm) camera. I'd not moved the arm at all at this point; I just put it up in the 'poised for capture' position. When we felt that the rates were pretty well null, or just about as good as we'd get them, he would disable the jets — go free-drift — and at that point I would start flying the arm off the end-effector camera. Actually I would glance out the windows — kind of a cockpit scan — but most of my focus was on that monitor that had the target in it, and was flying the arm towards the target.

"There's a trigger on the rotational hand controller that operated the snares inside the end-effector; when I had the right relationship of the target size and position in my monitor, I knew I was over the grapple fixture, then I would squeeze the trigger and I essentially captured the grapple fixture."

Jim Wetherbee describes the mood; "It was pretty tense in the cockpit: not a whole lot of people were saying very much. At the moment of grapple, again, not a whole lot was said. Mostly we realized we still had a long day ahead of us to do the photographic survey to document the condition of LDEF as soon as we grappled it — and we still had a lot of arm maneuvers to accomplish, and the latches in the payload bay had to work before we really were satisfied that that major objective had been accomplished."

With LDEF safely stowed, Day 5 saw the start of the 'mini-Spacelab' mission proper. The sheer diversity of secondary payloads makes it impossible for us to adequately describe them all here, but there was a combination of microgravity experiments, including protein crystal-growth, and medical objectives to undertake.

The latter took advantage of this extended mission's ability to allow more time to analyse the effects of prolonged exposure to weightlessness on the human cardiovascular system and, to a lesser degree, the vestibular system, and how it might affect future Shuttle crews bringing the Orbiter back to earth once the Extended Duration Orbiter program comes along, enabling missions up to 16 days long to become feasible.

Also of note was the so-called 'L-cubed'

instrument, which Jim Wetherbee describes as, "kind of a sextant in reverse"; its official title is Latitude-Longitude Locator. Instead of trying to locate their own position, as one might do aboard a ship at sea, the astronauts know with a high degree of precision where they were, and were trying to identify locations on the surface of the Earth in terms of their latitude and longitude. And it looked like it was accurate to within a couple of miles, which is quite impressive when one considers how high and how fast the Orbiter travels.

A series of AMOS optical site experiments were conducted once more, though the ground facility at Maui, Hawaii was obscured by cloud on every pass, so the

Briefly: Bonnie Dunbar

Born: 3 March 1949, in Sunnyvale, Washington.

Physical description: Brown hair; hazel eyes; height 5 feet 5½ inches; weight 117 pounds.

Education: Graduated from Sunnyside High School, Sunnyside, Washington in 1967; received bachelor of science and master of science degrees in Ceramic Engineering from the University of Washington in 1971 and 1975, respectively; and a doctorate in Biomedical Engineering from the University of Houston in 1983.

Family: Married to Ronald Saga of Monument, Colorado.

Recreational interests: Enjoys flying, running, softball, squash and sailing.

Organizations: Member of the American Ceramic Society, the National Institute of Ceramic Engineers, Keramos Honorary, the Society of Biomedical Engineering, American Association for the Advancement of Science, and _Tau Beta Pi_.

Special Honors: Graduated _Cum Laude_ from the University of Washington in 1975; awarded a NASA graduate research grant in 1973 and 1974; named Rockwell International Engineer of the Year in 1978, Group Achievement Award, Skylab Re-entry, 1979. Recipient of NASA Space Flight Medal in 1975.

Experience: Following graduation in 1971, Dr. Dunbar worked for Boeing Computer Services for two years as a systems analyst. In 1973, she started research for her master's thesis in the field of mechanisms and kinetics of ionic diffusion in sodium beta-alumina. In 1975, Dunbar was invited to participate in research at Harwell Laboratories in Oxford, England as a visiting scientist. Her work there involved the wetting behavior of liquids on solid substrates.

Following her tenure in England, Dunbar accepted a senior research engineer position with Rockwell International Space Division in Downey, California. Her responsibilities there included developing equipment and processes for the manufacture of the Space Shuttle thermal protection system at the company's Palmdale, California plant. She also represented Rockwell as a member of the Dr. Kraft Ehricke evaluation committee on prospective space industralization concepts. She has served as an adjunct assistant professor in Mechanical Engineering at the University of Houston.

Dunbar is a private pilot with over 200 hours in single-engined light aircraft, and has logged more than 700 hours flying time aboard T-38 jets as copilot.

NASA experience: Dr. Dunbar accepted a position as a payload officer/flight controller at Johnson Space Center, Houston in 1978.

She served as a guidance and navigation officer/flight controller for the Skylab reentry mission in 1979, and was subsequently designated project officer/payload officer for the integration of several Shuttle payloads.

Dr. Dunbar became a NASA astronaut in August 1981. Her technical assignments have included assisting in the verification of Shuttle flight software at the Shuttle Avionics Integration Laboratory (SAIL) and serving as a member of the Flight Crew Equipment Control Board.

Dunbar's first space flight was 61-A/_Challenger_, the Spacelab D-1 mission flown in conjunction with West Germany in 1985. She was a Mission Specialist for the seven-day flight, during which more than 75 scientific experiments were completed in the areas of physiological sciences, materials processing, biology, and navigation.

She was in training for the _original_ LDEF retrieval mission — 61-I/_Challenger_, scheduled for September 1986 — at the time of the _Challenger_ disaster. All flight crew assignments were subsequently disbanded, and she 'survived' to become the only member of that original crew to actually retrieve LDEF.

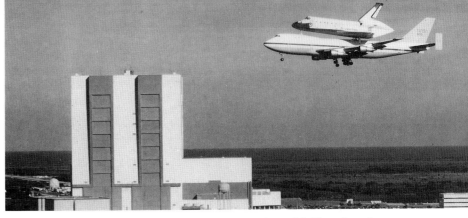

(Right) *Columbia* — poised atop NASA's Boeing 747 Shuttle Carrier Aircraft (SCA) — completes its two-day ferry flight from Edwards Air Force Base to Kennedy Space Center, with LDEF safely ensconsed in its payload bay.

(Below) **Syncom 4-F5 departs 'Frisbee-fashion'.**

camera was flown again: Marsha Ivins was the prime operator on that.

STS-32 had been scheduled to get within hours of the Shuttle mission-duration record established by the STS-9/*Columbia*/Spacelab 1 mission in 1983. The prospect of fog at the Edwards, California landing site resulted in a 'wave-off' for de-orbit, granting the crew crew limited its involvement to simply turning on the payload bay lights at the appropriate times. The famous IMAX '3-D' another day on-orbit. On 13/14 January — about midway through the mission — a weather system had moved in through Edwards, giving them over a half-inch of precipitation. The system moved through White Sands, depositing light precipitation there. On 17 January, another system moved into Edwards, giving them light precipitation and nearly an inch of *snow* on 18 of January. This made the lakebeds wet and unacceptable for landing.

That same system moved into White Sands on 18 January and dumped a couple of inches of snow on Northrup Strip on the 19th — making them *"No-go"* that day. Edwards wasn't much use either that day — the 19th — the day *Columbia* was waved-off a day because of the fog forecast. At the decision-time to close the payload bay doors, the observation

was *"Go"* but the forecast was *"No-go"* and not expected to change. The fog which had formed over the lakebed for the first landing opportunity had pulled visibility down to three miles by the second opportunity, so *Columbia's* payload bay doors were never closed.

Asked how she felt about breaking the Shuttle endurance record, Bonnie Dunbar was philosophical: "As I said to my mother, records are there to be broken — and that one will be. It's kinda nice to have, personally, that much time, but I wasn't looking to break any records. I was just glad to get another day."

RE-ENTRY & LANDING

On the 20th, mission controllers decided to go for the earliest opportunity to avoid fog. The weather was forecast to be *"Go"* for the first three landing opportunities, but *"No-go"* for the last.

While the crew were getting ready for the de-orbit burn, a problem arose with a General Purpose Computer (GPC). Experts on the ground were able to isolate the problem and relayed information as to how the astronauts could rectify the situation. They reprogramed one of the primary GPCs to accept backup software, but that absorbed some time and resulted in a 'wave-off' for de-orbit

burn on that orbit. They therefore came in yet another orbit later than originally planned.

Columbia was carrying more propellant in her OMS pods than any previous Shuttle flight. Extra propellant had been loaded aboard for the LDEF rendezvous, but Dan Brandenstein's deft handling of the tricky operation proved surprisingly economical and the reserves hadn't been used up. LDEF's presence in the payload bay was already set to make this the heaviest Shuttle landing yet, so to reduce gross weight, Brandenstein and Wetherbee performed the de-orbit burn 'out of plane' and used up some of the excess propellant.

"We were kinda flying sideways," said Jim.

Sheer weight considerations aside, *Columbia's* center-of-gravity was further forward than on any previous Shuttle mission, by a considerable margin. This provided some opportunites to analyse the Orbiter's behavior in this unique configuration, not only during re-entry, but also in hypersonic atmospheric flight, and on landing and rollout. The SILTS tail-mounted experiment payload, flown on missions 61-C and STS-28, was operating to record heating-profile data throughout re-entry.

I quizzed Jim as to the nature of nocturnal flight in the unpowered Orbiter, hurtling earthward with no second chance at landing. He accepted that it's a thoroughly demanding situation — "Certainly, at night, you have less visual cues coming into your brain: there's just not a whole lot to see"— but he tempered his response with an acknowledgement of the vital role the Shuttle Training Aircraft (STA) plays pre-flight, and was quick to point out that his Commander has had more night-time flying experience in the STA, and in the Shuttle Orbiter itself, than anyone else in the history of the program.

Brandenstein switched to manual (computer-aided) mode as *Columbia* went subsonic, and handed the controls to Wetherbee briefly as they entered the Heading Alignment Circle (HAC). Then came the landing itself. "He made it look easy, didn't he," said Jim with a smile. "I didn't even know that we had touched-down, with the exception that some of my displays changed."

Summing up STS-32, Jim Wetherbee was a contented man. Bonnie Dunbar, too, was more than happy — and not just because, through her efforts with LDEF, she's lived out Andy Warhol's adage about being famous for 15 minutes! "I really enjoyed the mission: I thought it was good team effort. I enjoyed eleven days and I'm looking forward to longer stays."

STS-32: RETRO — pages 72/73

STATISTICAL ANALYSIS: STS-32/ COLUMBIA

Crew:
Dan Brandenstein (Commander)
Jim Wetherbee (Pilot)
Marsha Ivins (MS1)
Bonnie Dunbar (MS2/EV1)
David Low (MS3/EV2)

Orbiter: *Columbia* (OV-102)
(Prior missions — 8; STS-1, STS-2, STS-3, STS-4, STS-5, STS-9/Spacelab 1, 61-C, STS-28)

External Tank: ET-32
(Splashdown zone: Latitude 10.43 degrees north/Longitude 157.22 degrees west — Pacific Ocean, 60 miles south of Hawaii)

SSME Position 1: Engine 2024
(Prior total firing time: 1,081 seconds: prior missions — nil)

SSME Position 2: Engine 2022
(Prior total firing time: 2,349 seconds: prior missions - 3; STS-26/*Discovery*, STS-29/*Discovery*, STS-28/*Columbia*)

SSME Position 3: Engine 2028
(Prior total firing time: 2,350 seconds: prior missions — 3; STS-26/*Discovery*, STS-29/*Discovery*, STS-28/*Columbia*)

Forward RCS: FRC-2
(Prior missions — 8, STS-1/*Columbia*, STS-2/*Columbia*, STS-3/*Columbia*, STS-4/*Columbia*, STS-5/*Columbia*, STS-9/*Columbia*, 61-C/*Columbia*, STS-28/*Columbia*)

Port OMS: LP-03
(Prior missions — 8; 41-C/*Challenger*, 41-D/*Discovery*, 51-A/*Discovery*, 51-C/*Discovery*, 51-D/*Discovery*, 51-J/*Atlantis*, 61-B/*Atlantis*, STS-28/*Columbia*)

Starboard OMS: RP-04
(Prior missions — 4; 51-B/*Challenger*, 51-F/*Challenger*, 61-C/*Columbia*, STS-28/*Columbia*)

Mobile Launcher Platform: MLP-3
(Pad 39A)

SRBs: Flight Set 8

SRB case use history:

Element	Left Booster	Right Booster
F. Dome	New	STS-26
Cyl.	DM-3, QM-3, STS-5, 51-A, 61-C	STS-2, STS-9, 61-A, STS-26
C.F. Cyl.	STS-26	STS-26
Cyl.	STS-6, 51-B	41-B, 51-I, STS-26
C.F. Cyl.	PVM-1	STS-26
Cyl.	STS-8, 51-G	41-G, 61-B, PVM-1
C.F. Cyl.	New	PVM-1
ET Attach	New	New
Stiffener	New	New
Stiffener	New	New
Aft Dome	STS-26	51-I, TEM-1

Launch:
12:35:00 pm GMT/09 January 1990
Kennedy Space Center, Florida

Landing:
09:36:36 am GMT/20 January 1990
Edwards Air Force Base, California

Orbits: 172.3

Distance:
4,509,972 nautical miles

Mission Elapsed Time:
10 days, 21 hours, 01 minute, 38 seconds
(261 hrs; 01 min, 38 secs)

Weights:
Take-off/4,523,534 pounds
Landing/229,526 pounds

Cargo bay payloads:
Syncom 4-F5
RMS (for LDEF retrieval)

Middeck payloads:
Characterization of Neurospora Circadian Rhythms (CNCR)
Protein Crystal Growth (PCG)
Fluid Experiment Apparatus (FEA)
American Flight Echocardiograph (AFE)
Latitude/Longitude Locator (L3)
IMAX

Orbital inclination: 58.5 degrees.

Major orbital maneuvers:

Date	Time (GMT)	Perigee (miles)	Apogee (miles)	Period (mins)
09 Jan	13:18	181	222	90.9
10 Jan	09:32	186	222	90.9
	14:05	198	222	91.1
	19:05	198	210	90.9
12 Jan	11:33	204	208	91.0
	16:06	204	211	91.0
13 Jan	15:45	206	209	91.0
	no further maneuvers			

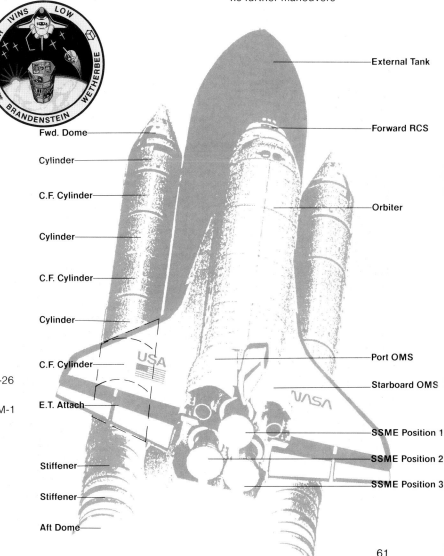

Fwd. Dome

Cylinder

C.F. Cylinder

Cylinder

C.F. Cylinder

Cylinder

C.F. Cylinder

E.T. Attach

Stiffener

Stiffener

Aft Dome

External Tank

Forward RCS

Orbiter

Port OMS

Starboard OMS

SSME Position 1

SSME Position 2

SSME Position 3

STS-36
ATLANTIS

(Top) **STS-36 crew self-portrait. Left to right; Commander John Creighton, Dave Hilmers, Mike Mullane, Pierre Thuot and John Casper.**

(Above) **Creighton's respiratory ailment delayed the launch. It was one of several frustrations pre-mission.**

After several delays, the STS-36/*Atlantis* mission got under way from Kennedy Space Center on Wednesday 28 February, at 02:50 am local time (07:50 am GMT). The launch was made possible by some clever weather reconnaissance and interpretation. By timing the passage of a weak band of showers, *Atlantis* was able to 'thread the needle' with five minutes remaining in the launch window. Use of the Shuttle Training Aircraft for weather-recce was instrumental in the *"Go"/"No-go"* decision.

LAUNCH

Transatlantic Abort Landing (TAL) site weather conditions posed problems as well. Moron, Spain was solidly down throughout the 'window', while the weather-check aircraft at Zaragoza couldn't see the landing-aids until six minutes before the launch.

The primary purpose of the secret Department of Defense-sponsored mission was to deploy a dual role AFP-731 reconnaissance/intelligence satellite into an average 110-nautical-mile low-Earth orbit.

STS-36 Commander was John Creighton, who was making his second space flight. He flew as Pilot of the 51-G/*Discovery* mission in June 1985. Seated alongside Creighton on *Atlantis's* flightdeck was Pilot

John Casper, one of two first-time space-farers on this mission, the other being Mission Specialist Pierre Thuot. Dave Hilmers and Mike Mullane, the other Mission Specialists on the flight, had each made two space flights; Hilmers on 51-J/*Atlantis* in October '85 and STS-26/*Discovery* in late-'88, and Mullane on 41-D/*Discovery* in mid-'84 and STS-27/*Atlantis* in December '88.

There were five scrubbed launch attempts for STS-36 — establishing an unenviable record for the post-*Challenger* era. Lift-off was originally scheduled for 22 February, but was postponed 24 hours when Creighton developed a respiratory ailment. Unfavorable weather conditions put paid to countdowns on the next two days. On none of these three occasions did the astronauts actually board *Atlantis*. On the

(Below) **Mission Specialist Dave Hilmers wields a large-format AeroLinhof camera during an Earth-imaging session.**

fourth attempt, on the 25th, the crew was in place, but a range-safety computer malfunctioned at T-31 seconds.

At this point, the crew was stood-down for 48 hours to enable them to get some proper rest. They didn't spend all their time relaxing, however. Creighton, Mullane and Hilmers flew back to Texas to undertake further simulator training at Johnson Space Center. Only Casper and Thuot remained at KSC.

Winds were not ideal on 26 February, but they were deemed good enough for *Atlantis* to go. The countdown was continued despite the presence of an icicle on the gaseous oxygen vent arm exhaust duct. Lift-off was perfect. Because *Atlantis* was launching to an extremely high inclination (62 degrees), several emergency landing sites were designated along the United States' eastern seaboard. These included Dover Air Force Base in Delaware.

ON-ORBIT

Deployment of the 37,300-pound AFP-731 satellite took place on *Atlantis's* 18th orbit, some 27 hours after lift-off. It is

Obituary: Sam Phillips

LIEUTENANT General Samuel Cochran Phillips died in California in February, aged 66. Although first and foremost a military man, he will probably be best remembered for the five years he spent with NASA as Director of the Apollo Moon landing program.

Sam Phillips, already a Major General, was recruited to NASA by the new Director of Manned Spaceflight, Dr George Mueller. He had previously been Director of the Air Force's Minuteman ballistic missile defence system. Phillips joined NASA in January 1964 as deputy director of the rapidly expanding Apollo program, but within nine months he was promoted to the position of Director. He was responsible for overseeing the design, construction and testing of flight and ground equipment, the training of thousands of technicians and the assembly of millions of parts into the mighty Saturn 5 launcher.

He and Mueller worked against time to meet President Kennedy's deadline of landing a man on the Moon before the end of the decade. There were many problems to be overcome, in particular delays and design problems with the flight hardware. Phillips warned of faulty design and workmanship on the first Command Modules as early as 1965, but his words went largely unheeded, resulting in the deaths of three astronauts in the January 1967 Apollo 1 pad fire.

The resultant halt in launches, hold-ups in completion of the first Lunar Module and fears of a Soviet Moon spectacular led to a revised program. Phillips announced to the press that Apollo 8 would circumnavigate the Moon over Christmas 1968. The bold gamble paid off, enabling the crew of Apollo 11 to set *Eagle* down on the Sea of Tranquility little more than six months later.

Sam Phillips left NASA after the glorious triumph of Apollo 11 to resume his military career. However, he briefly returned to the agency after the *Challenger* disaster in January 1986 to conduct a Shuttle program management review and make recommendations for changes in its organization. At the time of his death he was a member of the Committee for the Human Exploration of Space, an advisory body set up by the National Research Council.

P.B.

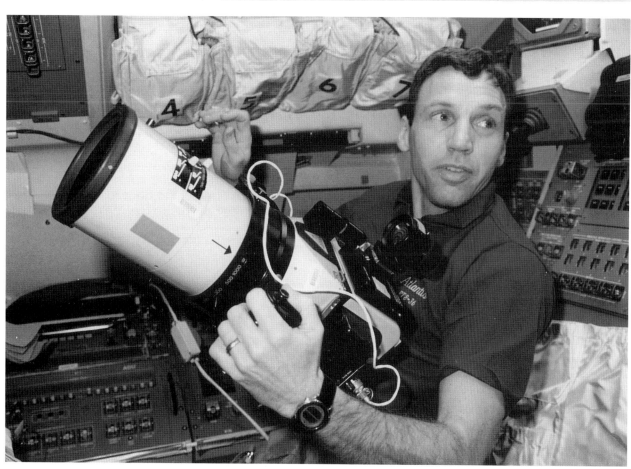

Prince Charles visits Kennedy Space Center

PRINCE CHARLES toured facilities at Kennedy Space Center while the STS-36/ *Atlantis* stack was in residence on Pad 39A. His guides included KSC chief Forrest McCartney and Shuttle astronaut Mike McCulley, who flew as Pilot on the STS-34/ *Atlantis* Galileo-deployment mission.

The heir to the British throne was accompanied by Greece's King Constantine, who was deposed in 1967 and now resides in Britain. Prince Charles arrived at KSC by air, alighting on the Shuttle Landing Facility (SLF). During his visit, he participated in the filming of segments of a BBC documentary film on the global environment: a project with which he was closely involved.

He also visited the Orbiter Processing Facility (OPF) and Firing Room 1 in the Launch Control Center (LCC), and viewed STS-36 pre-flight preparations.

(Left) **Prince Charles at KSC. In the background, in residence on Pad 39A, is the STS-36/*Atlantis* stack.**

(Below) **John Creighton became the self-proclaimed "world's fastest skier" — at 17,500 mph — during this mid-deck workout. While the claim may be questionable, one can't help but admire his effort at fashioning makeshift 'skiing' paraphernalia!**

thought that a new, lightweight deployment device known as the Stabilized Payload Deployment System (SPDS) was used to get the satellite out of the payload bay. The Rockwell-developed SPDS rolls the satellite over the side of the cargo hold, then sets it free with spring-loaded pistons at the appropriate time.

From its high-inclination orbit, which covered most of the populated area of the Soviet Union, AFP-731 was intended to monitor 'secure' transmissions. It didn't work out that way, however...

RE-ENTRY & LANDING

Atlantis landed at Edwards AFB, California at 10:09 am local time on Sunday 4 March. Surface crosswinds in excess of 25 knots threatened to delay the landing, and upper-level jetstream currents travelling at 115 knots caused some concerns about turbulance. An upper-level systen was expected to move through the Edwards area later in the day and cause some light precipitation, thereby making the lakebed unusable for several days.

There was more to come. Weather teams determined that if the landing did not take place on the 4th, the next opportunity would not occur until two days later, due to expected strong winds on the 5th. By landing on the 4th, those concerns were neatly circumvented.

Within days of being deployed, the AFP-731 spy-sat broke up in orbit. Some of the more sizable fragments re-entered the atmosphere on 19 March. It seems likely that the spacecraft's primary propulsion system failed to inject it into the correct orbit, at which point mission controllers issued a fragmentation command. Deliberate fragmentation, rather than explosive detonation, would be conducive to the generation of relatively little orbital debris.

While DoD were underplaying the AFP-731 issue, releasing very little in the way

(Bottom) **Creighton leads his crew down the steps, to be greeted by Bill Lenoir, Don Puddy and Mike Coats.**

(Below) **An STS-36 astronaut captured this glorious view of sunlight reflecting off ocean waters.**

of hard facts, authorities in the Soviet Union were displeased. There was, they said, a strong likelihood that debris would rain down on Soviet territory, and raised questions as to why agreed United Nations protocols pertaining to such situations were not complied with.

N.M.

FOR THE RECORD

- 129th manned spaceflight.
- 62nd U.S. manned spaceflight.
- 31st Shuttle space mission.
- 9th mission by Orbiter *Discovery*.
- Musgrave became 39th person, and 20th American, to make three space flights.
- Blaha and Gregory became joint 102nd persons, and joint 62nd Americans, to make two space flights.
- Carter and Thornton became joint 221st persons, and joint 132nd Americans, in space.

(Below) **Mike Mullane, making his third space flight, at work with a 70mm Hasselblad.**

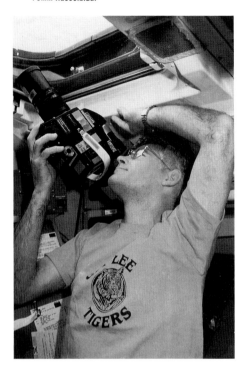

Obituary:
Ron Evans

RONALD EVANS, Command Module Pilot on the final Apollo mission to the Moon, died at his home on 17 April 1990. He was 56.

Evans was born on 10 November 1933 in St. Francis, Kansas. After graduating in Electrical Engineering from the University of Kansas, he received his commission as Ensign from the U.S. Navy in June 1957. He took part in two WESTPAC aircraft-carrier cruises, then became a combat flight instructor on Vought F-8 Crusader attack aircraft 1961/62. Evans gained a masters degree in Aeronautical Engineering from the U.S. Navy Postgraduate School at Monterey, California in 1964.

At the time of his selection as an astronaut in April 1966, Evans was involved in a seven-month tour of combat duty in the Vietnam war. He was one of 19 recruits to the fifth group of NASA astronauts, and went on to serve as a member of the astronaut support crews for Apollo 7 and Apollo 11, and as backup Command Module Pilot for Apollo 14.

Evans, by this time holding the U.S. Navy rank of Commander, was chosen as Command Module Pilot for the last manned lunar mission, Apollo 17, in 1971. The three-man crew for this historic mission were blasted into orbit from Kennedy Space Center on 6 December 1972. While his colleagues Gene Cernan and Harrison Schmitt explored the mountains of Taurus-Littrow, Evans spent more than three days alone in the Command Module *America*, establishing a record for solo lunar-orbital flight that looks set to stand for a long time. His only companions were five pocket-mice, which were carrying cosmic-ray detectors for an experiment known as Biocore.

During his epic solo adventure, Ron Evans was responsible for an extensive program of scientific investigations. These included visual observations of geological features, hand-held photography of lunar landmarks, and control of the automatic cameras and other scientific equipment carried in *America's* Scientific Instrument Module bay (SIMbay).

On 14 December, Evans was rejoined by Cernan and Schmitt, together with a record haul of nearly 250 pounds of Moon-rocks. By the time the return trip to Earth began two days later, Evans had spent a total of 147 hours, 48 minutes in lunar orbit.

On 17 December, Ron Evans clambered out of *America* to retrieve film-cassettes from the mapping and panoramic cameras and data from a lunar-sounder experiment in the SIMbay. During his 56-minute space-walk, he had time to pause and admire the crescent Earth, which loomed before him. The Apollo 17 mission ended with a perfect splashdown on 19 December.

Evans was promoted to Captain and awarded Distinguished Service Medals by both the U.S. Navy and NASA. He remained with the space agency for a time, acting as backup Command Module Pilot for the joint U.S./Soviet Apollo-Soyuz Test Project (ASTP) mission of July 1975. The following year, he retired from the Navy. At the time of his resignation from NASA in March 1977, he was involved in the development of the Space Shuttle.

Ron Evans moved to Scottsdale, Arizona, where he became Director of Space Systems Marketing for Sperry Flight Systems of Phoenix. He leaves a wife and two children, to whom we extend our sincere condolences.

P.B.

(Below) *Atlantis* **touches down at 'Eddie' on 3 March 1990.**

STATISTICAL ANALYSIS: STS-36/ ATLANTIS

Crew:
John Creighton (Commander)
John Casper (Pilot)
Mike Mullane (MS1)
Dave Hilmers (MS2/EV1)
Pierre Thuot (MS3/EV2)

Orbiter: *Atlantis* (OV-104)
(Prior missions — 5; 51-J, 61-B, STS-27, STS-30, STS-34)

External Tank: ET-33
(Splashdown zone: Latitude 61.46 degrees south/Longitude 145.11 degrees east — Antarctic Ocean, 1,140 miles south of Tasmania)

SSME Position 1: Engine 2019
(Prior total firing time: 7,080 seconds: prior missions — 5; STS-9/*Columbia*, 51-J/*Atlantis*, 61-B/*Atlantis*, STS-26/*Discovery*, STS-28/*Columbia*)

SSME Position 2: Engine 2030
(Prior total firing time: 2,376 seconds: prior missions — 3; STS-27/*Atlantis*, STS-30/*Atlantis*, STS-34/*Atlantis*)

SSME Position 3: Engine 2027
(Prior total firing time: 2,324 seconds: prior missions — 3; STS-27/*Atlantis*, STS-30/*Atlantis*, STS-34/*Atlantis*)

Forward RCS: FRC-4
(Prior missions — 5; 51-J/*Atlantis*, 61-B/*Atlantis*, STS-27/*Atlantis*, STS-30/*Atlantis*, STS-34/*Atlantis*.

Port OMS: LP-01
(Prior missions — 11; STS-6/*Challenger*, STS-7/*Challenger*, STS-8/*Challenger*, 41-B/*Challenger*, 41-G/*Challenger*, 51-B/*Challenger*, 51-F/*Challenger*, 61-A/*Challenger*, STS-27/*Atlantis*, STS-30/*Atlantis*, STS-34/*Atlantis*)

Starboard OMS: RP-03
(Prior missions — 10; 41-D/*Discovery*, 51-A/*Discovery*, 51-C/*Discovery*, 51-D/*Discovery*, 51-G/*Discovery*, 51-I/*Discovery*, 61-A/*Challenger*, STS-26/*Discovery*, STS-29/*Discovery*, STS-34/*Atlantis*)

Mobile Launcher Platform: MLP-1
(Pad 39A)

SRBs: Flight Set 9

SRB case use history:

Element	Left Booster	Right Booster
F. Dome	New	New
Cyl.	STS-2, STS-9, 51-J, 51-G	GTM-3, STS-3, 41-B, 51-I
C.F. Cyl.	New	STS-27
Cyl.	STS-8, 51-J, STS-26	61-A, QM-7
C.F. Cyl.	STS-26	STS-26
Cyl.	STS-26	STS-26
C.F. Cyl.	STS-27	STS-26
ET Attach	DM-7, STS-27	51-J, TEM-1
Stiffener	STS-27	61-C, QM-6, QM-8
Stiffener	STS-27	61-B, DM-9, STS-27
Aft Dome	51-J, STS-27	New

Launch:
07:50:22 GMT/28 February 1990
Kennedy Space Center, Florida

Landing:
18:08:44 GMT/04 March 1990
Edwards Air Force Base, California

Orbits: 70.4

Distance:
1,824,700 nautical miles

Mission Elapsed Time:
4 days, 10 hours, 18 minutes, 22 seconds
(106 hours, 18 mins, 22 secs)

Weights:
Launch/Classified
Landing/Classified

Cargo bay payloads: Classified

Middeck payloads: 'Phantom Head' (remainder classified)

Orbital inclination: 62.0 degrees

Major orbital maneuvers:

Date	Time (GMT)	Perigee (miles)	Apogee (miles)	Period (minutes)
28 Feb	08:50	122	130	88.6
	10:45	124	130	88.6
01 Mar	10:41	150	157	89.4
	19.11	148	150	89.4
03 Mar	12:00	134	149	89.1
	no further maneuvers			

Fwd. Dome
Cylinder
C.F. Cylinder
Cylinder
C.F. Cylinder
Cylinder
C.F. Cylinder
E.T. Attach
Stiffener
Stiffener
Aft Dome

External Tank
Forward RCS
Orbiter
Port OMS
Starboard OMS
SSME Position 1
SSME Position 2
SSME Position 3

STS-33: RETRO

STS-31 DISCOVERY

(Top) **McCandless *(left)* and Sullivan trained for a spacewalk, just in case.**

(Above) **Hubble at Lockheed's Sunnyvale, California facility.**

Deployment of what NASA officials were describing as the most important payload to be orbited since the Shuttle flight program began in April 1981 marked a true highpoint in U.S. space endeavor and was seen as evidence of a new renaissance in space science. That payload; the Hubble Space Telescope — the product of a $2.1-billion effort to place a large astronomical observatory high above the Earth's hazy atmosphere, the better to expand our knowledge of celestial phenomena and unlock long-kept secrets as to the origin and destiny of our Universe. Sadly, of course, there were big problems in store — but we'll look at them later.

LAUNCH

The Hubble Space Telescope (HST) was deployed by a close-knit team of five astronauts: the STS-31/*Discovery* crew, headed by Loren Shriver. STS-31 Pilot was Charlie Bolden, and Mission Specialists were Steve Hawley, Bruce McCandless and Kathy Sullivan. All five astronauts had flown space before. Hawley was making his third space voyage, having previously flown on the 41-D/*Discovery* and 61-C/*Columbia* missions, while Shriver, Bolden, McCandless and Sullivan had previously made one space flight apiece.

STS-31/*Discovery*'s first launch attempt took place on 10 April, and was scrubbed at the T minus 31-second mark when erratic indications were noted from an Auxiliary Power Unit (APU). Initially, the countdown went into an unscheduled hold for five or ten minutes pending investigation of the problem. When it became clear that there was no immediate solution, the launch attempt was scrubbed.

That was a pity, because the weather hadn't presented too many problems, with conditions at Kennedy Space Center and the various landing sites having been forecast and observed "*Go*". Banjul, one of the three Transatlantic Abort Landing (TAL) sites for this mission, stepped into line at the last minute, when NOAA's Steve Sokol called windspeed "*within limits.*"

The APU malady, which is described in detail in an accompanying panel, made all that academic, but Commander Loren Shriver was philosophical about the decision to scrub. Shortly after the flight, he told the author; "Obviously, when you start into the countdown two or three days before the planned lift-off date, you have to go into that assuming that everything's going to work properly and you're going to go.

"By the time we stepped in, you have a tendency to think that, definitely, it's gotten to this point and everything's OK, so there's a little bit left — it's a very critical part — but you're *about there*. Everything had progressed very, very well throughout the entire countdown, up through the starting of the APUs — then along came the problem with APU 1.

'We're just not in the business of taking chances like that, so even though the APU was running in its high-speed mode, it still was not functioning correctly, so rightfully the system chose not to launch with that. We were disappointed, but probably no more than anyone else."

After the 10 April scrub, a new launch target date was set for 25 April, although it was recognized that if preparations proceeded smoothly, an attempt might be feasible as early as the 24th. HST's batteries were removed and transferred to the 'battery lab' in the Vehicle Assembly Building (VAB) to be recharged. This, an eight-day operation, commenced late in the evening of Saturday 14 April.

STS-31's launch finally took place on 24 April at 07:34 local time (12:34 GMT), three minutes after the opening of the 'window'. The three-minute delay was due to a software problem which automatically stopped the ground launch sequencer at T minus 31 seconds. Prior to lift-off, there had been concerns that the Return To Launch Site (RTLS) abort contingency might be threatened by an out-of-limits crosswind — from easterly winds — and limited cloud ceilings. The cloud-cover went 'broken' for 20 minutes about one hour before launch, then came within limits.

All three STS-31 TAL sites — Banjul in The Gambia, Ben Guerir in Morocco and Moron, Spain — were marginal at forecast time, but two of the three came within limits by decision time.

The greatest weather threat to launch was the "*No-go*" forecast for the two prime landing sites (PLS), Edwards, California and White Sands Space Harbor, New Mexico. After much discussion amongst NASA decision-makers, the headwind rule was waived at 30 knots (it's usually 25 knots), accommodating the forecast at 28 knots.

Discovery performed a direct-insertion ascent: one OMS burn at apogee, performed so that the Orbiter would coast towards a record altitude for the Shuttle program of 330 nautical miles. Two factors — the flightpath angle at MECO and the velocity at MECO — determine the apogee. In the case of STS-31, both values were higher than usual.

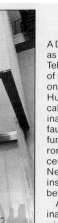

ON-ORBIT

The first two days of the flight were very busy, there being a lot to accomplish. On Day One, launch day, Steve Hawley undertook a thorough checkout of the Shuttle's RMS mechanical arm, assisted by Charlie Bolden. Bruce McCandless and Kathy Sullivan, again with assistance from Bolden, went through a checkout of the three EMU spacesuits (one was a spare) being carried to the support contingency EVA option. Soon after entering orbit, cabin pressure had been brought down to 10.2 psi to allow for a faster-response EVA on Day 2 if that were needed.

"We got all that done on flight Day One, so as to be ready and not to be behind on flight Day 2," said Loren Shriver. By the time the crew got to bed it was about about 11 hours into the mission, and about 19 hours after their awakening on launch morning.

Day One gave way to an even busier Day 2 — the day HST was to be deployed. I asked Shriver about the way in which the various crew tasks were allocated; "As Commander, I tried to avoid putting myself as prime operator of any of the experiments, and assigned them to other people — just monitoring them to make sure they all took place on time.

"I think that's a better way to do it. The Commander has a lot of latitude, as far as secondary payload activities and DSOs (Detailed Secondary Objectives — Ed.) go, to apportion the workload so no one person gets overburdened. That's not just the workload in flight, but also the workload in training, which is just as important."

Steve Hawley was the 'King of the RMS' on this mission, even though he hadn't actually operated arm on-orbit before. He jokes that his assignment to this task came about because the selection of Bruce McCandless and Kathy Sullivan to the contingency EVA roles left him as the only choice! That McCandless and Sullivan should be thus assigned was entirely logical, of course, because they'd both had actual EVA experience: on missions 41-B/Challenger and 41-G/Discovery respectively.

HST weighs 13 tons and measures 43 feet long by 14 feet in diameter. Disconnection of its umbilical links with Discovery took place on orbit 16 as scheduled. This is

Hubble trouble

A DREAM was looking distinctly nightmarish as we closed for press, the Hubble Space Telescope (HST) having been found incapable of performing as advertised. The news broke on 14 June, when it became clear that Hubble was suffering from what astronomers call a 'spherical aberration' — essentially, an inability to focus properly due to an inherent fault. That inherent fault appeared to be a fundamental design flaw in the primary mirror (pictured at left). The mirror was almost certainly manufactured (by Perkin Elmer of New York) according to the very precise instructions, but those instructions may have been wrong — if only by a tiny fraction.

A critical measurement may have been inaccurate by as little as one-fiftieth of the width of a human hair, but with the vast distances Hubble must look, that's enough to cause major degradation of images. In fact, one official involved in the program conceded that, in its present condition, Hubble's resolution is no better than that of a ground-based telescope.

Lew Allen, soon to retire as Director of the NASA/Caltech Jet Propulsion Laboratory (JPL) in Pasadena, California, was immediately drafted in to head an investigation board. The board's task was to determine how the dreadful error came to happen; some experts think the inaccurate calculation may have been made as long ago as 1980, while the primary and secondary mirrors were being designed and rough-cut prior to fine milling and polishing.

A Hubble rescue mission was being tentatively planned for 1992 or '93. Spacewalking astronauts will fit a device analogous to human spectacles to correct Hubble's vision. In the meantime, observation sessions will favor those instruments which stand to make the best scientific gains in light of the new-found disability. Astronomers with a positive outlook were saying that, with a little ingenuity, HST could still perform 50-60 percent of its originally-intended mission.

Hubble has five instruments on board; three of them are hardly affected by the 'spherical abberation'. Unfortunately, the JPL-furnished Wide Field Planetary Camera — which would have obtained the most spectacular Hubble images — is virtually useless in the telescope's present condition.

HST was named for the American astronomer Edwin P. Hubble, who refined the Belgian abbot Georges Lemaitre's theories relating to the 'Bang Big' concept of the origin of the Universe. It was built under the prime contractorship of Lockheed, of Sunnyvale, California.

The STS-31/Discovery stack was rolled out to Kennedy Space Center's Pad 39B on 15 March and HST was placed aboard the payload bay two weeks later. Extra-stringent cleanliness requirements characterized the STS-31 pre-flight processing flow; special measures were implemented in deference to HST's highly sensitive optics.

After the four-year delay caused by the Challenger disaster, members of the world astronomical community were relishing the moment when their opportunity came to

use HST. They were set to undertake observations of unprecedented scope and clarity.

In the words of English poet William Blake, "If the doors of perception were cleansed, everything would appear to Man as it is — infinite". Blake of course, was referring to the mind's eye, but the adage holds true for astronomical studies, which at present are limited by the Earth's hazy atmosphere. Air-currents and stray light smear and distort our view of the heavens.

Sailing high above the atmosphere, HST was intended to sharpen the astronomers' observations, enabling them to see stars and galaxies 50 times fainter than ever before. It was also to allow them to see seven times further than ever, and because of the time it takes light to travel, looking further out into space meant looking back into the past. Hubble could, one day, enable Man to look back some 15 billion years in time to the formation of the Universe, unlocking vital clues to its origin and history.

Acting like a time machine, it will reveal the Universe in different stages of its evolution, from its earliest days to the present, perhaps providing a glimpse forward to its ultimate fate.

HST is a 13-ton structure about the size of a city bus. It is a Cassegrain-type telescope and totes a primary mirror 2.4 meters in diameter. Five instruments to detect and analyse the light from distant objects are housed at the focus behind the primary mirror. Four are American-developed (a wide-field/planetary camera, two spectrographs and a photometer), while the fifth (the Faint Object Camera) was furnished by the European Space Agency.

The two cameras will electronically scan regions of the sky, while the wide-field planetary camera was intended to 'see' relatively large fields of view and photograph many objects at once. ESA's Faint Object Camera will produce images which exploit the maximum resolving and light-gathering power of the telescope's optics. It will image stars in ultraviolet light at high resolution, something which has not been done before.

HST is intended to operate for 15 years in low-Earth orbit. Almost of the major systems have been designed for on-orbit repair or replacement by astronauts. The Shuttle will visit HST in orbit about every five years, allowing obsolete or faulty items of hardware to be changed-out. Its British Aerospace-built solar-cell arrays, for example, are intended to last five years before being replaced.

The HST program is managed by NASA's Goddard Space Flight Center in Greenbelt, Maryland, with a specially-inaugurated body — the Space Telescope Science Institute in Baltimore — allocating observing time and scheduling the various astronomical activities. ESA is contributing 15 percent of the overall cost, in return for a proportional share of observing time. Europe's center for coordinating observations is the headquarters of the European Southern Observatory at Garching, West Germany.

how Steve Hawley described the deployment sequence to us; "The unloaded arm flew very much like it does in the simulators on the ground, and the grapple was easy and no surprise. We did not see any motion in the telescope when we released the latches. We didn't know whether we could expect any or not. We did not, so that meant that there weren't really any other forces on it other than the arm just holding it.

"When we started to lift it out, it came straight up out of the payload bay — but it's

known characteristic of the arm that you don't get pure motion when you command the loaded arm to do something. What we don't predict very well is how any particular payload is going to react, so the actual motion of the payload in detail was not what we had seen practicing on the ground — it's kinda sloppy.

"That's okay. The problem for the operator is whether or not you can predict ahead of time how it's going to behave so that you anticipate the motion that's actually going

■ continued on page 74

(Far-left) **Dan Brandenstein leads the STS-32 crew to** *Columbia.*

(Bottom-left) *You're* **coming home! The Canadian-built RMS mechanical arm, deftly operated by Bonnie Dunbar, has LDEF firmly in its grasp.**

(Left) **This unusual 'upstairs/ downstairs' view of the newly-refurbished Pad 39A reveals the flame-trench below. Note the operator in his cab at left, controlling the closing movement of the Rotating Service Structure.**

(Right) **Tropical Storm 'Sam' — known as 'Willy-Willy' in Australia — seen from** *Columbia* **over the eastern Indian Ocean, off Australia's west coast.**

STS-32: RETRO

(Left) **Marsha Ivins feigns bewilderment at the diversity of camera equipment floating around** *Columbia's* **middeck. Dr. Ivins was responsible for the painstaking LDEF photo-documentation effort.**

(Below) **The first nocturnal landing of the post-*Challenger* era.**

Training for the Hubble deployment

STEVE HAWLEY, who was regarded by many as the 'star' of the Hubble deployment due to his deft manipulation of the Shuttle's RMS mechanical arm, discussed his pre-flight training regime with us in some detail. "With a manual task like deploying the HST, you're particularly sensitive to getting the right amount of training in a facility that replicates what you're going to see — because, obviously, that's a task that requires some amount of precision: it's a big object and clearances are pretty small.

"We spent a fair amount of time, pre-launch on the ground, replicating what we thought the views would be like. That all took place in the computer-generated-image simulators, and at Lockheed's facility in Sunnyvale as the telescope was sort of on its way out

the door to go to Florida for launch. It was lying horizontally and we had them erect a little platform that simulated the eye-height aspect: we tried to simulate being at the proper physical location with respect to the telescope to see what we'd be able to see.

"We had digital image-generator scenes, we have a facility that actually generates line-drawings which are supposed to be representative, we've got a facility that's called the Manipulation Development Facility *(an RMS simulator in which inflatable mock-payloads are maneuvered in and out of of a full-scale payload bay representation).* In retrospect, I would say that none of those simulations were exactly like what we really saw — the TV views are different, the geometry is different.

"One of the things that was surprising, although I suppose we anticipated it to some extent, was the effect of sunlight on our ability to discriminate details in the scene.

HST, as you know, is highly reflective, and the sunlight would sometimes just produce overwhelming glare as it reflected from its surface. Although, intellectually, you know that's going to happen, as you train you don't always factor that in to the way you view the world.

"We had sunglasses, but although that helps a little bit as you look out the window, it doesn't help any on television. In fact, it's even worse on television, because you get a kind of bloom effect — and, in any case, you can't read the CRTs if you're wearing sunglasses. We decided that wasn't a very effective countermeasure. You just have to live with the scene that you get.

"If the glare became excessive, you just had to pick up a secondary cue until you could get your primary cue back. In that respect, it's analogous to when you're driving an automobile and become subjected to glare."

Briefly: Steve Hawley

Born: 12 December, 1951 in Ottawa, Kansas, but considers Salina, Kansas to be his hometown.

Physical description: Blond hair; blue eyes; height 6 feet; weight 165 pounds.

Education: Graduated from Salina (Central) High School, Salina, Kansas in 1969; received bachelor of arts degrees in Physics and Astronomy (graduating with highest distinction) from the University of Kansas in 1973 and a doctor of philosophy in Astronomy and Astrophysics from the University of California in 1977.

Family: Single (formerly married to astronaut Sally Ride).

Recreational interests: Enjoys basketball, softball, tennis, running, playing bridge, and reading.

Organizations: Member of the American Astronomical Society, the Astronomical Society of the Pacific, *Sigma Pi Sigma, Phi Beta Kappa,* and the University of Kansas Alumni Association.

Special honors: Evans Foundation Scholarship, 1970; University of Kansas Honor Scholarship, 1970; Summerfield Scholarship, 1970-1973; Veta B. Lear Award, 1970; Stranathan Award, 1972; Outstanding Physics Major Award, 1973; University of California Regents Fellowship, 1974; Group Achievement Award for software testing at the Shuttle Avionics Integration Laboratory (SAIL), 1981; NASA Outstanding Performance Award, 1981; Group Achievement Award for Second Orbiter Test and Checkout at Kennedy Space Center, 1982; Quality Increase, 1982; NASA Space Flight Medal, 1984.

Experience: Hawley attended the University of Kansas, majoring in physics and astronomy. He spent three summers employed as a research assistant: 1972 at the U.S. Naval Observatory in Washington, D.C., and 1973 and 1974 at the National Radio Astronomy Observatory in Green Bank, West Virginia. He attended graduate school at Lick Observatory, University of California, Santa Cruz. His research involved spectro-photometry of gaseous nebulae and emission-line galaxies with particular emphasis on chemical abundance determinations for these objects. The results of his research have been published in major astronomical journals.

Prior to his selection by NASA in 1978, Hawley was a post-doctoral research associate at Cerro Tololo Inter-American Observatory in La Serena, Chile.

NASA experience: Dr. Hawley was selected

as an astronaut by NASA in January 1978. Prior to STS-1, he served as a simulator pilot for software checkout at the Shuttle Avionics Integration Laboratory (SAIL). For STS-2, STS-3, and STS-4, he was a member of the astronaut support crew at Kennedy Space Center, Florida for Orbiter test and checkout, and also served as prime closeout crewman for STS-3 and STS-4. During 1984/85 he was Technical Assistant to the Director, Flight Crew Operations Directorate.

Hawley first flew as a Mission Specialist on flight 41-D which launched from the Kennedy Space Center, Florida on 30 August, 1984. This was the maiden flight of the Orbiter *Discovery,* during which the crew successfully activated the OAST-1 solar cell wing experiment, deployed the SBS-D, Syncom 4-F2, and Telstar 3-C satellites, and operated various experiments. During the seven-day mission, *Discovery* completed 96 orbits of the Earth before landing at Edwards Air Force Base, California, on 5 September 1984.

Hawley next served as a Mission Specialist on mission 61-C/*Columbia,* which launched from the Kennedy Space Center on 12 January 1986. During the six-day flight the crew deployed the Satcom Ku-1 satellite and conducted experiments in astrophysics and materials processing. 61-C made a successful night landing at Edwards Air Force Base, California on 18 January 1986. With the completion of his second spaceflight, Hawley had logged a total of 291 hours in space.

In 1985 Dr. Hawley was assigned to serve as a Mission Specialist for the Hubble Space Telescope deployment mission, originally designated 61-J/*Atlantis.*

Briefly: Loren Shriver

Born: 23 September 1944, in Jefferson, Iowa, but considers Paton, Iowa to be his hometown.

Physical description: Blond hair; blue eyes; height: 5 feet 10 inches; weight: 160 pounds.

Education: Graduated from Paton Consolidated High School, Paton, Iowa, in 1962; received a bachelor of science degree in Aeronautical Engineering from the United States Air Force Academy in 1967 and a master of science degree in Astronautical Engineering from Purdue University in 1968.

Family: Married to the former Susan Diane Hane of Paton, Iowa. They have four children, Camilla Marie (born 15 July 1969); Melinda Sue (born 27 September, 1970). Jered Loren, (born 19 December 1973); Rebecca Hane (born 24,January 1977).

Recreational interests: Enjoys softball, running and exercising, camping, backpacking, reading and sailboarding.

Organizations: Member of the Society of Experimental Test Pilots and the Air Force Association; life member of the Air Force Academy Association of Graduates and the Air Force Academy Athletic Association; and member of the American Institute of Aeronautics and Astronautics.

Special honors: Received the Air Force Meritorious Service Medal, Air Force Commendation Medal, two Air Force Outstanding Unit Awards, and the National Defense Service Medal; named High School Class Valedictorian, the USAF Academy Distinguished Graduate, a USAF Pilot Training Distinguished Graduate, a Squadron Officer's School Distinguished Graduate, and the USAF Test Pilot School Distinguished Graduate; recipient of the F-4 Combat Crew Training Academic Award.

Experience: Shriver was commissioned in 1967 upon graduation from the USAF Academy in Colorado Springs, Colorado, and subsequently attended graduate school for one year at Purdue University. From 1969 to 1973, he served as a T-38 academic instructor pilot at Vance Air Force Base, Oklahoma. He completed F-4 combat crew training at Homestead Air Force Base, Florida in 1973, and was then assigned to an overseas tour in Thailand until October 1974. In 1975, he attended the USAF Test Pilot School at Edwards Air Force

Base, California, and upon completion of this training was assigned to the 6512th Test Squadron at Edwards. He has completed Air Force Squadron Officer's School and the Air Command and Staff College correspondence course of study.

In 1976, Shriver began serving as a test pilot for the F-15 Joint Test Force at Edwards Air Force Base. He has participated in the Air Force development test and evaluation of the F-15 fighter aircraft and has participated in or conducted several follow-on systems tests on the same aircraft. He also took part in the Air Force development test and evaluation of the T-38 lead-in fighter. Shriver has been contributing author on six technical reports for these various programs.

Shriver has flown in 30 different types of single- and multi-engine civilian and military fixed-wing and helicopter aircraft, has logged over 4,500 hours in jet aircraft, and holds commercial pilot and private glider ratings.

Nasa experience: Shriver was selected as an astronaut candidate by NASA in January 1978. In August 1979, he completed a one-year training and evaluation period, making him eligible for assignment as a pilot on future Space Shuttle flight crews. In September of 1982 he was selected as pilot for the first Department of Defense mission, STS-10. That mission later became 51-J/*Atlantis*.

events — controllers at NASA/Goddard in Maryland commanded the various activities to take place. All five astronauts were watching to make sure those activities took place as they were expected to.

Deployment of the first 40-foot solar array was straightforward. The second array didn't deploy quite so smoothly, and stopped short in its cassette. That was cause enough for concern that mission controllers elected to order Bruce and Kathy to go downstairs, finish suiting-up and get in the airlock. While a remote fix mode was pondered for the second solar array, the EVA astronauts began to depressurize the airlock and had close to hand all the tools needed to deploy the solar array manually.

From that, it follows that the way tasks had been apportioned between the various astronauts was such that it could accommodate two of their number suddenly not being available to help on the flightdeck. Loren Shriver and Steve Hawley were primarily responsible for the flightdeck activities; Loren making sure that the Orbiter was positioned properly, and Steve operating the arm. Charlie was backup to both Loren and Steve on their functions, plus he was to support for EVA, so he

Lift-off scrubbed: the importance of APUs

DISCOVERY'S countdown was halted seconds before lift-off on 10 April, due to a fault in one of the Orbiter's three Auxiliary Power Units (APUs), which are housed in the vehicle's aft compartment, just behind the three main engines.

The countdown had reached the T minus 31-second mark when erratic indications were noted from APU No.1, which was running properly in the high-speed mode, but unevenly at low speeds. The APUs are started at T minus 5 minutes. All three APUs must be functioning properly before lift-off is approved, although the system is 'triple-redundant' and the Shuttle could, technically, run on just one APU in an extreme circumstance.

During ascent and re-entry, the APUs are absolutely essential. They run the engine gimbals and engine valves during ascent, and for re-entry they power the flight-control surfaces. On-orbit the APUs are not used at all, except for one fairly short test sequence. They are all shut down a couple of minutes after main engine cut-off (MECO), after they've helped to perform the main propulsion system venting and inerting of propellants, and then positioned the main engine aft-nozzles to the appropriate configuration for the remainder of the flight.

The criticality of the APUs to ascent and entry is why having triple-redundancy is so important. That way, there's the capability to sustain a failure and still have a fallback mode to rely on. Loren Shriver: "If you let yourself go to one APU, then you've got nothing left. If that APU fails, you're out of luck. The system says that we should be able to fly on one APU, but nobody's ever done that in a real live Space Shuttle.

"Probably, from a certain point on, you might be able to fly through ascent and end up somewhere on a safe orbit, but we hope we never have to."

After the 10 April scrub, APU No. 1 was removed and replaced over the Easter weekend. As a precautionary measure, the controller unit for APU No. 1 also was replaced (this subsequently proved to be unnecessary). An early-morning 'hot-fire' test was conducted on Wednesday 18th, clearing the unit for flight.

■ continued from page 71

to result. The upshot for the operator — with a big telescope in the bay and the complexities of the scene in terms of sunlight glare and so on — is how quickly can you recognize what it's really doing. That's the real challenge, and that was always the challenge we figured that we would face in trying to do this.

"Initially, all you're concerned about is collision avoidance. You're just getting it out of the payload bay. For launch, the telescope was positioned with the mirror located at the aft end of the payload bay: that's for structural reasons. When it's released, the mirror has to be pointed over the Orbiter nose, so you have to basicilly lift it out and then rotate it end for end. None of that needs to be precise.

"At the moment of release, there's a requirement for precision that's driven by several things — primarily the telescope's desire to communicate to the ground through TDRS, secondly to give the telescope a fighting chance of acquiring the sun with its sun-sensors before a sunset, and thirdly to get full illumination of the solar arrays, producing electricity.

"You can arrange the relative geometry between the telecope and the Orbiter pretty much at will to protect visibility, or clearances with solar-cell arrays, or whatever you want to protect."

The solar-cell arrays were deployed just prior to release by the RMS. In fact, the original plan was to have deployed the arrays and antennas *after* the release, but NASA intervened some years ago to suggest that, as long as the telescope was on the arm, it would be wise to deploy all the appendages to make sure they all worked. That, in turn, gave rise to most of the EVA procedures that were devised in support of this mission, the intention being to deploy the appendages manually if they did not deploy properly in an automatic regime.

As things turned out, there was very nearly a need for Bruce McCandless and Kathy Sullivan to perform just such a spacewalk...

Initially, they were with their colleagues on the flightdeck, monitoring the deployment of the first solar array. Once Hawley got the telescope to the position defined for the deployment of the appendages — a position devised to ensure the astronauts had a clear view of the various deployment

ended up scooting back and forth between the flightdeck and the middeck.

Bypassing some of the deployment sequence software resulted in the recalcitrant solar array being successfully unfurled, and all of the appendages were out and confirmed functioning prior HST's release by the mechanical arm. *Discovery* stayed 'on-call' about 40 miles away for about two days post-release: available to go back and rendezvous, regrapple and provide EVA support to the telescope.

Hawley: "The only credible case where you would want to do that would be if the aperture door closed for some reason, because that wasn't scheduled to be commanded open for 36 to 40 hours after release. If that had failed, we had agreed to go back and open it manually. Once we released the telescope the first time, we gave up the option to bring it home on that mission. We didn't have enough propellant."

The tardy second solar array wasn't the only problem experienced during Hubble's first few days in orbit. Difficulties with communications hampered initial check-out activities soon after the telescope's release. Controllers at Goddard bypassed the high-gain antennas and employed the low-gain antennas instead. After several time-consuming attempts, communications via the high-gain antennas were eventually established.

Several days later, various attempts to maneuver HST through 90 degrees to verify that NASA/Goddard had an attitude-control capability with the telescope prior to opening of the aperture door proved successful. However, initial commands issued to actually open the door proved fruitless and radio contact with the telescope was temporarily lost. During the communications problems, Hubble twice entered an automatic safety mode designed to prevent damage being inflicted to its sensitive instruments and overall structure.

On one such occasion, the aperture door automatically closed, as it would if the telescope were inadvertently pointed toward the Sun. By dint of some imaginative software reprograming, controllers at NASA/Marshall and Goddard were able to rectify the various problems, and the first test image was relayed by Hubble on 20 May. The region observed was centralized on the 8.2-magnitude star HD96755 in the open cluster NGC 3532, in the southern constellation Carina — near the Southern Cross.

As far as an overview on the deployment operation as a whole is concerned, Steve says it worked "pretty much as advertised — there were no real surprises," except of course that McCandless and Sullivan ended up in the airlock.

Loren Shriver, during our interview, em-

phasised that the astronauts did not have as great an insight as to how the telescope was progressing toward deployment as certain people on the ground did; "All the commands that were sent to deploy solar arrays, high-gain antennas, unlatch latches, unlatch the aperture door, came from Goddard."

A far as photo-documentation of the Hubble deployment went, Steve Hawley is in no doubt that it suffered as a result of two astronauts being ensconced in the airlock at the critical moment: "It was a matter of priorities. Under normal circumstances, where an EVA was not imminent, Bruce and Kathy would have been able to capture the moment of release. In fact, that was what we had planned to do — although we had also trained with them not being available. I think Kathy had planned to be looking over my shoulder, out the window, with various cameras at the time of release.

"I got some shortly after the release. I grabbed wherever camera was handy and started shooting."

In fact, the release *was* captured — on six minutes of film exposed by the payload bay-mounted IMAX '3D' camera.

RE-ENTRY & LANDING

For *Discovery*'s landing, the weather was as forecast all week — a strong upper-level low-pressure area was approaching on the

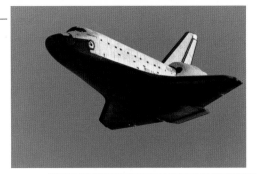

(Left) The moment of Hubble's release, captured by an IMAX '3-dimensional' camera mounted in Discovery's payload bay.

(Right) Discovery pictured moments before her landing gear deployed.

west coast. Strong surface winds were forecast to be barely out of limits for the first landing opportunity, worsening later that day and the next day. Closing of the payload bay doors was delayed for about an hour in hopes of an improvement in the weather, and shortly before deorbit burn, the forecast was amended to "Go" on concrete Runway 22 and "No-go" to the lakebed, so the landing runway was re-designated accordingly.

Other landing concerns were the cloud ceiling and turbulence. Landing observations showed that the concrete was well within limits, while every lakebed runway was out of limits, confirming the forecast.

The deorbit burn itself was quite lengthy, this being was one of lightest Shuttle missions to come back and land. There was very little residual weight after HST was deployed. The burn was 573 fps: the largest OMS burn ever by a Shuttle, due to the high altitude. There's a period of free-fall after the deorbit burn before reaching the point in space at the upper level of the atmosphere for 'entry interface'. That period of free-fall was extra-long on this occasion: 37 minutes, as compared to 30 or 31 minutes from a more normal altitude.

There was a series of eight aerodynamic PTIs (Program Test Inputs) to perform through re-entry. There are small inputs into the Orbiter's control system to see how it reacts, building knowledge as to how the vehicle responds to control inputs and perturbations from the atmosphere. Most of the re-entry took place at night, so the astronauts were treated to an excellent view of the ionospheric display in darkness.

Shriver echoed the praises heaped on the Shuttle Training Aircraft (STA) by other Commanders, saying that it helped considerably on both the Heading Alignment Circle (HAC), and then the glideslope; "The STA makes it very familiar, like you've done it many times before — although the partial-pressure suit and the G-loads against the suit make a difference."

Appraising this most historic of space-flights, Loren said; "It'll be a source of great pride for me in the future to look back and think that I had something to do with the mission that actually put it into space". Steve Hawley says he feels the same way, but placed more emphasis on the short-term aspect; "I'm looking forward to the results!"

Those results won't be as impressive as originally thought, however — at least for two or three years — because a major design fault was discovered about two months after Hubble's deployment. Further details appear in a separate panel at the end of this report, and Reginald Turnill discusses the wider implications of this most unfortunate development in his Review of the Year at the front of this edition.

N.M.

Shuttle's record altitude — the view from 330 nautical miles

STS-31'S ASCENT to a record altitude of 330 nautical miles (288 statue miles), provided American astronauts with their best view of our planet from Earth orbit since Gemini 11 in September 1966. We asked Mission Specialist Steve Hawley, who'd flown in space twice before, to describe the view…

"I was struck by the fact that, on previous flights, I had felt that the view was very much like flying — just that you were flying higher and faster. On this flight, I was struck by the sense that we were really in orbit and it was really a planet. It looked like a planet. The curvature was very apparent.

"The detail that I had seen on previous flights, I tended to overlook, because the panorama was so impressive. The grandure of it. Your ability to see half a continent at a time was so overwhelming that you tended to not pick up on the details so much as you picked up on global scale of things. I had said on previous flights that Earth observations is a little more challenging than you might imagine, because the world doesn't look like maps: you have to get used to where you are.

"Turns out that I just wasn't high enough. If you get high enough it looks like maps! Most maps are drawn on a scale that is more like flying higher than lower, because you can see 1,500 or 2,000 miles in any direction. I haven't done any calculations, so I don't know for sure, but that's probably about what it is. Most maps that you're used to seeing are drawn on scales such that you see several thousand miles at a time, so it's not surprising — but it was apparent to me that the geography was easier than it was on previous flights.

"I would say that we could see maybe four times as much of the Earth's surface as you do from a normal Shuttle orbit. You could see half of the United States from east to west, and you could see the whole north-south extent of the United States. You couldn't even see half-way across the United States from my previous flight altitudes.

"It was a little bit fuzzy — how to say it — in fact, you cannot really see in detail all that far because generally haze and clouds get you. If it were not hazy and cloudy, you'd be able to make a more accurate statement about the relative visibility. But you could convince yourself that you could see from the tip of Cuba to New York City. In fact, you can't really see New York City because it's too hazy."

STATISTICAL ANALYSIS: STS-31/ DISCOVERY

Crew:
Loren Shriver (Commander)
Charlie Bolden (Pilot)
Bruce McCandless (MS1/EV1)
Steve Hawley (MS2)
Kathy Sullivan (MS3/EV2)

Orbiter: *Discovery* (OV-103)
(Prior missions — 9; 41-D, 51-A, 51-C, 51-D, 51-G, 51-I, STS-26, STS-29, STS-33)

External Tank: ET-34
(Splashdown zone: Latitude 19.95 degrees north/Longitude 150.01 degrees west — Pacific Ocean, 386 miles east of Hawaii)

SSME Position 1: Engine 2011
(Prior total firing time: 5,280 seconds: prior missions — 4; STS-9/*Columbia*, 51-J/*Atlantis*, 61-B/*Atlantis*, STS-33/*Discovery*)

SSME Position 2: Engine 2031
(Prior total firing time: 2,142 seconds: prior missions — 2; STS-29/*Discovery*, STS-33/*Discovery*)

SSME Position 3: Engine 2107
(Prior total firing time: 2041 seconds: prior missions — 1; STS-33/*Discovery*)

Forward RCS: FRC-3
(Prior missions — 9; 41-D/*Discovery*, 51-A/*Discovery*, 51-C/*Discovery*, 51-D/*Discovery*, 51-G/*Discovery*, 51-I/*Discovery*, STS-26/*Discovery*, STS-29/*Discovery*, STS-33/*Discovery*)

Port OMS: LP-04
(Prior missions — 6; 51-G/*Discovery*, 51-I/*Discovery*, 61-C/*Columbia*, STS-26/*Discovery*, STS-29/*Discovery*, STS-33/*Discovery*)

Starboard OMS: RP-01
(Prior missions — 11; STS-6/*Challenger*, STS-7/*Challenger*, STS-8/*Challenger*, 41-B/*Challenger*, 41-C/*Challenger*, 41-G/*Challenger*, 51-J/*Atlantis*, 61-B/*Atlantis*, STS-27/*Atlantis*, STS-30/*Atlantis*, STS-33/*Discovery*)

Mobile Launcher Platform: MLP-2
(Pad 39B)

SRBs: Flight Set 10

SRB case use history:

Element	Left Booster	Right Booster
F. Dome	STS-8, 51-G; TEM-1	51-J, DM-9, STS-29
Cyl.	STS-27	QM-1, DM-3, 41-B, 51-I; STS-29
C.F. Cyl.	New	STS-29
Cyl.	61-A	ETM-1
C.F. Cyl.	New	STS-29
Cyl.	61-B	New
C.F. Cyl.	DM-9, QM-8	New
ET Attach	DM-3, QM-3, STS-5, 51-G	STS-8, DM-6, STS-27
Stiffener	QM-6, QM-8	STS-29
Stiffener	New	DM-4, STS-3, 41-B, ETM-1, STS-30
Aft Dome	DM-9, QM-8	51-F, TEM-2

Launch:
13:33:51 GMT/24 April 1990
Kennedy Space Center, Florida

Landing:
14:49:57 GMT/29 April 1990
Edwards Air Force Base, California

Orbits: 76

Distance: 2,068,213 nautical miles

Mission Elapsed Time:
5 days, 1 hour, 16 minutes, 6 seconds
(121 hrs, 16 mins, 6 secs)

Weights:
Launch/4,516,325 pounds
Landing/189,477 pounds

Cargo bay payloads:
Hubble Space Telescope
IMAX Cargo Bay Camera

Middeck payloads:
Ascent Particle Monitor (APM)
Investigations into Polymer Membrane Processing (IPMP)
Ion Arc (Student Experiment)
Protein Crystal Growth (PCG-111)
'Phantom Head'

Orbital inclination: 28.5 degrees

Major orbital maneuvers:

Date	Time (GMT)	Perigee (miles)	Apogee (miles)	Period (mins)
24 Apr	18:39	381	385	96.8
27 Apr	17:40	380	386	96.8
	19:57	378	383	96.7
29 Apr	06:45	378	383	96.7
	16:03	381	385	96.8
	no further maneuvers			

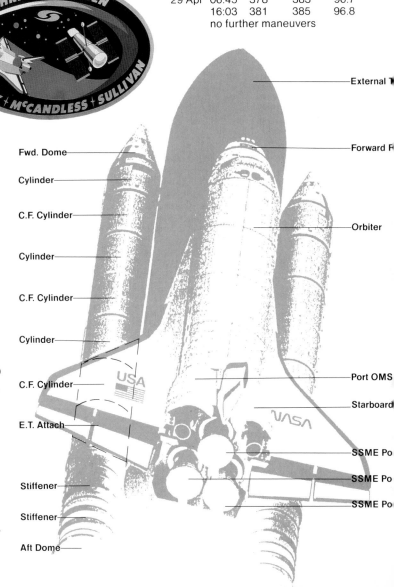

Fwd. Dome
Cylinder
C.F. Cylinder
Cylinder
C.F. Cylinder
Cylinder
C.F. Cylinder
E.T. Attach
Stiffener
Stiffener
Aft Dome

External T
Forward F
Orbiter
Port OMS
Starboard
SSME Po
SSME Po
SSME Po

SOVIET
MANNED
MISSIONS

SOYUZ TM-8

Problems with quality control, and consequent delays in the manufacturing process for the Kvant-2 module's electronics, led to a hiatus in manned activities aboard the Mir complex during the summer of 1989. Rather than keep a crew aboard the station on indefinite standby, mission planners chose to bring cosmonauts Aleksandr Volkov, Sergei Krikalev and Valeri Poliakov back to Earth, with the landing taking place on 27 April. Tightening of budgets as part of the *perestroika* credo had a direct bearing on the decision, which was to leave Mir empty for the first time in two years.

LAUNCH

Announced on Cosmonauts' Day, 12 April, the decision to mothball Mir was probably made towards the end of March. For nine months prior to that, Mir had been going through a regime of periodic 'boosts' of its 51.6-degree-inclination orbit to 350-360 kilometers altitude — with air-drag taking it down to around 330 kilometers before the start of the next cycle.

On 21 March, one of these maneuvers took the complex from of an orbit of 348 x 362 kilometers to one of 360 x 387 kilometers, with a period of 92 minutes, the record height for Mir up to that time. A further four major engine firings over the succeeding month — two using the Progress 41 engines, and two using Soyuz TM-7's — resulted in an orbit of 401 x 417 kilometers on 25 April; another record in terms of the overall altitude for

a Soviet manned spaceflight, though not the record distance from the Earth for a Soviet crew, as this distinction belongs to the crew of Voskhod 2, which flew in a 167 x 475-kilometer orbit in March 1965. The new orbit was sufficiently high to protect Mir from re-entering before the next crew arrival, then scheduled for August but subject to possible further delays.

Mir was by no means inactive during its four months of loneliness, as ground controllers continuously monitored its condition and tested its on-board systems. The lack of a crew actually had its plus side, because it increased the observation time available to experimenters using the 'Roentgen' observatory aboard Kvant-1.

The new occupation was signalled on 23 August, when Progress-M left Baikonur at 3:10 am GMT (7:10 am Moscow Time). It followed the standard two-day approach to Mir, before docking with Mir's forward-facing hatch at 5:19 am GMT on 25 August. It was the first Progress spacecraft to use the forward port; all previous missions to Salyut 6, Salyut 7, and Mir had used the aft port of the station or, in more-recent Mir missions, Kvant-1's rear port.

By the time Progress-M arrived, Mir's orbit had decayed to 382 x 397 kilometers, with a 92.3-minute period — still enough to claim a place in the record books as the highest orbit during a Progress approach and docking.

Compared with its predecessors, Progress-M featured a number of improvements, carried across from the Soyuz-TM design and aimed at providing a greater cargo capacity, and reducing overall weight to give more maneuvering freedom — as required on this particular mission. The Progress-M design also allows it to carry a small Earth-return capsule for sending back film and the products of Mir's microgravity 'factory'. Progress M-6, due late-1990, will be the first time it is used.

Immediately Progress-M's safe arrival was confirmed, mission planners gave the go-ahead to launch one of the two crews in training. The prime crew had been named in early-August as Aleksandr Viktorenko and Aleksandr Serebrov, both of whom had trained alongside Frenchman Michael Tognini in preparation for the 1988 'Aragatz' mission. Backups for the new flight were identified as Anatoly Solovyov, a seasoned cosmonaut, and Aleksandr Balandin, who was originally trained for space as part of the Soviet Shuttle program.

During April, though, some Soviet reports were giving the pairings in a different form, with Viktorenko and Balandin as the prime crew.

A couple of days before launch, the State Commission conducted its standard flight readiness review for the crew launch, and confirmed that Viktorenko and Serebrov would indeed fly the Soyuz TM-8

(Left) **The Soyuz TM-8 spacecraft pictured at a ceremony shortly before the TM-7 mission.**

(Left) Spacewalk-training in the hydrotank at Star City.

(Below) The Soyuz TM-8 stack is railroaded to the launch pad, tail-first.

him by Serebrov, completed the maneuver manually. Docking occurred at 10:25 pm GMT on 7 September (2:25 am on 8 September Moscow Time), and the two men boarded Mir at 11:46 pm for a sojourn scheduled to end on 19 February, 1990.

ON-ORBIT

The work program set out for Viktorenko and Serebrov was quite ambitious. The first major event was to be the 16 October launch of Kvant-2, a large airlock/workshop module containing seven tonnes of equipment and cargo, including water and air production equipment, and a shower unit, additional gyroscopic stabilisers for the complex, and the Ikar space bicycle — akin to America's Manned Maneuvering Unit (MMU). Expected in space on 30 January 1990 was a third module, 'Kristall' — fitted out with a microgravity laboratory, and equipped with a new docking unit capable of linking Mir to the Soviet Shuttle Orbiter vehicle.

It took only three days to bring Mir back into service by switching-on its internal systems and replenishing food and water stocks from Progress-M's cargo. Progress -M's hatch was opened on 10 September and on 13 September, a test-firing of its rocket motor system raised Mir's apogee by two kilometers. By the end of the month, several of the complex's scientific installations were in action, including the 'Roentgen' observatory, 'Gallar' (a semi-conductor production system), 'Circe' (a cluster of French-built sensors to measure radiation levels inside Mir), and medical-monitoring equipment including the Bulgarian 'Zora' installation designed to measure the body's psychophysiological reactions.

Much time was also devoted to replacing time-expired elements of Mir's onboard systems.

A solar flare occurred on 29 September, which increased the general radiation level in near-Earth space. Even though Mir's orbit is protected by the Earth's magnetic field, Viktorenko and Serebrov endured a radiation dose equivalent to an extra two weeks in orbit. Three more flares of similar intensity occured in the period up to 24 October, subjecting the crew to a radiation dose of 2.2 rem, in addition to the normal 1.7 rem 'background'.

October saw the start of a series of Earth -observation sessions, concentrating particularly on the atmosphere and its transparency. To this end, the cosmonauts took photographs with the KATE-140 camera, and used spectrometers to measure ozone levels in the tropics. This research was conducted under the joint Soviet-Cuban 'Atlantika-89' atmospheric study project. Complementary observations and measurements were conducted within the atmosphere by aircraft-borne sensors.

Progress-M's engine was fired three times more, on 13, 17 and 25 October, raising Mir's orbit from 372 x 389 kilometers to 390 x 405 kilometers. Propellant was also pumped from Progress-M into Mir's tanks during the week commencing 18 October.

On 13 October, mission control at Kaliningrad let the crew know that the two modules were being delayed, with Kvant-2 now due for lift-off on 28 November, and Kristall postponed until spring 1990 — after their return to Earth.

The cosmonauts were said to have reacted to the news in a "...reserved manner...". The Soviet daily newspaper Isvestiya immediately ran an editorial on the delay, hitting-out at the spacecraft designers, casting doubt on whether the Mir core-module would last-out long enough for the complex to reach its planned six-module configuration.

Isvestiya asked how it could be that Soviet microchips, manufactured as recently as 1985 for use in the rendezvous system computers, could possibly fail testing only one week before launch, while equivalent devices aboard America's Voyager 2 had been operating for twelve years in interplanetary space! The paper was extremely critical of the chips' manufacturer — the Voronezh Elektronika Production Association — pointing out, in highly derogatory tones, that the same plant produces microchips for video recorders, the quality of which "...speaks for itself...".

Kvant-2, all 19,565 kilograms of it, was ready for launch two days early, and left Baikonur at 1:02 pm GMT on 26 November to make a six-day chase intended to culminate in a docking with Mir. It didn't quite work out that way. Immediately, one solar

(Left) **Veteran cosmonaut Vladimir Dzhanibekov addressed fears that Kvant-2's microchip problem remained unresolved.**

(Below) **Close-up view of Mir's multiple docking unit.**

panel failed to open out, so the module was switched to a low power-consumption mode to conserve electricity supplies. A combination of rolling the module about its long axis at the same time as operating the panel's drive motor pulled the panel free from its latching mechanism. In case this action had proven unsuccessful, a specially-designed tool was added to the manifest for the upcoming Progress M-2 mission to support an emergency space-walk.

Progress-M was still part of the Mir complex at the time Kvant-2 was launched. Its engines were used on 25 November to adjust Mir's trajectory slightly in preparation for meeting Kvant-2. On 1 December, at 9:02 am GMT, Progress-M undocked and drifted away from Mir. Almost immediately, it performed a retrofire maneuver and re-entered the atmosphere in such a way as to burn-up.

During the final approach on 2 December, while still 20 kilometers from Mir, Kvant-2's computer aborted the rendezvous. Viktorenko and Serebrov tried unsuccessfully to take control of the operation. Naturally, there were fears that the microchip problem remained unresolved, but veteran cosmonaut Vladimir Dzanibekhov, speaking from mission control, said the problem lay in computer software. He said that mission managers were treading carefully because of their relative inexperience in controlling the docking of two such large spacecraft; the Mir/Kvant-1/Soyuz TM-8 complex at nearly 40 tonnes, and Kvant-2 at 20 tonnes.

A second attempt at docking was scheduled for 6 December, and all went perfectly. With Kvant-2 under automatic control and Mir's crew overseeing the stabilization of the space station, the two were locked together a few seconds before 12:22 pm GMT.

On 8 December, following a brief checkout, the new module was moved from the forward-facing port on Mir's multiple docking adaptor to the upper-facing port. The whole process was automated, and employed a 'Ljappa' manipulator arm attached to Kvant-2. It latched onto an anchor-point on Mir, pushed the module free and rotated it to a 90-degree angle with Mir, before pulling it back onto the second docking port. The whole process of reconfiguring Mir was completed on 12 December. At

8:23 am GMT, Viktorenko and Serebrov undocked Soyuz TM-8 from the rear of Kvant-1, and piloted it on a 20-minute flight along the length of Mir to redock it with the forward port, clearing the way for the cargo freighter Progress M-2.

Thursday 14 December saw the 100th day of the mission, and to mark it, Viktorenko and Serebrov held a press conference, answering questions from journalists at mission control, and taking them on a 'guided tour' of the inside of the station. They talked at length about the forthcoming spacewalks to test the Ikar-YMK 'space motocycle'. One piece of equipment they showed off was 'Inkubator', part of an experiment to see how birds might cope in microgravity. A quantity of Japanese quail eggs was manifested for Soyuz TM-9, so that 'Inkubator' could be used to produce chicks.

Progress M-2 left Baikonur at 3:31 am GMT on 20 December, carrying a cargo which included water, food, air supplies, reading material, film, fuel and new experiments, among them a number of biological specimens. It arrived at Mir on 22 December for a docking with the Kvant-1 end of the station at 5:41 am GMT.

A particularly significant item of cargo was an American payload, flown under the terms of a multi-mission commercial agreement, and devoted to studying the speed

Briefly: Aleksandr Viktorenko

ALEKSANDR Stepanovich Viktorenko was born on 29 March 1947 in the village of Olginka, in the Sergeyevski District, North Kazakhstan Region. After finishing school in 1965, he enrolled at the I.S. Polbin Higher Military Aviation School in Orenburg. He joined the CPSU in 1968, and upon graduating in 1969, served in the Soviet Air Force.

Viktorenko was posted to the Baltic Fleet, where he served as a Soviet Navy pilot until 1977. His commanding officer later recalled 'Aleksandr had flown a front-line Il-28 bomber to begin with. He subsequently retrained for a new aircraft, a heavy supersonic airplane. I recall no aircraft that was more difficult to pilot. Viktorenko flew it masterfully.'

In May 1977, Andrian Nikolayev visited Viktorenko's unit to actively recruit young pilots for cosmonaut training, and Viktorenko and Nikolai Grekov were both selected to join the cosmonaut team in 1978, reporting directly to Nikolayev. After being selected, Viktorenko was sent on a test pilot's course, where he mastered ten different types of aircraft, and was awarded the qualification of Test Pilot 3rd Class. He is also a Military Pilot 1st Class, and is a qualified parachuting instructor. He has logged over 2,000 hours flying time, and also has made over 150 parachute jumps.

Unfortunately, in 1979, Viktorenko was seriously injured during training, and was nearly dismissed on medical grounds. He was the victim of a freak accident during an exercise in an isolation chamber, when he unsuspectingly flipped a timer switch which had mysteriously come under an electrical charge of 220 volts. He badly burnt both hands in the accident and lost consciousness, seriously injuring his head in the ensuing fall, and remaining unconscious for six hours.

Apparently, when Viktorenko collapsed, doctors monitoring the exercise did not hurry to his aid, as they assumed he had merely collapsed from exhaustion! The injuries he sustained were grave enough to have him prevented from flying for the rest of his life, and the doctors tried to have him dismissed from the cosmonaut team. However, Viktorenko persevered, and through countless medical checkups fought his way back to the pilot ranks — and was eventually allowed to resume cosmonaut training.

He completed initial training, which would normally have only taken two years, in 1982, and was awarded the title of cosmonaut. His first assignment was as backup to Vladimir Vasyutin, the Commander of the original Soyuz T-13 mission. At the same time he was also assigned as the backup to Svetlana Savitskaya, Commander of the original Soyuz T-14 mission.

However, both missions were cancelled when Salyut 7 suffered a failure which left it without power. A repair mission became necessary, and the Soyuz T-13 backup crew was split-up. Once the complex had been repaired, mission planners wanted to get back to the original flight schedule, and Viktorenko's next assignment therefore became backup to Vladimir Vasyutin, who had been assigned as Commander of Soyuz T-14, launched on 17 September 1985.

Viktorenko, Aleksandr Aleksandrov and Yevgeni Salei should then have flown as the prime crew aboard Soyuz T-15, and should have replaced the Vasyutin crew. However, when Vasyutin became ill and had to be returned to Earth, the planned Soyuz T-15 mission was cancelled — for reasons that are as yet unclear.

Under normal Soviet crewing policy, Viktorenko and Aleksandrov should then have flown the next mission — the revised

Soyuz T-15, launched on 13 March 1986. However, in the event, they served as the backups, and the prime crew assignment was given to Leonid Kizim and Vladimir Solovyov; both very experienced cosmonauts who had previously worked together on the Salyut 7 space station.

In December 1986, Viktorenko was named as Commander of the joint Soviet-Syrian mission, Soyuz TM-3, launched on 22 July 1987. He, Aleksandrov and Muhammad Fares docked with Mir, joining the long-stay crew of Romanenko and Laveikin. There followed nearly six days of joint Soviet-Syrian experimentation.

The flight lasted seven days, 23 hours; Aleksandrov remained aboard Mir, and Viktorenko and Fares were accompanied back to Earth by Laveikin. The landing took place in high winds, and instead of alighting in open fields, the descent module was blown towards a village, finally touching down only two kilometres from the nearest buildings.

Upon his return, Viktorenko was awarded the title of Hero of the Soviet Union and received the Order of Lenin. He also was awarded the qualification of Cosmonaut 3rd Class, and the title of Hero of the Syrian Arab Republic — together with the Order of Military Glory. It was noted that Viktorenko had adapted particularly quickly and painlessly to weightlessness, and he attributed this to nearly ten years of training for a first space flight.

At some time following the Soyuz TM-3 mission, Viktorenko was assigned to the 'Rescuer' program — under which a Soyuz was always ready to be launched to rescue stranded cosmonauts from space. A team of experienced cosmonauts, including Viktorenko, was on constant standby to fly solo and then bring two cosmonauts back to Earth. The exact period of this assignment is unknown, but it appears that he combined it with active training for other missions.

As a result of Aleksandr Aleksandrov replacing Laveikin in orbit during the Soyuz TM-3 mission, the established Viktorenko/ Aleksandrov team was broken up. In addition, following doubts over Aleksandr Serebrov's health, he and Vladimir Titov were switched to the backup crew of Soyuz

TM-2 at the last minute, and Serebrov and Titov were subsequently split-up.

Mission planners, therefore, found themselves with two experienced cosmonauts, Viktorenko and Serebrov — both of whom had trained for a long-duration mission, and both of whom were without a partner. The obvious solution was to pair them, and it is believed that they may have served as the second backup crew for Soyuz TM-4, launched on 21 December 1987.

On 1 February 1988, Viktorenko was paired with Frenchman Michel Tognini, and they began training together as a crew. They were later joined by Serebrov, once he had completed his assignment as backup flight-engineer for the Soyuz TM-5 crew. The three were named on 26 September 1988 as the backup crew for the second joint Soviet-French spaceflight, Soyuz TM-7, launched on 26 November 1988.

Following the successful completion of the mission, Viktorenko was awarded the title of L'Officier de la Légion d'Honneur (Officer of the Order of the Legion of Honor).

His next assignment came in November 1988, when it was announced that he and Aleksandr Serebrov would be the prime crew for the forthcoming Soyuz TM-8 mission, and that the backups would be Anatoli Solovyov and Aleksandr Balandin. However, in late January 1989, Balandin replaced Serebrov as the flight-engineer, and Serebrov was switched to the backup crew with Solovyov. Although no reason was given for this switch, it appeared that it was due to the delay in the launching of the scientific modules to Mir. As one of the modules contained the 'Ikar' manned maneuvering unit to which Serebrov had been assigned the first test flight, there was no point in the latter flying until it had been safely delivered.

Viktorenko's next assignment, therefore, came when he and Balandin served as the prime crew for Soyuz TM-8, scheduled for launch on 19 April 1989. However, due to further delays with the modules, this mission was postponed — and Balandin and Serebrov again swopped roles. Soyuz TM-8 was finally launched on 6 September 1989, with Viktorenko and Serebrov aboard. The pair docked with Mir — whereupon Viktorenko became the first cosmonaut to visit Mir twice.

The docking was not without incident, as it had to be aborted when Soyuz TM-8 was only four meters from Mir. The space-station had suddenly shifted and moved out of the docking sight. Viktorenko therefore took manual control, and after a thorough systems check, completed the docking manually. Once aboard, the two cosmonauts settled down to a long program of scientific experiments and observations, and awaited the docking of the first major module, Kvant-2.

Two weeks after a series of five spacewalks, Viktorenko and Serebrov handed over the space-station to Anatoly Solovyov and Aleksandr Balandin. Shortly after undocking their Soyuz TM-8 ferry, it was found that the electrical power levels were very low, and the two cosmonauts had to switch off a number of instruments to conserve energy. However, re-entry was successful; the flight had lasted 166 days, six hours.

Viktorenko is married. He and his wife, Raisa, studied together in the same school from the first to the eleventh classes. They have a daughter, Oksana, and a son, Alexei, whom Viktorenko named after veteran cosmonaut Alexei Leonov. Viktorenko's hobbies include playing the bayan (a type of accordion).

Aleksandr Viktorenko was the 62nd Soviet cosmonaut to fly in space, and he has spent a total of 174 days, five hours, two minutes and 55 seconds aloft.

G.H.

(Below) **Nocturnal lift-off of Soyuz TM-8.**

at which protein crystals grow in microgravity. The agreement, negotiated between America's Payload Systems Inc. and Glavcosmos through the Soviet foreign trade organization Licensintorg, provided for the experiment to be sealed before ar-

rival in the Soviet Union, and to be returned to its owners in the same state. It was activated on 25 December and left to operate inside Kvant-1 until the end of the Soyuz TM-8 mission, when it was carried back to Earth.

Briefly: Aleksandr Serebrov

ALEKSANDR Aleksandrovich Serebrov was born on 15 February 1944 in Moscow. He enrolled at the Moscow Physical-Engineering Institute, and upon graduation in 1967, worked for nine years as a researcher at one of the departments of the Institute. He was awarded a Candidate of Technical Sciences degree in 1974.

In 1976, Serebrov joined the CPSU, and began work in the G.I. Petrov design bureau (now known as the Energiya Scientific Production Association). It is said that he soon showed himself to be a highly-qualified and resourceful worker, capable of solving complicated engineering and scientific tasks independently. At the bureau, he took part in the design and testing of spacecraft, including the development of the Soyuz-T — and met Gennady Strekalov, another future cosmonaut.

Serebrov was selected to join the cosmonaut team in 1978, and it is believed that he continued to be involved in Soyuz-T development work. It was his second attempt at joining the cosmonaut team, as he was unlucky when he first applied, having to undergo two separate operations (one was almost certainly a tonsillectomy) before being accepted.

His first spaceflight was as flight-engineer aboard Soyuz T-7, launched on 19 August 1982. The spacecraft docked with the Salyut 7 space station, and Serebrov, Leonid Popov and Svetlana Savitskaya joined the crew of Berezovoi and Lebedev already aboard. The visiting crew spent nearly seven days carrying out a program of experiments before returning to Earth after a flight lasting 190 hours.

Upon his return, Serebrov was awarded the title of Hero of the Soviet Union, and also received the Order of Lenin.

A problem then arose with Salyut 7's solar panels, resulting in a reduced flow of electrical power. This seriously affected the environmental-control system, producing cold, damp and uncomfortable conditions which threatened to make the station uninhabitable — and also posed a threat to the continued functioning of the station's electronics and other systems.

To overcome this serious problem, Vladimir Titov and Gennady Strekalov — who were in line as the next long-duration crew — were specifically trained in how to repair the faulty Salyut 7 solar array. Serebrov was assigned to their crew as research-cosmonaut for the mission; Soyuz T-8, launched on 20 April 1983. The three cosmonauts were supposed to dock with Salyut 7, but once in orbit the Soyuz rendezvous-radar antenna failed to deploy properly. Several attitude-control maneuvers were made at high rates, but they failed to swing the boom out (a postflight inquiry team later discovered that the whole of the antenna had been torn off when the Soyuz payload shroud separated).

The crew received permission from flight controllers to attempt a rendezvous using only an optical sight and ground-radar inputs for guidance. However, during the final approach — which was made in darkness — Titov believed that the closing speed was too great. He therefore attempted a braking maneuver, but felt that the two spacecraft were still closing too fast. He aborted the rendezvous to avoid a crash, and no further attempts were made before the threesome returned to Earth after a flight lasting just two days.

In 1987, Strekalov revealed that the aborted docking had been far more serious than previously thought. He described it as a "real brush with death" as the Soyuz had passed very close to Salyut 7 at high speed. Upon his return, Serebrov was only awarded the Order of Lenin, indicating official dissatisfaction with the failure of the mission.

Serebrov's next assignment came as flight-engineer on the second backup crew for the Soyuz T-14 mission, launched on 17 September 1985. During the docking operation, he acted as a commentator for Soviet TV!

Serebrov should then have served as backup for the original Soyuz T-15 mission. However, when Vladimir Vasyutin became ill and had to be returned to Earth, the planned Soyuz T-15 mission was cancelled — for reasons that are as yet unclear.

The cosmonaut's next assignment, therefore, was as flight-engineer for Soyuz TM-2. He and Vladimir Titov were intended to make a long-duration flight aboard Mir, but just six days before launch they were stood-down, due to doubts about Serebrov's health. The backup crew of Yuri Romanenko and Aleksandr Laveikin were given the prime crew assignment, and were launched on Soyuz TM-2 on 5 February 1987. Titov and Serebrov served as the backup crew.

Following the launch, Titov and Serebrov were split up, and in April 1987, Titov began training for a long-duration mission with Musa Manarov. In the same month, Serebrov again acted as a commentator for Radio Moscow, during the docking of the Kvant-1 module with Mir.

In July 1987, during the Soyuz TM-3 mission, Aleksandr Aleksandrov replaced Aleksandr Laveikin in orbit, due to doubts about Laveikin's health. This resulted in the breaking-up of the established Viktorenko/Alexandrov team. Mission planners therefore found themselves with two experienced cosmonauts, Viktorenko and Serebrov — both of whom had trained for a long-duration mission, and both of whom were without a partner. The obvious solution was to pair them, and it is believed that they may have served as the second backup crew for Soyuz TM-4, launched on 21 December 1987.

However, on that date, Serebrov was named by the Bulgarian press agency BTA as the backup flight-engineer for the forthcoming joint Soviet-Bulgarian Soyuz TM-5 mission — at the exact moment that Moscow was saying that assignment had been given to Andrei Zaitsev!

This is the source of more than a little confusion, as although Zaitsev was present at the press conference naming the crews, he was later stood-down — probably in late April 1988 — and Serebrov took his place, and therefore served as the backup flight-

engineer for Soyuz TM-5; launched on 7 June 1988. No reason has been given for this change of flight-engineers, although the Bulgarian press agency slip appears to indicate that Serebrov was always intended to be the backup.

He had actually been photographed practising splashdown procedures with the Bulgarian cosmonaut Aleksandr Aleksandrov and Vladimir Lyakhov in November 1987 — a month before the crews were named. At the time, it was assumed that this was the prime crew. However, Anatoli Solovyov, Viktor Savinykh and Aleksandrov were subsequently named as the prime crew, and Lyakhov, Krassimir Stoyanov and Zaitsev were named as the backup crew.

If Serebrov was paired with Viktorenko at the time, it made no sense to assign him to the Soyuz TM-5 mission, unless he stood in when Zaitsev was disqualified for some reason. But this does not explain why the Bulgarian press agency had prior knowledge, or why he was involved in the splashdown training.

Following the launch of Soyuz TM-5, Serebrov visited the USA and announced that he would be the flight-engineer on the forthcoming joint Soviet-French mission. However, when the crews were announced on 26 September 1988, he was actually named as the backup flight-engineer for the mission; Soyuz TM-7, launched on 26 November 1988. At the time, he was said to hold the title of Cosmonaut 3rd Class.

The French later awarded him the title of *L'Officier de la Légion d'Honneur* for his part in preparations for the joint mission.

At the Soyuz TM-7 pre-flight press conference, Aleksandr Volkov revealed that

Aleksandr Viktorenko and Serebrov would be the next long-duration crew to visit Mir, and that they would be the first to test the new 'Ikar' manned maneuvering unit. Serebrov later confirmed that he would be the first cosmonaut to use 'Ikar' in open space. However, in late January 1989, Serebrov was replaced on the prime crew for Soyuz TM-8 by Aleksandr Balandin, and was switched to the backup crew with Anatoly Solovyov. Although no reason was given for this switch, it appeared that it was due to the delay in the launching of the scientific modules to Mir. As one of the modules contained the 'Ikar' unit there was no point in Serebrov flying until it had been safely delivered.

Serebrov's next assignment, therefore, was as backup to Balandin on the Soyuz TM-8 mission, due to be launched on 19 April 1989. However, delays with the modules caused the mission to be postponed, and Serebrov and Balandin again swopped roles.

Soyuz TM-8 was finally launched on 6 September 1989, with Viktorenko and Serebrov aboard, and the pair duly docked with Mir.

Two weeks after a spectacular series of spacewalks, Viktorenko and Serebrov handed over Mir to Anatoly Solovyov and Aleksandr Balandin. Shortly after undocking their Soyuz TM-8 ferry, however, it was found that electrical power levels were very low, and the two cosmonauts had to switch off a number of instruments to conserve energy. Re-entry was successfully achieved; the flight had lasted 166 days, six hours.

At the time of the Soyuz TM-8 launch, it was reported that Serebrov had been a backup five times in the previous six years. Whilst four backup assignments in that period have been confirmed — Soyuz TM-2, Soyuz TM-5, Soyuz TM-7 and the original Soyuz TM-8 — the remaining one has not. However, it is believed that he served as the flight-engineer on the backup crew for the cancelled Soyuz T-15 mission. These assignments were in addition to the known and speculated second backup assignments; the cancelled Soyuz T-13 mission, and the Soyuz T-14 and Soyuz TM-4 missions.

Serebrov is a physician and designer, and is said to be a specialist on mass exchange and "everything connected with heat-transfer — from the heating of the station by the Sun to technological ovens." He is also President of the 'Soyuz' All-Union Young People's Aerospace Society, which is similar to the Young Astronauts organization in the USA.

A tall and athletically-built man whose interests include hunting and fast cars, Serebrov is known to his friends as Sasha, and his surname is apparently Russian for *silver's* or *of silver*. He is married, and he and his wife Yekaterina have two children — including a son, Kirill (born in 1969 or 1970), who in 1989 was studying Aerophysics at the Space Research Faculty of the Moscow Physical-Technical Institute.

Aleksandr Serebrov was the 52nd Soviet cosmonaut to enter space, and he has spent a total of 176 days, four hours, eight minutes and 12 seconds aloft.

G.H.

(Below) **The 'Chibis' lower-body negative-pressure ensemble played an important role in maintaining the cosmonauts' health during the six-month TM-8 mission, according to Valeri Poliakov** *(Below-right),* **a doctor who spent eight months aboard Mir in 1988/89.**

(Far right) **The underside of a Soyuz-TM capsule with the heat-shield jettisoned for landing.**

Six further flights of Payload Systems equipment aboard Mir are planned over the next few years. Before these opportunities arose, U.S. scientists had not had the opportunity to fly experiments on very long-duration microgravity missions since Skylab was aloft, over 15 years ago.

New Year was celebrated by Viktorenko and Serebrov, around a plastic fir tree with a 'banquet' of crispy pickles, fresh lemons, canned sturgeon, blackcurrant juice, and fruit candy. All that was missing was the champagne, but Mir is strictly off-limits for alcohol. As 1990 opened, they exchanged greetings with their families, who had been specially invited to mission control.

Much of January and February was occupied in preparing for, and carrying out, a series of spacewalks which culminated in tests of the Ikar-YMK maneuvering unit. Two of the spacewalk series came on 8 and 11 January and saw Viktorenko and Serebrov performing 'housework' on Mir's exterior (full details of the spacewalks appear in an accompanying section). Other tasks included routine work inside the station, including operation of its onboard experiments.

Mid-January saw a two-part maneuver to raise Mir's orbit, which had decayed to 385 x 388 kilometers by 16 January. A firing of Progress M-2's engine added eight kilometers to apogee, then two days later, another firing produced a 385 x 413-kilometer orbit.

A departure from normal practice took place on 28 January when, in memory of American teacher Christa McAuliffe, who died in the *Challenger* accident four years earlier, Viktorenko and Serebrov broadcast a 'space-lesson' to schoolchildren throughout the Soviet Union. They explained some of the workings of Mir and the Orlan-DMA spacesuits, and showed some of the laboratory equipment.

Four such lessons were broadcast from Mir in the fall of 1989, and together with this fifth one, Soviet educationalists produced a set of video-tapes for distribution, initially to American and Soviet schools, and then to other countries.

Friday 26 January, 1 February and 5 February, and much of the time between, was occupied with preparations for, and enactment of, spacewalks to test the new Orlan-DMA spacesuits and the Ikar-YMK maneuvering unit. These three excursions into raw space were great successes.

Meanwhile, on the ground, preparations were well in-hand for launching Soyuz TM-9 with the next Mir crew aboard. On 7 February, Anatoly Solovyov, Aleksandr Balandin, Gennady Manakov and Gennady Strekalov declared Soyuz TM-9 ready for flight. Two days later, it was on the launch pad, set to go.

Progress M-2 was still occupying the docking unit which would be needed by Soyuz TM-9. At 2:33 am GMT on 9 February, it was undocked and moved away from the space complex. As it did so, it was used for a series of communications tests throught the Soviet Union's Satellite and Data Relay Network (equivalent to NASA's Tracking and Data Relay Satellite System), using the Cosmos 2054/SDRN-west satellite, in geosynchronous orbit at 16 degrees west longitude. Soon after, a retrograde rocket-firing caused Progress M-2 to re-enter the atmosphere and incinerate.

On 10 February, Solovyov and Balandin, who had been relegated to backups for the Soyuz TM-8 flight, were confirmed as the TM-9 crew, and at 6:16 am GMT on 11 February, they set off on a relatively-un-

eventful trip to Mir. Docking took place at 6:38 am GMT on 13 February, heralding the start of a planned five and a half month stay.

For nearly a week, the four cosmonauts worked together aboard the complex. Solovyov and Balandin were briefed by Viktorenko and Serebrov on the finer points of living with Mir and were imparted with a working knowledge of its systems. Viktorenko and Serebrov went through re-adaptation exercises in preparation for returning to Earth gravity. A final series of experiments using the 'Gallar' microgravity furnace installation and the electrophoresis unit produced some last-minute samples to be brought back to Earth.

RE-ENTRY & LANDING

All that remained was to load-up Soyuz TM-8 with the results of five and a half months of experiments, and they were ready to depart. Weather conditions on the ground threatened to get in the way, and with just over 24 hours to go, meteorologists had still not given the go-ahead for landing. Eventually, an opening appeared above the area around the city of Arkalyk. Even so, the temperature was 30 degrees below zero on the Celsius scale. When approval for a re-entry on 19 February was given, everything went well as Soyuz TM-8 undocked. A normal retrofire was followed by an equally-uneventful passage through the atmosphere. Soyuz TM-8's landing capsule drifted down under its single orange and white parachute, and hit the ground at 4:36 am GMT, creating a flurry of snow.

Recovery teams were already on the ground, and they quickly hustled the two men into a warm tent. It took about one hour to unload the capsule, and the crew and the cargo were then flown to Arkalyk airport for an onward flight to Baikonur. With the active part of the Soyuz TM-8 mission completed, only the debriefing remained.

Viktorenko and Serebrov readapted quickly to full gravity. In fact, their in-orbit preparations for the return to Earth served them well, allowing the early stages of the adaptation program to be shortened. Cosmonaut Valeri Poliakov, a doctor who spent eight months on Mir during 1988/89, said that long space flights are now no longer a problem for Soviets, and that "...modern achievements of space medicine have made it possible to neutralize undesirable... influences on the human organism. Modern medical means not only guarantee the cosmonauts' health, but keep up their working capacity..."

Poliakov attributed the cosmonauts' ability to carry out five space-walks to the combined regimes of exercise and medical support.

R.D.C.

STATISTICAL ANALYSIS: SOYUZ TM-8

Spacecraft name: Soyuz TM-8
Crew:
Colonel Aleksandr Viktorenko (Commander)
Aleksandr Serebrov (Flight Engineer)
Launch vehicle: A-2 (Soyuz)
Launch: 9:38 pm GMT/05 September 1989. Baikonur, Khazakstan
Docking:
10:25 pm GMT/07 September 1989 (Kvant-1 port)
Re-docking:
9:03 am GMT/12 December 1989 (Mir forward port: 20 minutes in free-flight)
Undocking: Time unconfirmed/19 February 1990
Landing:
4:36 am GMT/19 February 1990 (55 kilometers northeast of Arkalyk)
Orbits: 2,588
Distance: 110,263,727 kilometers
Mission Elapsed Time: 166 days, 6 hours, 58 minutes
Initial orbit: 197 x 200 kilometers, 88.4 minutes, 51.6 degrees

Docked orbit: 381 x 395 kilometers, 92.3 minutes, 51.6 degrees

---

Spacecraft name: Progress-M
Crew: nil
Launch vehicle: A-2 (Soyuz)
Launch:
3:10 am GMT/23 August 1989 Baikonur, Khazakstan
Docking:
5:19 am GMT/25 August 1989
Undocking: 9:02 pm GMT/01 December 1989
Re-entry: 01 December 1989
Orbits: 1,566
Distance: 66,575,000 kilometers
Mission Elapsed Time: 100 days
Initial orbit: 187 x 217 kilometers, 88.5 minutes, 51.6 degrees
Docked orbit: 382 x 397 kilometers, 92.3 minutes, 51.6 degrees

---

Spacecraft name: Kvant-2
Crew: variable
Launch vehicle:
D-1 (three-stage Proton)
Launch: 1:02 pm GMT/26 November 1989. Baikonur, Khazakstan
Docking: 12:22 pm GMT/06 December 1989
Re-docking:
08 December 1989 (Mir upper port, using Ljappa)

Orbits: 3,391 (to midnight/30 June 1990)
Distance:
142,202,072 kilometers (to midnight/30 June 1990)
Mission Elapsed Time:
214 days, 10 hours, 58 minutes (to midnight/30 June 1990)
Initial orbit: 215 x 321 kilometers, 89.8 minutes, 51.6 degrees
Docked orbit:
394 x 398 kilometers, 92.4 minutes, 51.6 degrees

Spacecraft name: Progress M-2
Crew: nil
Launch vehicle: A-2 (Soyuz)
Launch:
03:31 am GMT/20 December 1989 Baikonur, Khazakstan
Docking:
5:41 am GMT/22 December 1989
Undocking:
02:33 am GMT/09 February 1990
Re-entry: 09 February 1990
Orbits: 798
Distance: 33,950,000 kilometers
Mission Elapsed Time: 51 days
Initial orbit:
187 x 212 kilometers, 88.4 minutes, 51.6 degrees
Docked orbit:
392 x 395 kilometers, 92.4 minutes, 51.6 degrees

Spacewalk spectacular

DURING THEIR six-month occupation of Mir, cosmonauts Aleksandr Viktorenko and Aleksandr Serebrov undertook a spectacular series of five spacewalks. They performed a wide variety of tasks on Mir's exterior, tested a new spacesuit, Orlan-DMA, and shook-down the long-awaited Soviet 'space motorbike', Ikar-YMK — named for Icarus, the legendary flyer — designed for use on satellite-repair or space-station construction missions.

Problems with one of the Kvant-2 solar panels led to another spacewalk being hurriedly planned, but in the event this proved unnecessary. The unscheduled EVA would have taken place over Christmas. A specially designed tool was a provisional addition to the manifest for Progress M-2, launched on 20 December 1989; it would have been used to free the still-folded right solar panel.

In the event, a combination of sudden movements by the spacecraft and activation of the panel's electric drive-motor eventually freed it.

EVA 1

Kvant-2's arrival resulted in the Mir complex taking-on an 'L-shaped', boot-like, appearance, making life difficult for the orientation-control system. Part of upgrading this system involved installing a pair of new star-sensors on Kvant-1's hull, at the aft end of the complex. The 150-minute spacewalk was planned for 8 January using one of the side exits of Mir's forward, multi-way docking unit. Hatch opening was scheduled for 7:24 pm GMT (10:24 pm Moscow Time).

When used for spacewalks, the forward docking unit acts as an airlock and is depressurised for the crew to exit. When the cosmonauts started to reduce pressure, ground control noted a corresponding pressure drop in the Soyuz TM-8 orbital module. There followed a delay as Viktorenko and Serebrov checked-out, and closed, a pressure equalization valve.

The hatch was eventually opened at 8:23 pm GMT. According to Deputy Manned Spaceflight Director Viktor Blagov, the blame for the problem was shared equally between the crew and mission control, as the latter had failed to spot the cosmonauts' error.

Each of the two sensors weigh 80 kilograms (176 pounds), and the cosmonauts manhandled them the full length of the complex before fixing them to appropriate attach points on Kvant-1 and plugging-in the connecting cables. On the way, Mir obligingly flew out of the Earth's shadow, causing one of its solar panels to rotate towards the Sun, thereby clearing their path. Work completed, they went back to the hatch, stopping-off to clean an area of Mir's hull and retrieve some material samples left outside by Aleksandr Volkov and France's Jean-Loup Chretien 13 months earlier. The samples were originally intended for only a six-month stay outside, but their collection was delayed by the mid-1989 hiatus in Mir activities.

In total, the cosmonauts were in vacuum for two hours and 56 minutes. They travelled a total of 35 meters around the exterior of Mir; not a great distance in itself, but new entry for the Soviet space record-books.

EVA 2

On 11 January, Viktorenko and Serebrov went out into space for a second time. During this excursion, they affixed samples of plastic and polymer materials to Mir's hull, to be collected by subsequent teams of spacewalkers. One of the spin-offs of having Mir in orbit is that it is the Soviets own, near-permanent equivalent of NASA's LDEF, with the extra advantage that the payload can be added-to or retrieved almost at will.

Making their way to the rear of the complex once again, they attached 'Arfa', a package of charged-particle and radiation detectors for studying the Earth's ionosphere. They then moved to another area of the station visited by Volkov and Chretien. Here, an attachment device for the Soviet-French ERA folding-structure was still in place. Viktorenko and Serebrov removed it and carried it back to the hatch to be stowed away inside Mir.

Back at the airlock, one major task remained; reconfiguration of two of its hatches. In order to minimise weight at launch, only two of the five hatches on the forward docking unit had been fitted with cone-type docking receptors; the forward and upper ones. With Kvant-2 safely docked at the upper port, its cone served no further use in that position.

Viktorenko and Serebrov had the task of moving the complete hatch to the lower port, and swapping it with the corresponding 'door'. This was accomplished relatively easily, and Mir was then ready to receive Kristall with its microgravity laboratory and Shuttle docking unit.

The hatch was closed and latched to complete the EVA after two hours and 54 minutes.

Orlan/Ikar test 1

Two weeks later, on 26 January, Viktorenko and Serebrov began a series of three spacewalks planned as the centerpiece

YMK MMU comparision		
	USSR Ikar-YMK	**USA MMU**
Mass (kilograms)	200	150
Thrusters	32	24
Propellant	compressed air	compressed nitrogen
Delta-V capability (meters/second)	30	20
Stabilization	gyroscope	gyroscope
Endurance	6 hours	6 hours

of their stay aboard Mir. They were charged with testing the new Orlan-DMA space suit and portable life-support system, and the Ikar cosmonaut mobility unit.

According to Soviet Manned Space Flight Director Valery Ryumin, the Orlan-DMA spacesuit is easier to don than its predecessors, and the arms and legs are removable, making for a better fit. It is good for a total of ten spacewalks, each lasting up to six-and-a-half hours. The suit is fitted with a two-way radio for communications between cosmonauts and mission controllers, and a telemetry transmitter to provide mission control with up-to-date information on the well-being of the suit's occupant.

Ikar (Icarus) is fitted with a total of 32 compressed-air thrusters; 16 primary thrusters and as many backups. Eight point forward, eight back, and four each are pointed in the 'up', 'down', left and right directions. The unit has eight more thrusters than the American nitrogen-gas-propelled Manned Maneuvering Unit (MMU) developed for NASA by the Martin Marietta company.

Development of Ikar began in earnest in 1985, under the direction of Chief Designer Gai Severin. Production was undertaken by Zvezda, a manufacturing organization better known for producing aircraft ejector seats and pressure suits for the manned space program.

At nine minutes past noon GMT, Kvant-2's hatch was opened for the very first time. More than half as big again as any of Mir's existing hatches, Kvant-2's one-meter diameter unit is now Mir's permanent 'front door', facilitating all cosmonaut exits and entrances.

The purpose of the latest excursion was given as "...to assemble additional science equipment and to test new spacesuits...". At the head of the list was installing a magnetic attachment point for parking Ikar. Both Ikar and the attachment device had been carried into orbit inside Kvant-2. This done, they moved away from the hat-

ch to perform a series of tasks on the outside of Kvant-2. They removed one of the dish antennas from its Kurs (Course) rendezvous system. By then, the antenna had served its purpose and was simply 'in the way'.

A TV camera was then attached to a moveable, Earth-pointing platform mounted outside Kvant-2, while elsewhere on the module's exterior, they affixed two small packages of scientific instruments called 'Ferrit' and 'Danko', and yet more material samples for exposure to the rigors of raw space.

Following a visual inspection of the outside of Kvant-2, Viktorenko and Serebrov went back inside, closing the hatch after a total of three hours and two minutes.

Orlan/Ikar test 2

Aleksandr Serebrov got the first opportunity to fly Ikar on 1 February, during a four-hour, 59-minute session which started with Kvant-2's hatch being opened at 8:15 GMT.

Leaving Kvant-2, he and Viktorenko first attached Ikar to its newly-installed docking unit. Serebrov prepared the vehicle for flight by lifting its arm-rests to the horizontal (operating) position, switching on its internal systems, and running a series of checks. He then released it from the docking unit and backed away under the watchful eye of a television camera held by Viktorenko. Another camera carried by Serebrov looked back at his colleague as he travelled initially about five meters from the station. Later in the test, he moved as far as 33 meters away, all the time remaining attached by a line which was unreeled from an electrically-powered winch under Viktorenko's control. The winch arrangement served as a safety device in case Serebrov, for some reason, was unable to pilot Ikar back to Mir.

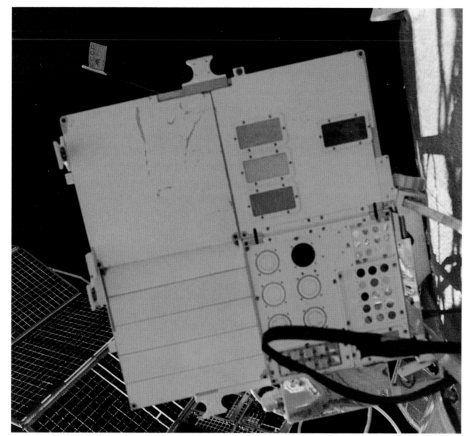

(Above) **Serebrov rides the 'space motorcycle'.**

(Left) **The French 'Echantillons' material-samples experiment, retrieved during the first spacewalk.**

(Right) **Detail shot of an Ikar attitude-control 'quad'.**

(Below-right) **An Ikar hand-controller, complete with range-meter.**

A tether was deemed necessary because of Mir's inability to 'chase after' a cosmonaut who might drift off into space. Later flights of Ikar, possibly using the Soviet Shuttle as a base, will dispense with it.

The test was an unqualified success, and Serebrov piloted Ikar back to Kvant-2. He parked it on its docking unit in anticipation of the next stage of testing, then both cosmonauts made their way back through Kvant-2's big hatch.

Orlan/Ikar test 3

Four days later, on 5 February, it was Viktorenko's turn to take a ride on Ikar. Exiting from the Kvant-2 hatch at 6:08 am GMT, he climbed into Ikar, went through the power-up/test routine and released the catch which had held it face-forward on the exterior of Kvant-2.

Remaining attached by tether, he backed away to a distance of 45 meters, putting Ikar through a regime of rotations in all directions. He travelled 200 meters through the space around Mir, using both manual control and semi-automatic operation of Ikar's thrusters.

Fitted on the front of Viktorenko's space suit was a gamma-ray/X-ray spectrometer called 'Spin-6000' which had been taken into orbit aboard Progress M-2. Designed by the Radium Institute of Leningrad, its purpose was to measure radiation emitted by the Mir complex. Prolonged exposure to the harsh environment in Earth orbit results in the absorption of solar radiation, causing a satellite itself to become a secondary radiation source. For designing scientific equipment, and understanding the effects of prolonged spaceflight on individuals, scientists need to quantify the amount and nature of such radiation. After completing the spacewalk, the spectrometer was set-up inside Mir to measure radiation levels within the station.

When Viktorenko and Serebrov climbed back inside Mir, they completed an outing which had lasted a total of three hours and 45 minutes.

R.D.C.

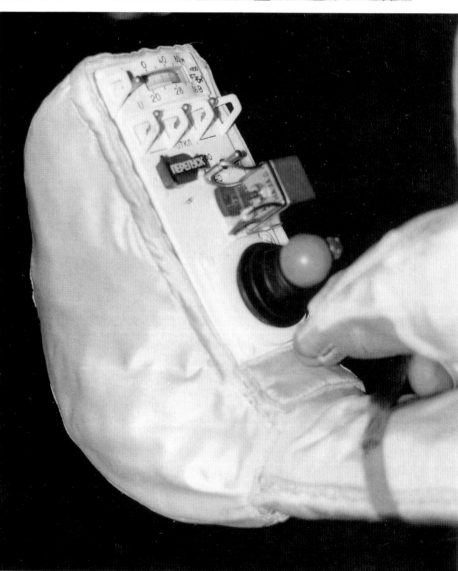

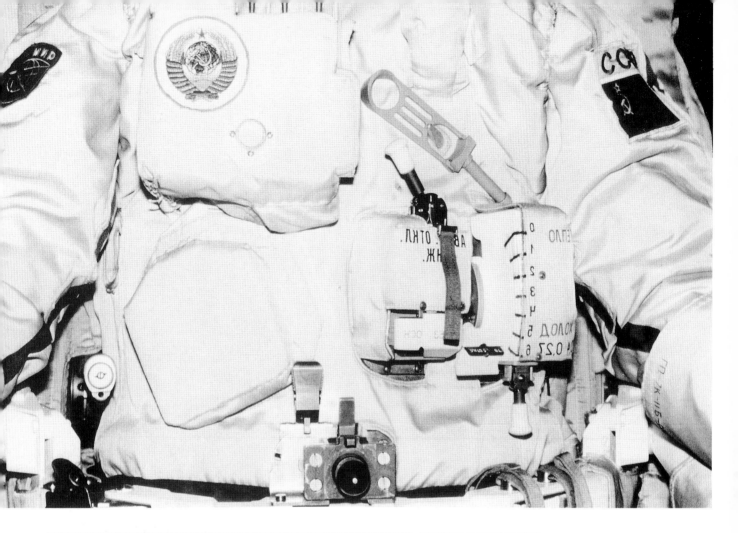

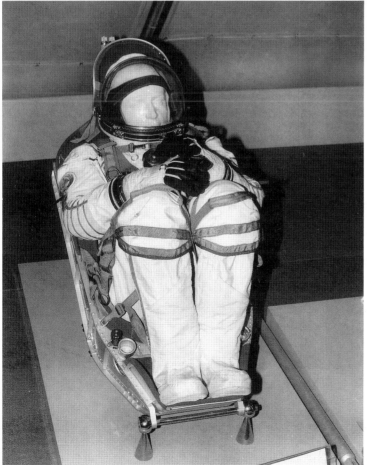

(Above) **Close-up view of the midriff of the new Orlan-DMA spacesuit. We haven't got the photo back-to-front! The operating instructions and associated numerals applied to the suit are reversed so that the wearer — unable to look straight down — can read them via wrist-mounted mirrors.**

(Left) **The other spacesuit: Soyuz ascent and re-entry suit and 'couch'.**

(Below) **Official Mir crew patch.**

PROGRESS M-3/PROGRESS 42/KRISTALL

SOYUZ TM-9

Cosmonauts Anatoly Solovyov and Aleksandr Balandin formally took charge of Mir on the morning of 19 February 1990, when they closed the hatch between themselves and their colleagues, the *other two* Aleksandrs — Viktorenko and Serebrov. Following a final check of Mir's air-tightness, Soyuz TM-8 departed — leaving the new crew to get on with its six-month stint aboard the complex.

LAUNCH

This latest crew had blasted-off from Baikonur at 6:16 am GMT (9:18 am Moscow Time) on 11 February, aboard Soyuz TM-9. Space veteran Solovyov was making his second space flight, while Balandin was a 'space rookie'.

Starting out from a 185 x 219-kilometer orbit, the spacecraft followed the standard two-day 'chase' trajectory before catching Mir, which was orbiting between 374 and 419 kilometers and completing a circuit of the Earth every 92.4 minutes. Its 'Kurs'

rendezvous system guided Soyuz TM-9 to a docking with the Kvant-1 module. The maneuver was completed at 6:38 am GMT on 13 February, eight minutes later than planned because of the unexpected need for a visual inspection of Soyuz TM-9's external condition.

The flight had gone well, but on the final run-in to Mir, it became apparent from television views of the approaching craft that there was a problem. Somehow, some of Soyuz TM-9's thermal insulation material had become detached from the body of the vehicle and was 'flapping' loose. The

material may have snagged on the launch vehicle's protective shroud as it separated during ascent to orbit. Viktorenko and Serebrov — and the staff in mission control at Kaliningrad — could see three panels of the material standing out like flower petals around the periphery of the descent module/orbital module interface.

The loose insulation made temperature-control difficult. For the next six months, Mir's attitude in space had to be monitored carefully, and constantly adjusted to avoid the Soyuz becoming too hot or too cold. There was also concern about the effects there might be on the descent module's metal skin as the regular cycle of thermal activity took it through a 300-degree range from 150 degrees Celsius to minus 150 degrees, and back, every one and a half hours.

ON-ORBIT

After the departing Soyuz TM-8 undocked, Viktorenko and Serebrov flew a tour of inspection round Mir to check the condition of the station's outer surfaces, and took photographs of the loose insulation on Soyuz TM-9 so that mission control would be able to assess the situation more fully and decide on the best course of action. Subsequently, the offending panels were clipped out of the way by Solovyov and Balandin during a spacewalk in mid-July.

Controllers felt this to be necessary because the projecting panels could have cast shadows during final preparations for retrofire at mission's end, and confused the horizon- and sun-sensors.

One of the major tasks assigned to the new crew was to oversee the docking of Mir's next add-on module, Kristall, which was due for launch in April. In the event, Kristall's arrival was delayed until June. Other tasks included operating in the 'Ruchei' electrophoresis experiment, aimed at producing very pure insulin samples, experiments with the 'Gallar' materials-processing installation, and conducting and undertaking geophysical studies, medical research, and Earth-observations.

Before Soyuz TM-8 departed, all four cosmonauts took part in the ongoing series of 'Resonance' experiments to check the vibrational characteristics of the Mir complex. These experiments are relatively simple to perform — they involve nothing more than bouncing off Mir's walls to create the necessary vibrations!

Soyuz TM-9 was occupying the rear docking port of Kvant-1, but this had to be cleared to allow the first of the mission's Progress resupply visits to take place. On 21 February, two days after Soyuz TM-8 departed, Solovyov and Balandin climbed into their own transport vehicle and undocked it. Soyuz TM-9 then backed-off from Mir for a 19 minute fly-round of the station,

which culminated in a docking with the forward-facing port of Mir's multiple docking unit at 4:15 am GMT.

In the course of the trip, Mir's cameras were used to take another look at Soyuz-TM-9's loose insulation. Soon after, the pictures were shown publicly on Soviet television.

The way was now clear for Progress M-3 to depart Baikonur, and it did so at 11:11 pm GMT on 28 February (2:11 am on 1 March, Moscow Time). Initially placed in an orbit of 183 x 228 kilometers, it gradually maneuvered up to Mir's 378 x 402-kilometer orbit for an automatic docking with Kvant-1 on 3 March at 1:05 am GMT. It delivered 2,500 kilograms of cargo, including fuel, food, water, mail for the crew, replacements for some of Mir's worn-out instruments — including parts for the computer — and a new set of storage batteries.

It took the two cosmonauts nearly two months to remove everything from Progress M-3 and pack their own trash inside it. They were in no hurry, though, as the docking port was not needed until early-May, when Progress 42's arrival was expected. During the last week of April, they pumped fuel and oxidizer into Mir's attitude-control system storage tanks.

March and April were two very routine months, occupied by operation of the on-board technical and experimental equip-

(Left) **One of the new-specification 'androgynous' docking units fitted to the Kristall module. They will permit the Soviet Shuttle to join with Mir.**

(Preceding spread) **The Mir/Kvant-1/Kvant-2/Soyuz TM-9 complex, as seen by the departing TM-8 crew. Note the 'petal-like' protuberances of loose thermal-insulation at right.**

ment, and maintenance activities. Maintence takes up a significant amount of a Mir crew's time, to the degree that it has actually brought complaints from some cosmonauts that too little time is left for conducting the important work of space research.

On 4 March the cosmonauts commenced the experiment to hatch quail eggs and grow the chicks in microgravity. 'Inkubator 2,' a device developed jointly by Soviet and Czechoslovak scientists, was used to provide the eggs with a suitably warm environment.

Originally, the experiment was intended to run for eight months, but in the event it was cut short by the chicks' inability to adapt to the absence of gravity. The first group of chicks, which hatched on 21 March, were shown to Soviet television viewers being fed by the crew. Eventually they were _"put to sleep"_ because they were never able to feed properly and rapidly grew very weak.

Had the experiment been successful, it would have represented a breakthrough in the study of the effects of weightlessness on living creatures. The intention had been to produce a steady supply of chicks to be returned to Earth for analysis.

On 30 March, Mir's core-module passed a major milestone — 1,500 days in space. Twenty-eight days later, it passed another when it became the oldest permanently-orbiting spacecraft to carry a crew. Up to that point, this distinction had belonged to Salyut 7, launched on 19 April 1982 and finally vacated by the Soyuz T-15 crew on 25 June 1986.

On 31 March came an announcement that there would be a nine-day delay in the launch of Kristall — putting it back to 18 April. In the event, further problems led to another six weeks' wait. Kristall was originally intended to enter space during the fall of 1989, but production problems led to a series of delays. The latest postponements were due to difficulties with onboard computer software.

The 'L-shaped' orbital complex — consisting of Mir, the two Kvants and Soyuz-TM-9 — was proving awkward to maneuver, because its center-of-gravity was not on the axis of the core-module.

Progress M-3 departed Mir around midnight on the night of 26/27 April, after a brief rocket-motor firing to check the system's operation and raise Mir's orbit by a few kilometers. The Progress completed a retrofiring about 24 hours later and burned up in the upper layers of the atmosphere.

Meanwhile, back on Earth, final preparations for the launch of Progress 42 were under way. It soared away from Baikonur at 8:44 pm GMT on 5 May (12:44 am on 6 May, Moscow Time) atop a Soyuz booster. Within ten minutes it was in a

Briefly: Anatoly Solovyov

ANATOLY Yakovlevich Solovyov was born on 16 January 1948 in the town of Riga, in the Latvian Soviet Socialist Republic. After finishing school in 1964, he began work as a fitter at a factory in Riga, then served as a locksmith at Rumbula airport in Riga. He also studied at night-school, and wanted to become a pilot, but initially could not decide whether to enter the Soviet air force or the realm of civil aviation.

In 1968, Solovyov enrolled at the Higher Air Force College in Chernigov, and following graduation in 1972, served in the Air Force in the Soviet Far East. He joined CPSU in 1971. Selected to join the cosmonaut team in 1976, he completed his final exams in 1979. In 1977, he graduated from a test pilot school, having learned to fly more than ten different aircraft types. He was awarded the qualifications of Military Pilot 1st Class and Test-Pilot 2nd Class.

It is believed that Solovyov's first assignment was as Commander of the second backup crew for the original Soyuz T-13 mission. However, that mission was cancelled when Salyut 7 suffered an onboard failure which left it without power. Once the complex had been repaired, Solovyov was assigned as Commander of the second backup crew for Soyuz T-14, launched on 17 September 1985.

Viktorenko, Aleksandrov and Salei should then have flown as the prime crew aboard Soyuz T-15, and Solovyov should have served as the backup Commander. However, when Vladimir Vasyutin became ill and had to be returned to Earth, the planned Soyuz T-15 mission was cancelled — for reasons that are as yet unclear.

Solovyov's next assignment came in December 1986, when he was named as the backup to Aleksandr Viktorenko, the Commander of the joint Soviet-Syrian mission, Soyuz TM-3, launched on 22 July 1987. For his part in preparations for the mission, Solovyov was awarded Syria's Order of Military Glory. He was also named in

December 1987 as the Commander of the second joint Soviet-Bulgarian mission, Soyuz TM-5, launched on 7 June 1988.

In November 1987, the Bulgarian cosmonaut Aleksandr Aleksandrov had been pictured practising splashdown procedures with Vladimir Lyakhov and Aleksandr Serebrov, and it was assumed that this was the crew that would actually fly to Mir. However, when Solovyov was named as Commander of the mission, Lyakhov and Andrei Zaitsev were assigned to the backup crew with Krasimir Stoyanov — although Serebrov later replaced Zaitsev.

Aleksandrov, Viktor Savinykh and Solovyov docked with Mir and joined the resident crew of Vladimir Titov and Musa Manarov. They then spent nearly eight days carrying out a program of joint Soviet-Bulgarian experiments, before returning to Earth after a flight lasting nine days, 20 hours.

Upon his return, Solovyov was awarded the title of Hero of the Soviet Union, and received the Order of Lenin. He also was promoted to the rank of Colonel.

Having served together on the Soyuz TM-3 backup crew and on the prime Soyuz TM-5 crew, Solovyov and Viktor Savinykh were split-up — possibly because Savinykh had completed three space flights — and Solovyov was paired with a new flight-engineer, Aleksandr Balandin.

In November 1988, it was announced that Aleksandr Viktorenko and Aleksandr Serebrov would be the prime crew for the forthcoming Soyuz TM-8 mission, and that the backups would be Solovyov and Balandin. However, in late January 1989 Serebrov was replaced by Balandin, and was switched to the backup crew with Solovyov. Although no reason was given for this switch, it appeared that it was due to the delay in the launching of the scientific modules to the Mir. As one of the modules contained the 'Ikar' manned maneuvering unit to which Serebrov had been assigned the first test flight, there was no point in the latter flying until it had been safely delivered.

Solovyov's next assignment, therefore, came when he and Serebrov served as the backup crew for Soyuz TM-8, due to be launched on 19 April 1989. However, delays with the modules caused this mission to be postponed, and Serebrov and Balandin again swopped roles. Soyuz TM-8 was finally launched on 6 September 1989, with Solovyov and Balandin serving as the backup crew.

It was then announced that the pair would constitute the next long-duration crew to fly, and they were subsequently launched aboard Soyuz TM-9 on 11 February 1990. They docked with the Mir complex, joining Viktorenko and Serebrov. After six days of handing-over operations, Viktorenko and Serebrov returned to Earth.

Solovyov, whose name is Russian for _nightingale's_ or _of a nightingale_, is married. He and his wife Natalya Vasilyevna — who works at the Yuri Gagarin Cosmonaut Training Center — have two sons.

Anatoly Solovyov was the 65th Soviet cosmonaut to fly in space.

G.H.

188 x 243 kilometer orbit, and started its two-day race to catch the Mir complex. It reached the station at 10:45 pm GMT on 7 May, docking with the Kvant-1 port; its cargo was reportedly similar to its recently-departed predecessor.

Progress 42 was the last of the 'old-style' Progress vehicles in the Soviet

spacecraft inventory. It was actually the 43rd vehicle of its type, and the series had a 100-percent operational success record, reaching back to 1978 and Salyut 6 — an impressive statistic by any standards.

Less than three weeks were available for loading and unloading activities, a relatively tight schedule in terms of recent

(Left) Soyuz TM-9 spears skyward from Baikonur on 11 February 1990.

(Below) Spectacular rendezvous image, captured from Mir.

(Right) Controls and couches compete for space in the Soyuz-TM cockpit. The primary instrument panel is off top-frame.

Progress missions. The first day of June had been set for launching the Kristall module, and the forward docking port had be clear by then. As things turned out, orbital mechanics dictated that Kristall leave the ground a day earlier, squeezing time even more.

On 26 May, propellant was pumped from Progress 42 into Mir's tanks. The freighter undocked at 7:09 am GMT on 27 May and was almost immediately commanded into a downward trajectory and the inevitable destructive re-entry.

The next day, Solovyov and Balandin went out on their third trip in Soyuz TM-9, this time maneuvering it back to the Kvant-1 docking unit where it had first arrived at Mir. Undocking occurred at 11:48 am GMT, and re-docking just 24 minutes later. Mir was then ready to receive Kristall.

On 31 May, at 10:33 am GMT (2:33 pm Moscow Time), a three-stage Proton rocket blasted-off from Baikonur, carrying the latest 20-tonne addition to the Mir complex. Ten minutes later it was in space, flying between 215 and 326 kilometers above the Earth, and circulating once every 89.9 minutes in a 51.6-degree-inclination orbit. Docking with Mir was set for 11:30 am GMT on 6 June, some six days after launch.

All went well during Kristall's approach, with orbit adjustments on 3 and 4 June to edge it nearer to Mir's 380-kilometer circular orbit. The first was a two-part maneuver, raising both the perigee and apogee. The result was a 278-kilometer perigee and a 368-kilometer apogee. Then, a third engine-firing raised perigee to 292 kilometers, and the docking approach was established.

As Kristall closed-in on Mir, difficulties in maintaining its orientation were traced to a faulty thruster, and the rendezvous was called off while controllers decided how to proceed without using it. Late on 6 June (early on 7 June, Moscow Time), the go-ahead was given for a second — ultimately successful — try. A couple of minor orbit adjustments by Kristall using backup engines (on 7 June and 9 June) ensured the necessary low-speed approach. Mir and Kristall came together at 10:47 am GMT on 10 June, with Kristall attaching itself to the extreme forward-facing hatch of the station's multiple docking unit. Now the complex's total mass was 83 tonnes.

Mir's orbit at the time of docking was 376 x 391 kilometers, with a 92.2-minute period.

Kristall had been outfitted with a microgravity 'factory' capable of producing quantities of a variety of semiconductor crystals for use in microelectronics, and further equipment for experimental pharmaceut-

Briefly: Aleksandr Balandin

ALEKSANDR Nikolaievich Balandin was born on 30 July 1953 in the town of Fryazino, near Moscow. After finishing school, he enrolled at the E.N. Bauman Moscow Higher Technical School, from which he graduated in 1976. He then began work at the Energia Scientific Production Association, where he proved to be a competent specialist capable of handling elaborate engineering tasks.

Balandin was selected to join the cosmonaut team in 1978, and enrolled in the CPSU in 1981. He underwent the usual cosmonaut training, then in 1985 he was transferred to the Soviet Shuttle flight-engineer training group. He was subsequently transferred back to the Soyuz training group, and in November 1988 it was announced that he and Anatoly Solovyov were to serve as the backups for the forthcoming Soyuz TM-8 mission (Aleksandr Viktorenko and Aleksandr Serebrov would be the prime crew).

However, in late January 1989, Balandin replaced Serebrov as the flight-engineer, and Serebrov was switched to the backup crew with Solovyov. Although no reason was given for this switch, it appeared that it was due to the delay in the launching of the scientific modules to Mir. As one of modules contained the 'Ikar' manned maneuvering unit to which Serebrov had been assigned

the first test flight, there was no point in the latter flying until it had been safely delivered.

Balandin's next assignment, therefore, came when he and Viktorenko served as the prime crew for Soyuz TM-8, due to be launched on 19 April 1989. However, delays with the modules caused the mission to be postponed, and Balandin and Serebrov again swopped roles. Soyuz TM-8 was finally launched on 6 September 1989, with Solovyov and Balandin serving as the backup crew.

It was then announced that the two cosmonauts would constitute the next long-duration crew to fly, and they were subsequently launched aboard Soyuz TM-9 on 11 February 1990. They docked with Mir and joined the crew of Viktorenko and Serebrov, already on board. After six days of handing-over operations, Viktorenko and Serebrov returned to Earth.

Balandin is married, and he and his wife Lidiya Vasilievna have a daughter, Yulia (born in 1984) and a son, Alexei (born on 31 January 1990). Only a week before the launch of Soyuz TM-9, Balandin's place on the mission was said to be under review due to the birth of his son, as he would not see him for six months.

Aleksandr Balandin was the 68th Soviet cosmonaut to enter space.

G.H.

ical-processing. One experiment was to involve producing solar-cell components for quality comparison with Earth-based manufacturing processes. Kristall also doubled as a cargo-carrier, bringing consumables to Mir's crewmembers, and equipment for an EVA to repair Soyuz TM-9's torn insulation.

One end of the Kristall module is fitted with a pair of new-type docking units for use by the Soviet Space Shuttle. One will be used by the second *Buran* orbiter during an unmanned mission scheduled to take place in 1991. Like the special docking unit built for the 1975 joint Soviet/U.S. Soyuz-Apollo mission, the new unit is 'androgynous'; any two vehicles equipped with it can join together.

The Soviets may be hoping to set a new standard for the other space agencies. Like the 'door' added to the complex by Kvant-2 at the end of 1989, the hatch diameter is one meter — over half as wide again as existing units. A matching unit for use with *Buran* has already been built.

Kristall was transferred to Mir's lower forward docking port — opposite Kvant-2 — on 11 June, making the complex 'T-shaped'. To achieve this, a short hinged-arm named 'Ljappa' latched-on to a fixture on Mir; the docking latches were released so an electric motor could move Kristall round to the side of Mir. Its docking gear then engaged in the side hatch, and a second hard-docking followed. After checking for air-tightness, the cosmonauts opened the hatches between Mir and the module, and after an initial tour of inspection they had Kristall's material-production system — Krater-5 — on-line and operating by 15 June.

Solovyov and Balandin had completed the major elements of their planned program aboard Mir. It was now left to them to carry out a spacewalk to fix Soyuz TM-9's torn insulation before attempting a return to Earth. The spacewalk was set for mid-July as this edition closed for press, and the landing was due in early-August, following the arrival of Soyuz TM-10.

Along with a replacement two-man crew for the station will come a 'hitch-hiker'. Rimantas Stankiavichus, a *Buran* Shuttle pilot, would be getting his 'space-legs' by undertaking a short, nine-day mission. On returning to Earth he would fly a simulated Shuttle re-entry profile in a Tu-154 airline, as 'Shuttlenaut' Anatoly Levchenko did in December 1987.

R.D.C.

STATISTICAL ANALYSIS: SOYUZ TM-9

Spacecraft name: Soyuz TM-9
Crew: Lt-Colonel Anatoly Solovyov (Commander)
Aleksandr Balandin (Flight Engineer)
Launch vehicle: A-2 (Soyuz)
Launch:
6:16 am GMT/11 February 1990
Baikonur, Khazakstan
Docking:
6:38 am GMT/13 February 1990 (Kvant-1 port)
Re-dockings:
4:15 am GMT/21 February 1990 (Mir forward port: 19 minutes in free-flight)
12:12 pm GMT/28 May 1990 (Kvant-1 port: 24 minutes in free-flight)
Orbits:
2,183 (to midnight/30 June 1990)
Distance:
92,658,037 kilometers (to midnight/30 June 1990)
Mission Elapsed Time:
139 days, 17 hours, 44 minutes (to midnight/30 June 1990)
Initial orbit:
185 x 219 kilometers, 88.5 minutes, 51.6 degrees
Docked orbit:
374 x 419 kilometers, 92.4 minutes, 51.6 degrees

Spacecraft name: Progress M-3
Crew: nil
Launch vehicle: A-2 (Soyuz)
Launch:
11:11 pm GMT/28 February 1990
Baikonur, Khazakstan
Docking:
1.05 am GMT/03 March 1990
Undocking:
around midnight/26/27 April 1990
Re-entry: 27 April 1990
Orbits: 904
Distance: 38,460,000 kilometers
Mission Elapsed Time: 58 days
Initial orbit:
183 x 228 kilometers, 88.6 minutes, 51.6 degrees
Docked orbit:
378 x 402 kilometers, 92.3 minutes, 51.6 degrees

Spacecraft name: Progress 42
Crew: nil
Launch vehicle: A-2 (Soyuz)
Launch: 8:44 pm GMT/05 May 1990
Baikonur, Khazakstan
Docking:
10:45 pm GMT/07 May 1990
Undocking:
7:09 am GMT 27 May 1990
Re-entry:
27 May 1990
Orbits: 338
Distance: 14,390,000 kilometers

Mission Elapsed Time: 22 days
Initial orbit:
188 x 243 kilometers, 88.8 minutes, 51.6 degrees
Docked orbit:
384 x 398 kilometers, 92.3 minutes, 51.6 degrees

Spacecraft name: Kristall
Crew: variable
Launch vehicle:
D-1 (three-stage Proton)
Launch:
10:33 am GMT/31 May 1990
Baikonur, Khazakstan
Docking:
10:47 am GMT/10 June 1990
Re-docking:
11 June 1990 (Mir lower port, using Ljappa)
Orbits:
479 (to midnight/30 June 1990)
Distance:
20,263,996 kilometers (to midnight/30 June 1990)
Mission Elapsed Time:
30 days, 13 hours, 27 minutes (to midnight/30 June 1990)
Initial orbit:
215 x 326 kilometers, 89.9 minutes, 51.6 degrees
Docked orbit:
292 x 366 kilometers, 91.1 minutes, 51.6 degrees

Spacecraft name: Mir
Crew: variable
Launch vehicle:
D-1 (three-stage Proton)
Launch:
9:29 am GMT/19 February 1986
Baikonur, Khazakstan
Orbits:
25,026 (to midnight/30 June 1990)
Distance:
1,059,658,351 kilometers (to midnight/30 June 1990)
Mission Elapsed Time:
1,592 days, 14 hours, 31 minutes (to midnight/30 June 1990)

Spacecraft name: Kvant-1
Crew: variable
Launch vehicle:
D-1 (three-stage Proton)
Launch:
12:06 am/31 March 1987
Baikonur, Khazakstan
Docking:
12:36 am/09 April 1987 (Mir rear port)
Orbits:
18,631 (to midnight/30 June 1990)
Distance:
788,882,601 kilometers (to midnight/30 June 1990)
Mission Elapsed Time:
1,187 days, 23 hours, 56 minutes (to midnight/30 June 1990)
Initial orbit:
171 x 300 kilometers, 89.1 minutes, 51.6 degrees
Docked orbit:
344 x 363 kilometers, 91.6 minutes, 51.6 degrees

PLANETARY MISSIONS

NEPTUNE

(Above) **The Voyager spacecraft bristle with scientific instruments, and Neptune provided a surfeit of data for them! At left is the RTG nuclear powerplant, amidships is the gold-plated disc** Sounds of Earth, **and at right are the cosmic-ray detector, plasma detector, wide- and narrow-angle TV cameras, ultraviolet spectrometer and other instruments.**

(Overleaf) **The 85-foot antenna at Goldstone, California — part of NASA's Deep Space Network (DSN).**

Hundreds of scientists and reporters flocked to the NASA/Caltech Jet Propulsion Laboratory (JPL) in Pasadena, California in late-August 1989 to witness the end of an era — Mankind's final first-time, close-up look at another world this century. The 12-year odyssey of NASA's Voyager 2 interplanetary explorer reached a magnificent climax just after midnight on 25 August, when the automobile-sized craft sped silently over the north pole of the giant planet Neptune. Four hours, six minutes later, observers gazed in awe and delight as signals relayed by Voyager 2 were translated into stunning images on their monitor-screens.

Voyager 2 skimmed just 3,000 miles above Neptune's cloud-tops — its closest encounter with any body in the Solar System since leaving Earth in 1977. It was a breathtaking demonstration of celestial navigation, comparable to a golfer sinking a putt from 2,250 miles. At that time, Neptune was some 2.7 billion miles from Earth, but Voyager 2 arrived within 20 miles of the point it was aimed at. "That's not bad

shooting!," said Project Manager Norman Haynes. "The navigation team nailed it right down the middle."

The excitement had been rising all week at JPL as Voyager 2 raced towards its target at 11 miles per second. After seeing the somewhat bland atmosphere of Uranus on the craft's previous encounter, scientists were surprised by the amount of atmospheric activity visible on its planetary

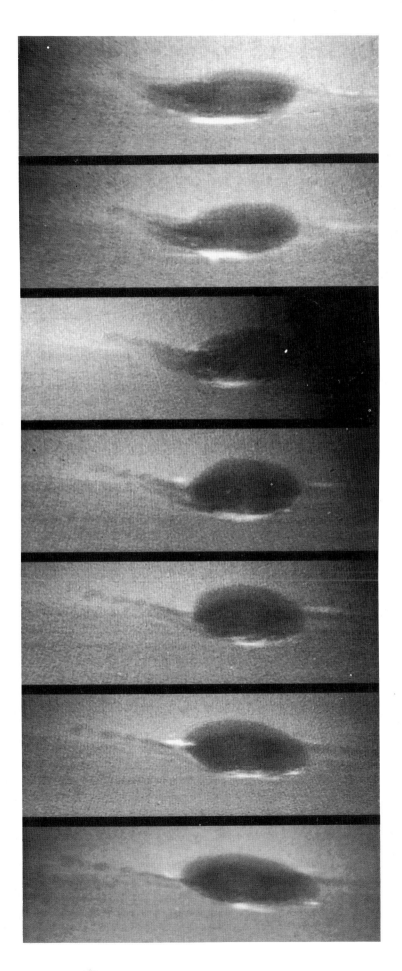

twin. Voyager 2 discovered super-hurricane-force winds on Neptune, with maximum speeds of about 1,200 mph recorded near 20 degrees south latitude. This makes Neptune the windiest planet in the entire Solar System.

These winds generally blow from east to west (the opposite direction to the planet's rotation). There is also evidence of large-scale convection; rising air in middle latitudes spreads out before descending at the equator and the poles.

A blue world

Pictures captured by the spacecraft's wide-angle and narrow-angle cameras revealed an amazing variety of cloud features in the planet's sky-blue atmosphere. Atmospheric scientist Andrew Ingersoll described for us a bright polar collar and broad bands of different shades of blue extending around Neptune's southern hemisphere. The blue coloring results from the present of methane in the atmosphere, which absorbs red light.

The most distinctive of the cloud-features at Neptune was the so-called 'Great Dark Spot', an oval storm system as wide as the Earth. Voyager project scientists had been watching this feature since its discovery in January, comparing it with Jupiter's famous 'Great Red Spot'. Imaging team leader Brad Smith commented, "It's in about the same proportion to the planet's size and at the same latitude."

Close-up images of the 'Great Dark Spot' revealed bright cirrus-like clouds of frozen methane rapidly forming and changing shape above and around it. Detailed study of their motion indicated that the spot has a counterclockwise rotation — again comparable to the Jovian spot. However, the energy-source for the 'Great Dark Spot' remains a mystery: Neptune receives only one-twentieth as much energy from the Sun and from its internal heat as Jupiter.

Other, smaller spots and white clouds were also visible. One patch of bright cloud was nicknamed 'The Scooter', because it sped around the planet much faster than the other clouds. Scientists were also amazed by Voyager 2's first-ever discovery of cloud shadows. Analysis of the shadows indicated that the long, narrow banks of white cloud were situated between 30 and 60 miles higher than the main cloud deck.

Beneath its thick atmosphere, Neptune is believed to consist of an 'ocean' of melted ice overlaying a rocky core. Scientists expected to find evidence of a magnetic-field generated deep inside the planet. The first confirmation of such a field came several days before closest-approach, when Voyager 2's instruments detected radio-waves emanating from the planet. Analysis of these signals revealed to scientists that Neptune is rotating once

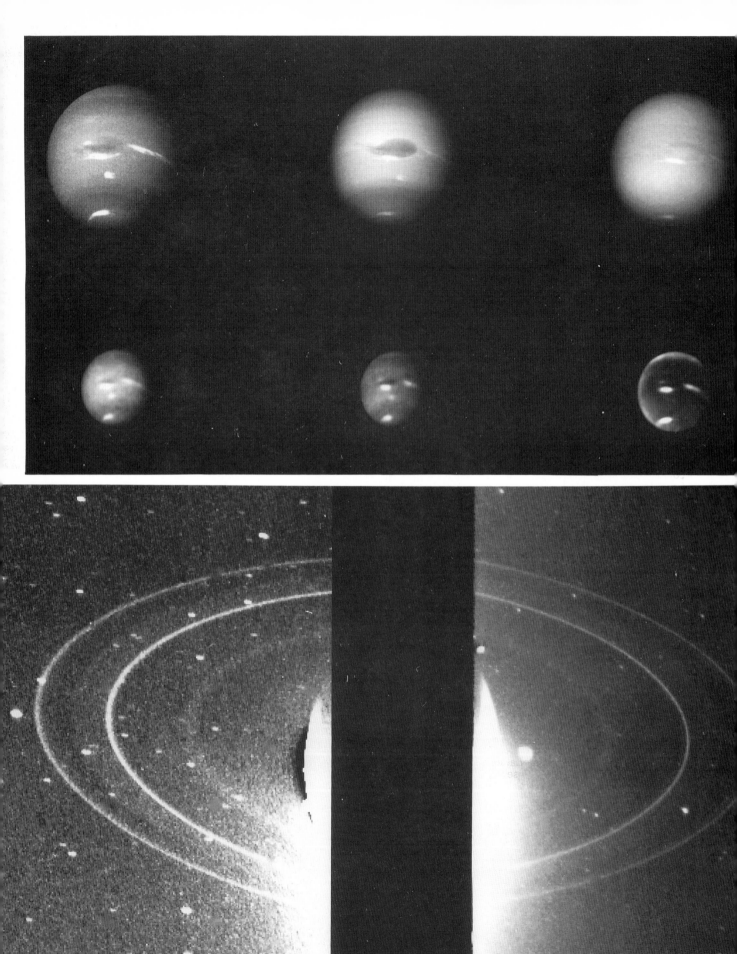

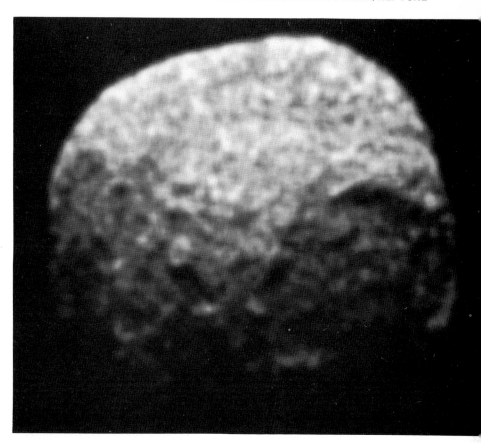

every 16 hours, three minutes.

Voyager 2 passed into Neptune's magnetic-field on 24 August, whilst still more than 375,000 miles from the planet. However, the nature of the magnetic-field was quite unlike anything the scientists had expected. It proved to be variable in strength, but generally weaker than the magnetic-field of the Earth — or any of the other outer planets — and is tilted at an angle of 47 degrees to the axis of rotation.

An equivalent situation here on Earth would put our magnetic pole in New York instead of northern Canada! At the time of the Voyager 2 flyby, the planet's south magnetic pole was very nearly pointed at the Sun.

Even more surprising has been the discovery that the field originates well away from the planet's center, at a point near the south magnetic pole. Like all the other outer planets, Neptune's magnetic polarity is the reverse of that on Earth. A compass needle would point *south* on Neptune.

Scientists thought Voyager 2 would be in a trajectory favorable to the detection of auroras around Neptune's north pole, but the discovery that its magnetic-field was so tilted altered the situation dramatically. In the event, however, auroras were found over wide regions of the planets, as well as on the large moon Triton, which Voyager 2 encountered some five hours after the primary flyby.

Observations made from Earth when Neptune passed in front of bright stars (occultation) suggested that the planet had several partial rings, or ring-arcs, around it. However, Voyager 2's cameras revealed the presence of two *complete* — though very narrow — rings, located 23,000 miles and 17,700 miles above the cloud-tops. A broad sheet of fine, dusty material lies between the two, while a third diffuse ring could be seen at an altitude of about 10,600 miles. Scientists suspect that this may extend all the way to Neptune's cloud-tops.

The two main rings are so thin (no more than 30 miles across at their maximum) that they were impossible to detect from Earth. Voyager 2 pictures confirmed that there are three clumps of material spread around the outer ring like long beads on a string. At first, scientists believed they may be caused by gravitational interaction with four newly-discovered moons which orbit between the rings. However, Voyager 2's cameras then detected at least six 'moonlets' — each just a few kilometers across — which may also play a major role in shepharding the beads of string material together.

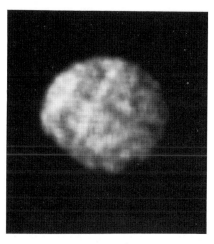

More moons

Before the Voyager 2 encounter, two Neptunian moons had been discovered during 140 years of Earth observations; Triton and Nereid. NASA's bold mission confirmed that both are highly-unusual. Triton moves in a circular, inclined path well outside Neptune's ring system, but it is the only large moon known to orbit in the opposite direction to its host planet's rotation. Nereid is much smaller and takes nearly a year to complete one circuit of its host, due to its very elongated orbit. Unfortunately, Voyager 2 was unable to pass any closer than 2.9 million miles of Nereid, so only a few blurred pictures were returned.

In total, Voyager 2 discovered six 'new' moons. They are all as black as soot, and among the darkest objects in the Solar System. Most of them are small, irregular-shaped bodies less than 200 kilometers

across. However, 1989 N1 — the first to be discovered — was found to be larger than Nereid, with a diameter of about 250 miles across. Scientists succeeded in pointing Voyager 2's cameras so that it could image this moon. They revealed a battered potato-shaped object, darkened with age. Scientists say 1989 N1 is about as large as a satellite can be without being pulled into a spherical shape by its own gravity.

Of the other new discoveries, only 1989 N2 was imaged with reasonably high resolution. It is an irregular-shaped object about 120 miles across and orbits outside the ring system. 1989 N4 lies just inside the outer ring and seems to be a 'shepherd' moon, keeping the ring particles in position. The remaining three are smaller still, and lie between the second main ring cloud-tops. They streak around Neptune once every seven to eight hours.

Exactly as planned, Voyager 2 flashed

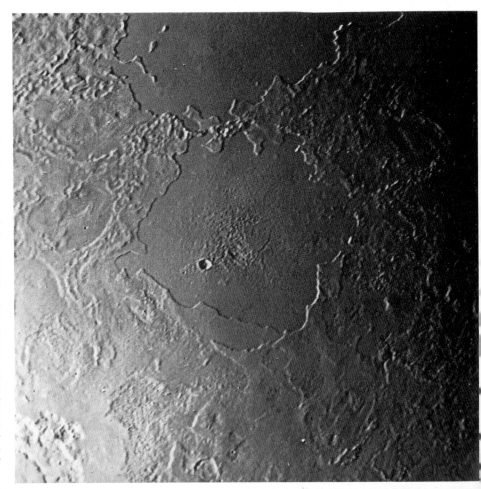

(Right) **An area of Triton 300 miles across. It has been extensively modified by flooding, melting, faulting and collapse.**

(Below) **This perspective rendering of one of Triton's caldera-like depressions was obtained by geometrically reprojecting part of a high-resolution frame.**

over the surface of Triton — the planet's largest moon — a few hours after its closest-approach to Neptune. This was regarded as a 'planetary' encounter in its own right, so great was the potential scientific harvest. For this reason, details of the Triton flyby appear in a separate panel.

Voyager 2's observations of Neptune and Triton ended on 2 October 1989. The remarkable 12-year-old spacecraft sent back more than 9,000 images of the planet, its rings and satellites, as well as a wealth of other data which will require many years of detailed analysis.

When Voyager 2 flew past Neptune, the planet's gravity bent the craft's trajectory so that it is now travelling away from the plane of the ecliptic (the plane in which all the planets in the Solar System, except lonely Pluto, lie) at an angle of 40 degrees. Most of the instruments on the venerable spacecraft were switched off to conserve power as it heads away from the Sun at the start of the Voyager Interstellar Mission (VIM) — a never-ending journey to the stars which it 'shares' with three other NASA spacecraft, all engaged in the search for the illusive edge of our Solar System.

P.B.

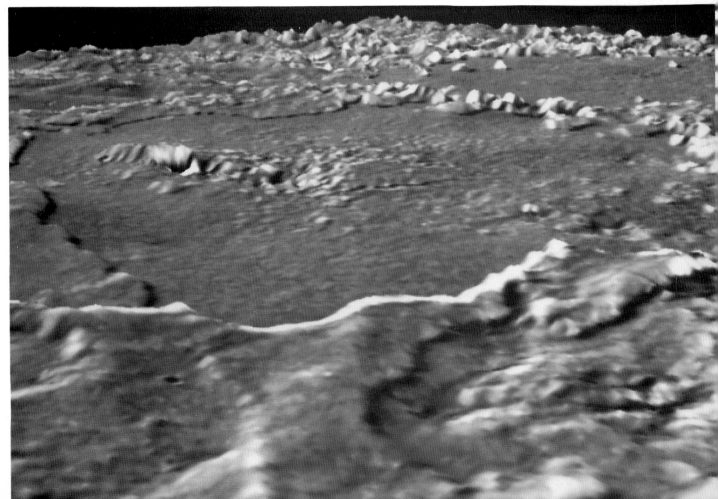

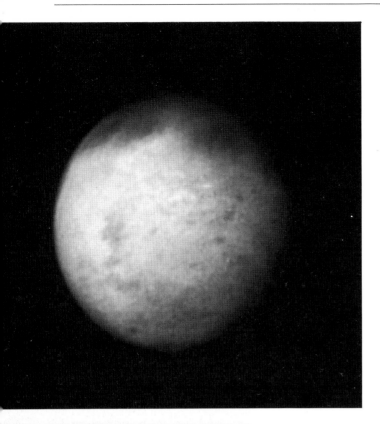

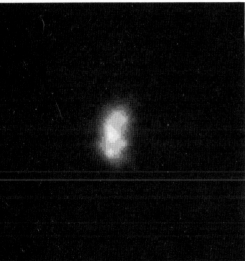

(Above) **Nereid was the last moon of Neptune to be discovered before Voyager 2's arrival. First seen by the American astronomer Gerard Kuiper in 1949, it is about 105 miles across.**

(Top) **A tantilizing taste of things to come. This image of Neptune's largest satellite, Triton, was captured by Voyager 2 on 24 August 1989, from a distance of 1.7 million miles.**

(Top-right) **A pre-encounter artist's impression of Neptune 'seen' from Triton — with methane existing as ice on the surface, and liquid nitrogen lakes. Five years later, speculation became fact.**

Unlocking the secrets of Triton

A FEW hours after its closest-approach to Neptune, Voyager 2 relayed stunning images of the Neptunian moon Triton, which had even hardened scientists gasping in admiration and bewilderment. "All we can say is, 'Wow! What a way to leave the Solar System,'" commented Dr. Larry Soderblom.

Triton was thought to be one of the largest moons in the Solar System, and was known to have a thin atmosphere. However, Voyager 2 revealed that it is smaller than expected, and brighter. "Triton has been shrinking as we approached," joked imaging team chief Brad Smith, "until we feared that by the time we arrived it might be gone."

Although Triton turned out to be only 1,680 miles in diameter (considerably smaller than our Moon), the presence of a thin atmosphere — composed of methane and nitrogen — was confirmed. The sheer variety of surface features left experienced analysts struggling for explanations. Triton's southern hemisphere is covered by a veneer of frozen methane and nitrogen, colored pink as a result of chemical reactions with solar radiation. Beyond the edge of the melting ice-cap there's a bluish area of icy crust, probably made of rock-hard water ice. This is pockmarked with interlocking cellular features.

It was likened to "melted chain-mail" by one reporter.

Criss-crossing this frozen wasteland are long, straight ridges with central furrows, which may be material pushed up from below through fractures in the crust. The lack of impact craters indicates to scientists that Triton's surface must be quite young in geological terms — not more than 500 million years old. Triton must have been resurfaced through a melting process, despite holding the record as the coldest known place in the Solar System; the surface temperature is -235C, just 38 degrees above absolute zero!

Further evidence of resurfacing are the smooth frozen lakes, similar to those found in volcanic craters on Earth.

Scientists suggest that Triton was once much warmer than it is today. Tidal heating could have resulted as the moon's orbit changed after it was captured by Neptune. Internal heat could also have been produced as the moon's denser material sank towards its center and decay of radioactive elements took place. Impacts from comets will also have caused wide-scale melting of the surface.

Perhaps most astounding of all is the revelation that Triton may still be volcanically active today. "This is a crazy idea," admitted Larry Soderblom, "but it's the best we have at the present time." Evidence for dozens of ice 'geysers' has been found in a very young region near Triton's south pole. Scientists believe that liquid nitrogen beneath the surface can seep through weak spots in the crust and erupt clouds of gas and dark organic material to an altitude of one to five miles. Dark streaks near the vents suggest that winds in the rarefied atmosphere can carry the particles more than 30 miles before depositing them on the surface.

With the exceptions of the Jovian moons Io and Europa, Triton has the highest density of any satellite of an outer planet. Curiously, it seems to closely resemble the planet Pluto both in size and density, and it may be that Triton can teach us a lot about that mysterious, far-distant world.

P.B.

BEYOND NEPTUNE

As Voyager 2 was beginning its search for the edge of the Solar System — joining the Voyager Interstellar Mission (VIM) — the cameras on its sister craft, Voyager 1, sprung into action for one last look back at the Sun and its planetary retinue. On 14 February 1990 — Valentine's Day — Voyager 1's imaging system, operating through both its wide- and narrow-angle lenses, was able to capture a series of 64 images through different filters. The images were recorded aboard the spacecraft and then transmitted to Earth in late March.

Released by NASA in mid-June after intensive image-processing, the resulting Solar System mosaic takes in the Sun and all the planets, except Mercury (which was lost in the Sun's glare), Mars (which was a mere sliver of a crescent, just beyond the threshold of current imaging capabilities), and mysterious Pluto (which was too far away and too small to be distinguished).

Displayed in its true glory, the mosaic would cover a wall measuring 100 by 150 feet. Because each planet is a mere picture-element (pixel) across — except Jupiter, which occupies four pixels — scattering inside Voyager's 1,500-millimeter focal-length TV camera reduces the mosaic's scientific value. "It's more of an historical event than a scientific endeavor," says Voyager Project Scientist, Professor Ed Stone. "It will remain unique for decades to come."

Mission scientists hope that Voyager 1 and Voyager 2 will continue to send back data for 25 to 30 years; data on changes in the solar wind and magnetic field, as well as ultraviolet observations of stars, active galaxies and quasars. The craft are heading away from the Sun in opposite directions; Voyager 1 is rising above the ecliptic plane, while Voyager 2 is plunging steeply below it. They are not alone in exploring deep space. In their search for the elusive boundary of our Solar System, the heliopause, they are supported by two other NASA spacecraft, Pioneer 10 and Pioneer 11; veterans of Saturnian and Jovian exploration, and now well-accustomed to life beyond the planets.

As the Sun moves through space, it emits a stream of charged particles which carry its magnetic influence far beyond the orbits of Neptune and Pluto. This solar wind forms the heliosphere, a bubble-like feature within the surrounding interstellar medium. No-one knows where the influence of the Sun comes to an end and interstellar space begins, but there should be a measurable discontinuity at that demarcation-line. Current thinking places it between 100 and 150 Astronomical Units (1 AU is the distance between the Earth and the Sun), although a recent report has suggested that it may be as close as 50AU.

However, most scientists think the heliosphere is shaped like a tadpole, with a long tail pointing away from the center of our galaxy.

Pioneer 10 is probably least likely to detect the shock-wave which marks the heliopause, since it is travelling along the tail. Pioneer 11 is headed along a shorter axis, but it is travelling relatively slowly compared with the Voyagers and its power supply is weaker. Voyager 1 is the favorite to make the historic breakthrough into interstellar space, since it is taking the most direct route as it heads towards the constellation Hercules.

Voyager 2 has further to go, and even travelling at a velocity of ten miles per second, it will probably run out of electrical power before it reaches the boundary.

(Left) **Pioneer 10 gets attention from TRW technicians prior to mating with its Centaur upper-stage. It was launched atop the Atlas-Centaur combination in March 1972, followed 13 months later by Pioneer 11.**

(Above) An artist's concept of Pioneer 10 passing beyond the orbit of Neptune on 13 June 1983, thus becoming the first spacecraft to do so. Pioneer 10 had also been the first craft to visit Jupiter.

There are four basic limitations which will directly affect the two Voyagers' performance; decreasing power margins, inability to lock onto the Sun for navigation, depletion of attitude-control fuel, and passing out of range of the Deep Space Network (DSN). By far the most worrying in the immediate term is the decay in power output from the spacecrafts' RTG nuclear

A cut above the rest

SHOULD ANY members of an alien civilisation come across either of the Voyagers on its galactic travels (shades of *Star Trek — The Movie*!), they will be able to learn some of its secrets from a gold-coated copper disc and stylus stashed aboard both craft. The location of our smallest planet is shown on a special star map, and each record contains spoken greetings in 54 languages; 120 images of the sights and inhabitants of Earth; and two hours of music and sounds ranging from Beethoven to Chuck Berry.

By that time, of course, the Voyager project will be almost forgotten — a topic to be studied, perhaps, as part of ancient 20th-century, history.

P.B.

generators. At present, Voyager 1 has roughly 380 Watts of power at its disposal, losing six to seven Watts per year due to radioactive decay of the plutonium power source. "We can only guess whether the decay rate will continue linearly," says William Kosmann, JPL's Manager for Mission Planning for the Voyager Interstellar Mission, "but power gets to be a problem around 2015."

Instruments will have to be switched off because there is ultimately a lower limit to the rate at which data can be returned to Earth.

To save power now, some of the scan-platform instruments have already been switched off: the photopolarimeter and infrared spectrometers are remote-sensing instruments, requiring a planet or moon to target. The camera systems have also been switched off, though their heaters have been left on so that they could conceivably be switched on again. The Voyagers' ultra-violet spectrometer remain operational, taking data on emissions from the interstellar medium. "Our uniqueness in the ultraviolet has gone with the launch of Hubble Space Telescope," Kosmann says. "But our perspective is certainly unique."

Apart from the plasma-wave instruments, which have been switched off, all the other fields-and-particles instruments remain functioning. "We're still sampling the solar-wind and measuring cosmic rays — like we've been doing all along," Kosmann says.

By the turn of the century, the other difficulties outlined above will become more readily apparent. To navigate through

But what about the dinosaurs?

NASA'S FLOTILLA of unmanned space probes might discover evidence for the existence of the so-called death star', which some scientists theorize caused the extinction of the dinosaurs 65 million years ago. This theory suggests that the Sun has a small companion star that orbits around it every 26 million years. The orbit is elliptical, and when the star comes close to the Sun, it could disrupt the Oort Cloud, a great mass of debris that exists in the outer reaches of the Solar System.

This, the theory contends, would sent an enormous shower of comets into the Solar System.

Some scientists are convinced that the extinction of the dinosaurs was caused by a 'death shower' of comets and asteroids that bombarded the Earth and kicked up so much dust and debris that the Sun was completely obscured. The resulting darkness and cold were lethal to the dinosaurs and many other life-forms.

N.M.

space, the Voyager uses the star Canopus and the Sun as references. "Our problem is that the Sun is getting dimmer, while the other stars aren't," says Kosmann. Though the Voyagers have gyro-control mechanisms, the power criticality means that it may not be possible to run them. Similarly, depletion of attitude-control fuel means that the craft run the risk of losing their three-axis stability and tumbling uncontrollably. There also remains the possibility that the Voyagers will pass out of

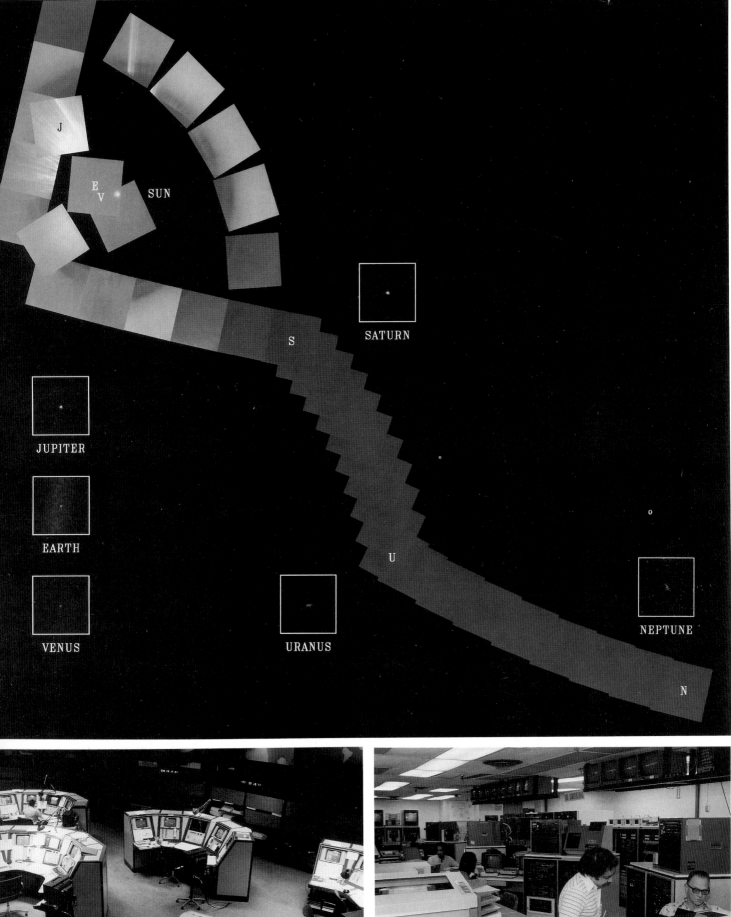

J

E
V   SUN

SATURN

S

JUPITER

EARTH

U

VENUS   URANUS

NEPTUNE

N

(Left) **Carl Sagan:** *"This is where we live — on a small dot".* On 14 February 1990, Voyager 1's cameras were pointed back toward the Sun to make the first-ever 'portrait' of our Solar System as seen from beyond the orbits of all the planets. A total of 64 frames make up a mosaic taking in the Sun and all the planets, except Mercury (which was lost in the Sun's glare), Mars (which was a mere sliver of a crescent , just beyond the threshold of current imaging capabilities) and mysterious Pluto (which was too far away and too small to be distinguished).

(Bottom-left) **The dimly-lit control room at the Jet Propulsion Laboratory (JPL),** where extraordinary interplanetary missions are guided and monitored.

(Bottom-right) **JPL** personnel maintain a watch on the unending flow of data from our interplanetary emissaries.

(Right) **JPL basks in the sun beneath the San Gabriel Mountains.**

range of the DSN; an event expected around the year 2030 if there are no other major setbacks.

"Our communication ability is increasing faster than the rate of Voyager's recession," Kosmann says. Major improvements with the DSN, including the addition of beam waveguides on the 34-meter dishes, mean that there is little chance of the Voyagers' signals falling on deaf ears for a long time to come.

Voyager 1 is travelling at 3.5 AU per year, heading up and out of the Solar System, while Voyager 2 is travelling at 3.13 AU — slower, because of the additional trajectory-bending manuevers needed at Uranus and Neptune (Voyager 1 didn't visit those planets). It is impossible to predict beyond 2030 what fates will befall the two long-dead spacecraft. In 40,000 years, Voyager 1 will make a relatively close flyby of the star known as AC +79 3888 in the constellation Camelopardus. Voyager 2 will likewise continue on its lonely way — towards the constellation Sagittarius, passing within two light-years of the 'nearby' star Ross 248 some 38,00 years from now.

N.B./P.B.

A primer on Pioneers 10 and 11

NASA's Pioneer 10 and 11 were launched a year apart in the early 1970s as pathfinders for the Voyagers in the outer Solar System. Both craft are travelling faster than 25,000 mph, the velocity needed to escape from the Sun's gravitational influence. After nearly two decades in space, both Pioneers are still in fine fettle according to project officials. Built in the late 1960s, both craft are spin-stabilized and much less sophisticated than the Voyagers.

To give an idea of their positions, Pioneer 10 is nearing the 50 AU mark, while Pioneer 11 is nearly 40 AU away. Powered by RTGs like the Voyagers, both craft transmit back to Earth with a signal only eight Watts in strength. Both carry a dozen fields-and-particles detectors — precursors of those carried on the Voyagers — but because they are spinning at 5 rpm, celestial-mechanics investigators can learn a great deal more about the outer Solar System environment. "Over a period of years, we can measure very small forces affecting the spacecraft," says Dr. John Anderson of JPL, principal celestial mechanics investigator for Pioneers 10 and 11. "We're 100 times more sensitive to these forces than the Voyagers. They aren't as gravitationally 'clean' because of their sophisticated three-axis control."

One unusual effect already observed on both Pioneers 10 and 11 is that their spin-rates seem to be slowing down, as measured against the star sensors on the spacecraft. "We're not exactly sure why," Dr. Anderson says, "but maybe it has to do with charge build-up on the craft causing magnetic braking." Ultimately Dr. Anderson's team is hoping that Pioneers 10 and 11 will solve one of astronomy's greatest riddles — the whereabouts (or otherwise) of 'Planet X'.

"What we've learnt so far is where 'Planet X' isn't," Anderson says. It has been known for many years that Pluto — the outermost planet, with its large moon Charon — cannot account for perturbations in the orbits of Uranus and Neptune. So since the 1930s, astronomers have been searching for a tenth planet, usually known by its roman numeral.

Historical observations have shown that the perturbations were more pronounced a century ago. To shed light on this riddle, Dr. Anderson says that his team "uses twentieth-century technology with nineteenth-century physics." As Pioneers 10-11 head away from the Earth, the apparent wavelength of their radio transmissions increases (as measured on the ground); the well-known 'Doppler-Shift'. "We then convert the Doppler-Shifts to model the accelerations, and hence any external forces on the spacecraft."

This gravitational book-balancing accounts for the Sun, the outer planets and the motions of the spacecraft itself — but there's an unaccounted acceleration of 10 million millionths of a kilometer per second every second, "There is a shortfall, but we can't explain its source by 'Planet X'," says Anderson. Perhaps an unseen disc of material at the edges of the Solar System is the cause — or else it's more exotic causes such as a black hole or a halo of cosmions. "We are staying alert to these possibilities as we have unprecedented sensitivity," he adds. "But we haven't seen anything that's set off any alarms yet!"

Both Pioneers have relegated 'Planet X' to a highly-inclined orbit virtually at right angles to the plane of the ecliptic.

Unlike the Voyagers, both Pioneers are rapidly running out of power. Pioneer 11 will probably 'fade from view' of the Deep Space Network in 1995, and Pioneer 10 will suffer the same fate five years later, assuming there are no major hardware failures. "When we loose contact, it'll be like a bereavement," Dr. Anderson says. "There's been a great sense of *camaraderie* on the project." His team could be consoled by the thought that if and when humans do eventually travel to the stars, the 'road map' will have been sketched first by Pioneers 10 and 11.

N.B.

MUSES-A/HITEN AT

THE MOON

One of the highlights of this *Space Year* was Japan becoming the third nation to mount a lunar-orbital mission, joining the United States and the Soviet Union. The mission is dubbed MUSES-A, for Mu-launched Space Engineering Satellite-A: 'Mu' being the generic title of the all-solid-propellant launch vehicle employed. Later in the decade, Japan hopes to stage complex lunar and/or interplanetary and cometary missions — having already dispatched two spacecraft, Sakigake and Suisei, to Halley's Comet in 1985. Missions to Venus and Mars, and a voyage to recover some cometary samples are mooted, and MUSES-A is serving as the technological pathfinder.

Contrary to some over-zealous Western media reports, this and projected medium-term future Japanese planetary missions are intended as purely scientific endeavors, hence their assignment to Tokyo University's ISAS space research division. ISAS — the Institute of Space and Astronautical Science — is a small organization, even compared to the mainstream national space agency, NASDA. Its ambition to tread in the 'celestial footprints' of the Voyager probes — developed, launched and guided by all the vast resources of NASA — is worthy of high praise indeed!

The MUSES-A mission got under way from Kagoshima Space Center atop its M3S2-5 booster on 24 January 1990. The 'Mu' vehicle's twin-spacecraft payload was directly injected into a highly-eccentric translunar orbit. The primary spacecraft, Hiten, weighed 197.4 kilograms at launch. This included 42 kilograms of RCS hydrazine fuel and a 12.2-kilogram lunar-orbital sub-satellite. Hiten is spin-stabilized with a nominal 20-rpm spin-rate. It totes various sensing devices — including a star-scanner, a pair of sun-sensors, an horizon-crossing detection scanner and some accelerometers — and twelve RCS thrusters.

One of the main objectives of the MUSES-A mission was to employ a gravity-assist regime for orbital maneuvering, and what better place to do it than at the Moon — our nearest celestial neighbour. In order to accomplish history's first lunar swingby, a multiple 'delta-V' (trajectory-bending) strategy was carefully investigated, using newly-developed software.

Compared with the pre-launch plan, however, the actual orbital sequence was drastically different, due to an error in the prescribed injection velocity. According to an ISAS report issued soon after, "The difference in the apogee altitude corresponded to a 50 meters-per-second error in the expected injection velocity of about 7,250 meters-per-second."

After successful correcting maneuvers, the Hiten (Japanese music goddess) spacecraft encountered the Moon on 19 March, 54 days after lift-off. On reaching perilune, the small sub-satellite was inserted into a near-circular lunar orbit. At the moment of its release into independent orbit around the Moon, the sub-satellite was dubbed Hagoromo (beautiful veil).

"From that point on, our music goddess

was without clothing!," quipped Dr. Kuninori Uesugi, the ISAS professor in charge of the program, during an interview with *Space Year*.

Long before the deployment, it was known (from telemetry relayed by the mother-craft in late February) that Hagoromo's transmitter had malfunctioned, and thus that no data could be obtained from it. In any case, the instrumentation aboard Hagoromo was only for gathering 'housekeeping' (internal temperature and voltage) data. Japan's first orbiter around a celestial body was not equipped to return scientific data.

Very fortunately, in view of the transmitter failure, the instant of Hagoromo's separation-motor 'burn' was observed from the Earth using the University of Tokyo's Schmidt camera. "We therefore estimated, or supposed, that Hagoromo was successfully inserted into lunar orbit — accomplishing the major objective of the mission," said Uesugi.

Hiten is employing a near-sun-synchronized double lunar-swingby orbit whose apogee is disposed in the Earth's geomagnetic tail; this type of orbit was ori-

(Above) **The tiny Hagoromo lunar-orbiter is just visible atop its Hiten 'mother-ship' in this photo, taken shortly before stacking on the M3S2 booster.**

(Left) **Sharp shadows highlight the pockmarked lunar surface in this (Apollo 11) view of the Japanese probe's barren destination.**

SOLAR ORBITERS

(Above) **Dr. Kuninori Uesugi of ISAS, who described the MUSES-A mission to** *Space Year.*

ginally introduced by NASA/Goddard's Drs. Farquhar and Dunham in 1980. Japan's Geotail mission — scheduled for launch in mid-1992 — will employ a similar double lunar-swingby orbit because of its efficient geomagnetic tail coverage, and Hiten is as a Geotail precursor, evaluating the technological aspects of such maneuverings.

The Geotail mission will be a constituent element of the International Solar Terrestrial Physics (ISTP) program, formed jointly by NASA, ESA and Japan's ISAS.

Hiten's systems are in very good condition, according to Dr. Uesugi. All the onboard experiment packages are functioning as planned, and should continue for more than a year. One of the experiments is an indigenous optical navigation device, which images the Moon and the Earth to determine its position in space. NASA's Voyagers have a similar system, but this is Japan's first attempt to fly one, and Hiten is claimed to be the first spin-stabilized satellite to feature optical navigation (the Voyagers have 'despun' buses).

The lunar images are transmitted to Earth, but since they are not intended for geological analysis, their definition is vastly inferior to the images returned by the Apollo astronauts.

Among the other technological goals of the MUSES-A mission is evaluation of a 'fault-tolerant' on-board computer, and exercising overall control of Hiten itself is a major objective of the ISAS technical team.

N.M.

When Richard O. Fimmel was assigned to the Pioneer project in 1963, he had no idea that most of the spacecraft concepts he was evaluating would still be in operation — in vast solar orbits — two decades after they were launched. These were the interplanetary missions which numbered 6 to 9 in the series launched at roughly yearly intervals from 1965 to 1968.

Now head of the Pioneer project office at NASA's Ames Research Center near Palo Alto, California, he fondly recalls all the subsequent Pioneer missions — to Venus, Jupiter, Saturn, and (with numbers 10 and 11) to the stars. But most fondly recalled are those early days. "I've been with the Pioneer Project since May 15th 1963," he recounts — a date etched in his memory because it was his wedding anniversary! "I've got kind of attached to the Pioneers, as I've had some of the most exciting times in my professional career."

Pioneers 6 to 9 were planned to investigate the solar wind and its interation with the Earth. In effect, they became 'solar weather stations' and their data is made available to meteorologists today via the National Oceanic and Atmospheric Administration (NOAA) in Boulder, Colorado. Planned to operate for six months, only Pioneer 9 has been declared 'dead' in — March 1987. All four are drum-shaped and spin-stabilized, electrical power being provided by the thousands solar-cells covering their exteriors.

In November 1988, Pioneer 6 passed within a million miles of Earth still returning particles-and-fields data.

Due to the press of subsequent missions, tracking time on NASA's Deep Space Network (DSN) is limited. But from time to time, Pioneer Operations Control makes contact with their distant charges, particularly when they pass through the Earth's geotail. "We do get a few select tracks per year," Dr. Fimmel says. Pioneer 8 returned "uneventful" data in late June, whilst Pioneer 6 was observed on Independence Day. Fimmel hopes that NASA will have a tracking ceremony on 16 December 1990, the 25th anniversary of its launch. "There may be problems, because the DSN will be heavily-subscribed at this time," he adds.

How long will the illustrious Pioneers continue to operate? "At the rate they've been going, indefinitely," Fimmel quips. Joking apart, he warns that the rate of solar degradation, which increases during periods of increased activity on the Sun, will be the root of their demise, but that's impossible to predict accurately.

N.B.

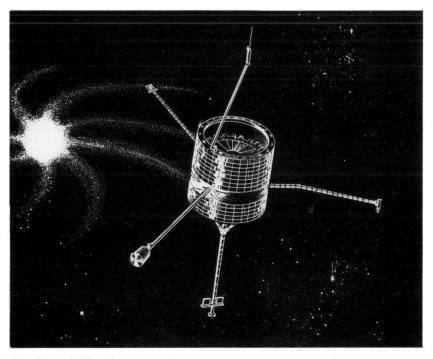

(Above) **Pioneers 6, 7, 8 and 9 share the same basic configuration. Only Pioneer 9 has ceased functioning, being declared 'dead' in March 1987.**

COMETARY EXPLORERS

In March 1986, five unmanned spacecraft visited perhaps the most famous celestial visitor — Halley's Comet. Of the five, only the two Soviet Vega probes have failed. ESA's Giotto has been retargeted for an encounter with Comet Grigg-Sjkellerup, and the two Japanese Halley probes, Sakigake and Suisei also are heading back to Earth for gravity-assists to take them to further comets. NASA's International Cometary Explorer (ICE), which flew through the tail of Halley after passing by Comet Giacobini-Zinner in September 1985, is also in commission.

All these Cometary probes are on orbits that roughly match the Earth's, so at various times they will automatically head back to where they were launched. The Earth thus provides sufficient energy to reach the inner Solar System portion of cometary orbits. The reason scientists are so interested in comets is that they have changed little since they were formed when the Solar System was born. They represent pristine material from which the planets and moons were formed.

In the night sky, comets can appear spectacular — though it is often difficult to predict how bright they will eventually be. As they approach the Sun, their ice nuclei are heated and give off dust, which causes a long tail to flow behind them. As they move around the Sun, their tails point away from it. Some appear once never to return again, so vast are their orbits. But others are periodic, and Halley is the brightest — plus its orbit the most predictable.

It is for this reason that five space probes were launched to it for its return in 1986.

Giotto: Comet Grigg-Skjellerup

Exactly four years to the day after being launched, ESA's Giotto spacecraft returned to Earth. Passing within 23,000 kilometers on 2 July 1990, Giotto has been given an extra lease of life by the first-ever gravity-assist to use the Earth. "The spacecraft wasn't designed to do this, but every indication is that we can," said ESA's Mannfried Grensemann, project manager for the Giotto Extended Mission (GEM).

On 2 July 1985, Giotto was launched from Kourou on its 700-million-kilometer journey to the icy nucleus of Comet Halley. The accuracy of its injection into the correct transfer orbit was such that Giotto's extended mission became possible even before it was planned! Giotto did not require as many mid-course corrections as anticipated. "As a result, *en route* to Halley we used far less fuel than expected," says Hugh Mooney of British Aerospace, prime contractor for the Giotto spacecraft. "This meant that Giotto could use its onboard propulsion system to head towards another comet."

Just after midnight on 13 March 1986, Giotto flew within 600 kilometers of the dark, icy nucleus of Halley's Comet. This unrivalled feat of interplanetary navigation has been likened to hitting a dinner plate in London with a rifle fired in Edinburgh. As expected, the spin-stabilized spacecraft was badly damaged by the Halley encounter. Travelling at 70 kilometers per second into the dust and gas surrounding the comet, this was inevitable. At such speeds, dust grains have the energy of hand-grenade explosions, so an ingenious 'bumper shield' was developed to protect the craft — which was penetrated a few seconds before closest-approach.

Preliminary damage analysis suggested that of Giotto's ten scientific instruments, four are fully functional and four partially so. A few hours after the Halley encounter, Giotto was powered-down and left in 'survival mode', as its experiments were designed to operate inside the cometary environment, not in deep space. Giotto continued to orbit the Sun, with a period five-sixths of the Earth's. So, in the past five years it has intersected the orbit of the Earth six times — reaching its starting point exactly five years after launch.

In February of this year, ESA enlisted the help of NASA to employ the Deep Space Network to 'waken' Giotto out of hibernation. Using the 70-meter antenna near Madrid, controllers got Giotto to respond to the tentative communication commands within hours. A few days later, Giotto began a powered-up phase to check its 'health' from the ground. Though there have been thermal problems caused by impact damage, the spacecraft seems to be in good health. Sadly, the Halley Multicolour Camera is damaged — a light baffle was destroyed, and part of the mechanism is blocking its field of view.

In January 1986, an ESA committee identified Comet Grigg-Skjellerup as a possible follow-on target for Giotto. Interestingly, the multiple gravity-assists using Earth (which will be used by the remaining cometary probes) were rejected. Because Giotto passed closest to the nucleus of Halley, the wear and tear it suffered made an extension of the mission to 1996 pointless. So all being well, Giotto will reach Grigg-Skjellerup on 2 July 1992, where its instruments will have another chance to reveal mysteries of the cometary kind.

Grigg-Skjellerup is an older comet,

(Above) **Comet Giacobini-Zinner, seen from Earth. Japan's Sakigake and Susei probes will hurtle past it in November 1998. NASA's ICE probe flew through its tail in September 1985.**

(Right) ICE is destined to return to Earth in August 2014. In this artist's rendering, it is undertaking its fifth and final lunar flyby — on 22 December 1983 — to target Comet Giacobini-Zinner.

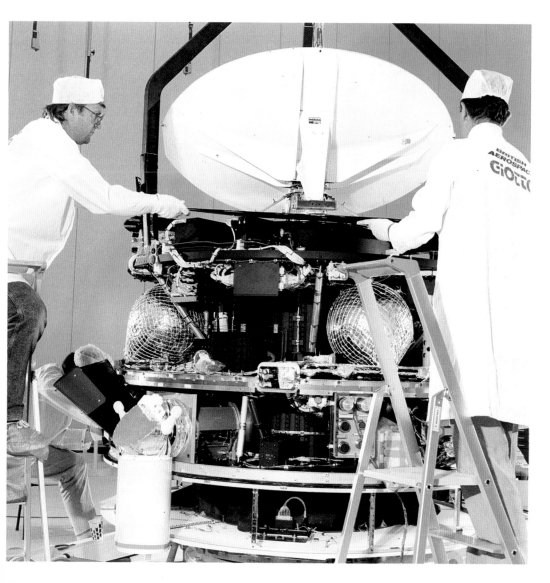

(Left) Giotto naked! British Aerospace technicians preparing the celebrated cometary explorer for a test in 1985. Having performed spectacularly at Halley's Comet, it undertook the first-ever Earth gravity-assist on 2 July 1990 and is now *en route* to Comet Grigg-Skjellerup.

(Above) **Sakigake's payload platform. Japan's other cometary explorer, Susei, is all-but identical.**

whose 5.1 year orbit is primarily the cause of Jupiter's gravitational influence. "The chief characteristics of Grigg-Skjellerup's trajectory are its low orbital inclination and its frequent encounters with Jupiter," says Dr. Gerhard Schwehm scientist for the Giotto Extended Mission. This means that its next encounter won't be as 'suicidal' as comet and probe will approach each other with a relative velocity of 'only' 14 kilometers per second.

After its pioneering Earth gravity-assist, the final hurdle for Giotto is financial. ESA has given its tentative approval for the Grigg-Skjellerup flyby, but extra funding will be required. As we went to press, it appeared that the Giotto Extended Mission would be made an optional program requiring around £10 million to cover tracking and operation costs, plus the analysis of the scientific results. "It would be a great pity to lose this opportunity while the spacecraft is still operational," says David Dale, Giotto's original project manager, now Head of Scientific Projects at ESA.

ICE: Earthbound

What will you be doing on 10 August 2014? Scientists at NASA's Goddard Space Flight Center just outside Washington D.C. have already marked this date down in their diaries, as on that day, the International Cometary Explorer (ICE) will return to Earth. Ownership of the spacecraft has already been formally handed over to the National Air and Space Museum, where it will doubtless become a star exhibit one day.

ICE was the third in a series of spacecraft launched to investigate interplanetary environment, placed in so-called 'halo orbits' around the point in space where the gravitational forces of the Sun are balanced with those of the Earth and Moon — the point known as Libration Point One. It is some 1.6 million kilometers from Earth.

In 1982, Dr. Bob Farquhar at Goddard proposed that by altering the trajectory of the craft — then known as the International Sun Earth Explorer, ISEE-3 — it could be caused to head towards Comet Giacobini-Zinner. So, by a series of complex maneuvers in 1982, the spacecraft sped within 120 kilometers of the Moon's surface to head off towards the distant comet. The craft was renamed the International Cometary Explorer, and it literally chased the comet as it headed towards the Sun, passing within 8000km of the nucleus of Giacobini-Zinner on 11 September 1985. The spacecraft's energetic particle and plasma detectors observed the comet's interaction with the solar wind, and dust impacts were noted from changes in the plasma density.

ICE subsequently passed within 25 million miles of the Sunward side of the nucleus of Halley's Comet (on 28 March 1986), and a subsequent propulsion system firing placed the craft in a similar orbit to that of Earth. ICE is now in an orbit ten days' shorter than the Earth's. It is 90 degrees ahead of the Earth, a figure which will increase to 180 degrees by 1999.

"It's still being tracked and it is returning useful information," says Dr. David Dunham, who works on the project for Computer Sciences Corporation. "There's no active control, but it isn't in hibernation." On 10 August 2014, it will have come full circle and be captured by the Moon. Though there is an option to use a further gravity-assist, most project officials believe that ICE will be brought back to Earth. "We'll answer the critics of the Giacobini-Zinner encounter," Dr. Dunham says, "as we can truthfully say we just borrowed the craft!"

Suisei: Comet Tempel-Tuttle

Japan's contribution to the flotilla of Halley-bound craft were its first deep space probes, known as Sakigake (Pioneer) and Suisei (Comet). They were identically-built, both being spin-stabilized and cylindrical in shape, though carrying different suites of scientific instruments. Sakigake carries a magnetometer, a solar wind ion measurement instrument and a plasma wave measuring instrument; Suisei carried an ultraviolet imaging instrument plus a solar wind experiment.

Sakigake was first to be launched (by a Mu-S2 solid-propellant booster), on 7 January 1985, eventually passing within seven million kilometers of Halley's nucleus. Suisei was launched (on another Mu-S2) on 18 August 1985, eventually passing within 151,000 kilometers of Halley's nucleus. Neither craft had the luxury of a dust protection device, so they passed on the Sunward side.

Since their Halley encounters, Japan's deep space tracking center at Usada has continued to track the craft with the 64-meter dish built for them. Both craft have two blocks of hydrazine-fuelled attitude-control thrusters; half of their supplies were used up by the Halley maneuvers. The remaining propellant has been used for 'braking burns' to increase the longevity of both probes. Sakigake will make an unprecedented four close passes by the Earth each year from 1992 to 1995. Suisei will pass within 900,000 kilometers of Earth on 20 August 1992. Both probes will then make further cometary encounters in the late 1990s.

Sakigake: Comet Honda Mrkos-Pajdusakova

Interestingly, Sakigake will become part of the International Solar Terrestrial Physics (ISTP) program, dedicated to investigating Sun-Earth interactions. The Inter-Agency Consultative Group which coordinated the Halley missions has continued with this program in mind. Sakigake will play tag with the Earth's geotail, the 'wake' behind our planet in the interplanetary medium. Enough energy will be imparted to Sakigake to place it on a transfer orbit to encounter comet Honda Mrkos-Pajdusakova on 4 February 1996, passing within 10,000 kilometers of its nucleus. In the meantime, Suisei will reach Comet Tempei-Tuttle on 28 February 1998. During that year, both probes will hurtle past Comet Giacobini-Zinner within five days of each other in November 1998, Suisei first.   N.B.

VENUS

Towards the end of 1990, Venus will be the focus for Mankind's insatiable curiosity. The first data from NASA's Magellan spacecraft will be ready for analysis, as will the full return of data from Galileo's Venusian fly-past in February '90. Since the very first successful interplanetary spacecraft — Mariner 2 — was sent there in December 1962, our perception of the veiled planet has come full circle. To the ancients, Venus represented the goddess of beauty, so attractive was its appearance in the twilight skies before dawn or after dusk. To science fiction writers, its cloud-enshrouded surface took them to unscaled heights of speculation and hyperbole; to visions of seas of soda water and dinosaurs chomping on swamp-like vegetation.

To today's space scientists, Venus represents a missing link in planetary evolution and reveals important information concerning the effects of a runaway greenhouse effect.

Fifteenth months after launch, Magellan reached Venus on Friday 10 August — firing its solid rocket motor at 5:31pm GMT to insert itself into orbit around the planet. "The spacecraft is doing very well," said Dr. Ed Sherry of the Magellan Project Office at the Jet Propulsion Laboratory (JPL) shortly before the big day. "We've experienced a little extra solar warming as we've passed inside the orbit of Venus to catch up with the planet."

Some weeks prior to orbital insertion, Magellan passed a major 'dress rehearsal' with flying colors. It was a four-day sim-

ulation of the operations it needed to execute in Venusian orbit. Data-gathering and communications with JPL were simulated for one hundred hours. Magellan Project Manager Anthony J. Spear reported that both spacecraft and ground systems performed flawlessly.

Because of the geometry of Magellan's approach and the communications time lag which results from Venus' distance from the Earth, observers didn't know until 6:04 pm GMT that Magellan was in orbit safely. Over the following days, Magellan's synthetic-aperture radar system will be tested so that it can start its epic mapping exercise by the start of September. "We've optimized the radar parameters so we can get as much data as quickly as possible," Dr. Sherry says.

Magellan was placed in an elliptical orbit around Venus with a period of 3.15 hours. Periapsis was at 250 kilometers around 10 degrees north, with apoapsis at 1,900 kilometers. Magellan will take radar images of the planet for 37 minutes on each pass. The rest of the time will be spent reorientating the craft to transmit this freshly recorded data back to Earth. JPL hopes that 90 percent of the surface will be mapped during the nominal 243 days of operations — an exercise likened by one Magellan official to wrapping a noodle around the planet.

Magellan was launched on 5 May 1989 on a standard transfer orbit to Venus. The mathematics of this were worked out as long ago as 1925 by Walter Hohmann, a German with a penchant for mathematical puzzles. One cannot simply fire a spacecraft towards Venus: it has to wait for a 'launch window' which will enable it to fly an energy-efficient route to the planet. The trajectory is a long sweeping curve meeting Venus at a specific time dictated by the energy limitations of the spacecraft's booster.

Originally, Magellan was slated to be launched to Venus in the October 1989 launch window, but this was eventually used by Galileo in the wake of the disruptions caused by the *Challenger* accident.

Though Magellan was launched before Galileo, it arrived at Venus later because

■ continued on page 118

The 'Goldilocks' question

ASTRONOMERS have known for many years that Venus is a very strange place. Enveloped in a dense, broiling carbon dioxide atmosphere, its surface is so hot that lead would actually melt. A Soviet Venera probe in the late 1970s recorded lightning discharges and a thunderclap which reverberated for fifteen minutes, possibly caused by volcanic discharges. Answering the question as to whether Venus does have active volcanoes is a task hampered by the dense Venusian atmosphere — but here, radar comes to the rescue. The most recent Venus probes have been equipped with radar devices to penetrate the thick clouds and map the underlying terrain. Plains, continents and vast mountainous regions have been observed — but the resolution has been such that the resulting maps are no more detailed than those in a school atlas of the Earth.

In 1983/84, Veneras 15 and 16 made detailed radar maps, but they were limited to the polar regions. Magellan, equipped with the most powerful radar sent to Venus, will increase this resolution by one hundredfold. By examining surface features in detail, geologists will try to piece together why Venus evolved so differently from Earth. That knowledge may help answer the so-called 'Goldilocks' question: why conditions were just right for life to form on Earth, but too hot on Venus.

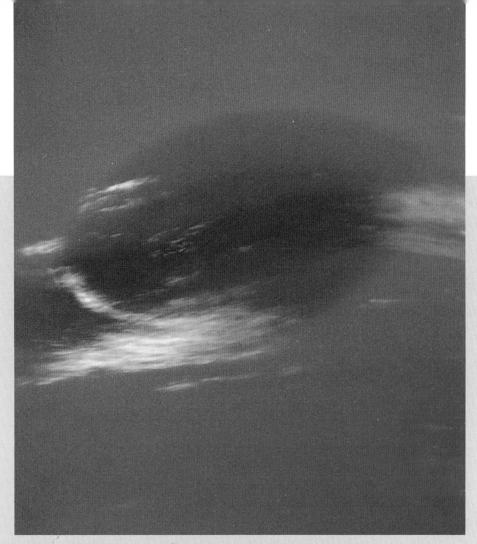

(Right) Shuttered 45 hours before closest-approach, this image of Neptune's swirling 'Great Dark Spot' shows feathery white clouds overlying the boundary of the dark and light blue regions.

(Below) Bright cloud streaks on Neptune, seen two hours before closest-approach — from a distance of 98,000 miles.

NEPTUNE: RETRO

(Right) Great variety in surface features is apparent in this photo-mosaic of Triton, assembled from 14 individual frames. Long fractures have opened, allowing some icy material to ooze up and form ridges which criss-cross the terrain.

(Below) Neptune imaged through the ultraviolet, violet and green filters of Voyager 2's wide-angle camera for better definition of cloud formations.

■ **continued from page 115**

(Right) **Earthlings lend scale to Magellan.**

it was travelling much slower. This meant it didn't have to decelerate as much at Venus as it would have had it been launched later. "It's all in the orbital geometry," says Dr. Sherry. "Because our approach velocity to Venus is smaller, we need less retrofire fuel in effect. That mass difference means we can carry more payload."

The all-important solid rocket motor only needed to fire for 83 seconds for Magellan to enter its correct orbit around Venus. During that time, the spacecraft's automatic control system ensured that it was correctly aligned by firing hydrazine-fuelled attitude-control thrusters. Every solid rocket system suffers from 'coning', an unpredictability in the smoothness of thrust-delivery caused by impurities building up around the exhaust nozzle. Magellan engineers were confident that any errors resulting from this phenomenon could be effectively 'dampened' by the hydrazine firings. Magellan was built by Martin Marietta, using 'spare' flight-qualified components from earlier missions. Its main 3.7-meter diameter antenna is a spare from the Voyager project, and its main control electronics are housed in a spare from the Galileo project. That Magellan was built 'on the cheap' was all too strong a reminder of NASA's budgetary problems in the early 1980s. What no-one doubts is the quality of the data it will return about our sister planet.   N.B.

Pioneer Venus

Eleven years separate the launches of the Pioneer Venus Orbiter (PVO) and Magellan. When the latter arrived on 10 August, the former was still operating. Only one instrument in the orbiter's total complement of a dozen has failed; the infrared radiometer. The Pioneer Venus Extended Mission has enabled scientists to observe Venus from close range during a solar cycle, the eleven-year period of activity on the Sun. "We've increased our knowledge of Venus immeasurably by our *in situ* data," says Dr. Richard Fimmel, a long-term mainstay of the program.

For a spacecraft which was designed to last for at most two years, Pioneer Venus has notched up some tremendous achievements. "We've discovered some pretty remarkable things," Fimmel says. For example, in 1986 PVO's ultraviolet imaging instrument was used to scan Halley's Comet as it sped by the Sun. "The glow of ionised hydrogen around its coma appeared like a vast cloud, the largest object in the sky," Dr. Fimmel recalls.

But for PVO, the end is nigh. Towards the end of 1992, it will suffer a fiery death as it burns up in the atmosphere of Venus. "The exact date depends on how much reserve gas there is," says Fimmel. "We intend to hold it at 150 kilometers above the surface for as long as possible. We'll have to fire the jets every other day." Scientists with research interests in aeronomy are eager to take as many samples as possible from the upper Venusian atmosphere.

                N.B.

GALILEO EN ROUTE TO

JUPITER

"It's an odd thing to say, but everything on Galileo is going boringly well," says the project's Mission Director, Neil Ausmann, of the Jet Propulsion Laboratory (JPL). "And that's just the way we'd like to keep it!" The relief of Galileo project personnel is self-evident, considering the problems and delays which continually affected the program during the 1980s. After launch from the Shuttle *Atlantis* in October 89, Galileo has headed inwards towards the Sun with Venus as its first destination. Because of the energy limitation imposed by its IUS upper stage, Galileo has had to take a 'circuitous' route to Jupiter known as the Venus-Earth-Earth-Gravity Assist (VEEGA) trajectory.

Galileo is now heading back towards the Earth (it will pass us in December '90) before heading out to the asteroid belt. In October 1991 it will fly past asteroid Gaspra before making another Earth pass in December 1992, so that it can pick up sufficient energy to head out to Jupiter. On its second pass through the asteroid belt, it will encounter asteroid Ida on 27 August 1993.

What this flightpath gains in energy efficiency, it loses in time; the journey to Jupiter will take six years. The target date for arrival at Jupiter is 7 December 1995.

Galileo was originally designed to go straight to Jupiter courtesy of the much more powerful Centaur upper-stage, cancelled in the wake of the *Challenger* accident. The VEEGA trajectory and use of an IUS forced a dramatic change on the mission. "At Venus there is twice as much energy from the Sun," says Dr. Torrence Johnson, Galileo project scientist at JPL. "But by time we get to Jupiter, there's 25 times less. We spent the three years after *Challenger* reconfiguring the craft to withstand this range of temperatures."

The range of modifications includes carrying additional thermal shielding to protect its delicate electronics from excessive heating. In particular, the bonding of the ribbed structure of the main antenna was of great concern, so as an extra precaution that won't be unfurled until early 1991.

For communications with Earth, a small low-gain antenna has been used. In late February '90, Galileo reached its closest point to the Sun — 64 million miles. "Everything's been perfect so far as the shields and shades are concerned," Ausmann says. "They've made sure the original thermal design of the spacecraft has been met." Galileo flew within 3,200 miles of the Venusian cloud-tops in February. Because of the limitations of low-gain data transmission, it took six hours to transmit one image. "We thought it would be unbelievable to have a planetary encounter," Ausmann says. The rest of the data has been stored on an onboard tape recorder, for playback as Galileo nears Earth in December. In the meantime — during the so-called mission cruise mode — data from the magnetometer, dust de-tectors and two ultraviolet spectrometers are being read out twice a week.

"We could only get ten bits of data per second at Venus," Ausmann says. "Now we're up to 40 bits of data per second."

Galileo continues to execute trajectory-correction maneuvers: the interplanetary equivalent of navigational fine-tuning. "It's a continual process of moving the aim point closer and closer to the Earth," Dr. Ausmann says. Short firings of the retro-propulsion motor system on the Galileo orbiter were made over a period of a day. The last maneuver was made on 17 July,

(Below) **Galileo rests at the NASA/ Caltech Jet Propulsion Laboratory (JPL) in Pasadena, California prior to the VEEGA modification effort. The eleven-meter boom, prominent from this angle, totes fields-and-particles instruments.**

so that present plans envisage Galileo passing within 1,000 miles of the Earth's surface (over Africa) at 08:59:38 GMT on 8 December. "We'll come whipping by," Neil Ausmann says. "On this first pass of the Earth we're not going to get a good view of the Moon. The second Earth pass two years later is more Moon favorable."

A post-Earth trajectory correction maneuvers will take place nine days after closest-encounter, placing Galileo on the correct trajectory for Gaspra and Mankind's first close look at an asteroid. This prospect, coupled with the promise of a low pass over the Moon's north pole next time around — *and* a further asteroid encounter — has more than whetted the appetites of scientists assigned to the Galileo program. "These encounters will keep us busy until we reach Jupiter in October 1995," Torrence Johnson says.

N.B.

(Left) **An artist's impression of the Galileo orbiter element streaking low over an erupting volcano on the Jovian moon Io. In the background are the turbulent clouds of Jupiter itself, which will at this stage have been plumbed by Galileo's probe element.**

(Below) **Venus was overflown by Galileo in February 1990 as part of the complex VEEGA route to Jupiter — though this particular image of our sister planet was captured eleven years earlier, by our old friend PVO.**

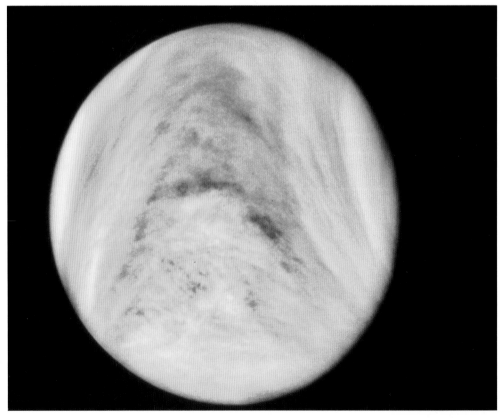

UNMANNED
MISSIONS

INTERNATIONAL

This *Space Year* featured several historic 'firsts' in the unmanned sphere; the Pegasus air-launch of Pegsat and GLOMR-2, and the relaunching of Westar 6/Asiasat 1 and Palapa B-2/R — to name but two. There were also graphic demonstrations of the incontravertible fact that, despite the apparent routinism of it all, satellite launches *do* occasionally go wrong. McDonnell Douglas went commercial with their Delta range, the final Titan 34D left the Cape, and Japan became the third 'Moon nation'.

The following are brief launch-by-launch accounts of every non-Soviet orbital unmanned mission conducted during the relevant period, plus details of the two might/should-have-beens; Ariane V36 and Commercial Titan 02. All of these missions could be described in far greater depth if space permitted. To illustrate this fact, we have selected one 'typical' flight — Ariane V32/Olympus 1 — for more detailed coverage in a separate sub-section.

Olympus 1/Ariane V32
12 July 1989

Weighing-in at 1,450 kilograms, with huge solar arrays spanning 26 meters, Olympus is the world's largest three-axis stabilized civilian communications satellite. Dubbed the 'Big Communicator' by it's makers, British Aerospace, Olympus is a European Space Agency (ESA) satellite designed to facilitate research and development in several new areas of communications satellite technology. It totes the most powerful direct-broadcast TV system ever carried on a satellite.

Olympus was originally called L-Sat when it was given the go ahead by ESA in 1979.

The 'Big Communicator' was launched three years later than planned, and sat on the ELA-1 launch pad at Kourou for two weeks — when last-minute problems with the Ariane 3 third stage cancelled the lift-off. All went well on 12 July, however, and Arianespace bade farewell to its last Ariane 3, which safely delivered Olympus into geostationary transfer orbit.

This was the eleventh Ariane 3 to fly since the maiden launch in August 1984. One failed in September 1985.

For further details, see panel.

TV-Sat 2 + Hipparcos/Ariane V33
8 August 1989

This fifth launch of the Ariane 4 — the fourth with two solid and two liquid strap-on boosters (designated the 44LP) — was also the 15th consecutive success for Arianespace, which had now delivered 24 satellites into orbit in 23 months.

ESA's V33 passenger, Hipparcos, ran into a problem. The West German TV-Sat 2 was being launched to replace TV-Sat 1, which failed in orbit in 1988.

For further details, see panel.

Navstar 2-3/Delta 186
18 August 1989

The third Navstar Block 2A Global Positioning System (GPS) satellite was launched by a Delta 2 from Pad 17B at Cape Canaveral. On the nearby Pad 17A, British Satellite Broadcasting's Marcopolo 1 was being prepared for its Delta launch.

McDonnell Douglas commercial launch operations were now getting into full swing, having already despatched two Navstars and an SDI payload in 1989, and boasting a bulging orderbook. The lighter-weight Block 2A Navstars are being launched by the Interim Delta 2, while later (heavier) versions — Block 2Bs — will require the fully-fledged Delta 2 variant.

Marcopolo 1/Delta 187
27 August 1989

British Satellite Broadcasting (BSB) was awarded the UK government license to operate a national direct-broadcast TV satellite system after the proposed Unisat project collapsed. The privately-funded company had to invest nearly £600 million to establish a two-satellite service by 1990, but conceded that its chances of making a profit before 1995 were rather slim.

The intense competition between TV channels was hotting up. The Astra 1 satellite had already provided Sky TV with a chance to establish itself in Britain before BSB. On 27 August, nervous BSB executives stood at a viewing stand at sunny Cape Canaveral to view the launch of 'their baby' — the first of two Hughes 373 spin-stabilized communications satellites designed to transmit with 110 Watts to very small dishes, hopefully to be fixed by the million to homes across the nation.

Their delight and relief as the 'old style' Delta 3945 blasted away was clear to see, and photos of the happy customers were later featured in McDonnell Douglas's commercial satellite launch-services advertisements.

USA-43 + 44/Titan 34D
4 September 1989

Cape Canaveral reverberated to the unique sound of a Titan 34D blast-off from Pad 40 on 4 September. To observers, the

(Above) **Delta 186 on Cape Canaveral's Pad 17B, poised to launch Navstar 2-3.**

(Overleaf) **Fiery ascent of the General Dynamics Atlas-E vehicle from Vandenberg, California, carrying the triple-element Stacksat payload.**

USA-45 (NTS-3)/Titan 2
5 September 1989

This third Navigation Technology Satellite (NTS), descended from the original Timation and Navstar 1 spacecraft, was boosted into orbit from Pad SLC-4W at Vandenberg Air Force Base by a Titan 2, also designated the Titan 2-23G.

The launch vehicle was the second of 15 out of 56 retired Intercontinental Ballistic Missiles (ICBMs) refurbished by Martin Marietta for the Department of Defense and national agency launches, to replace the Atlas E. Titan 2s will launch DMSP meteorological satellites, NOAAs and Landsats in the 1990s. The first refurbished Titan 2 flew in 1988, 22 years after lofting the Gemini 12 astronauts into orbit. The new-specification launcher is 37.5 meters tall and is equipped with a bulbous Titan 34D payload fairing.

Titan 34D makes a humming rather than numbing departure before the sound of the twin five-segment solid rocket boosters really hits the eardrums. It was a sound they would hear no longer, since this was the last Titan 34D to be launched. The type was introduced into service in 1982, as the latest in a line of thrust-augmented Titan 3 boosters, which first flew in 1965.

The 34D had had a mixed career, failing twice in 15 launches; one being the classic explosion above the skies of Vandenberg Air Force Base two months after the *Challenger* disaster in the fateful year of 1986. The payloads on the final Titan 34D were DSCS military communications satellites, although this was not confirmed officially.

Himawari 4/H-1
5 September 1989

In keeping with national tradition, the fourth Japanese Geostationary Meteorological Satellite (GMS) was not named Himawari 4 until it was safely delivered into orbit, a month later than scheduled. It had remained just plain GMS-4 on 8 August after a rather weird and rare launch abort at the Tanegashima Space Center. The H-1 was primed go and the countdown had reached zero, then — just before main engine ignition — one of two vernier stabilization engines failed to light and the launch was scrubbed.

GMS satellites are based on the Hughes GOES satellites, which with the European Meteosats, each play a part in the World Weather Watch program from various positions in geosynchronous orbit. Japan's brief is to cover the region between India and Hawaii.

The H-1 was the fifth Delta-based vehicle to be launched since 1987. A further four launches remained before the H-2 was slated to take over.

(Left) 'Star Wars' research continued with the LACE/RME mission in February '90. With six of its nine solid rocket boosters spewing flame, Delta 192 springs away from Complex 17 at CCAFS. At altitude, these six strap-ons are jettisoned and the remaining three ignite.

(Right) The UK Ministry of Defence's Skynet 4A satellite prior to a test in the anechoic chamber at British Aerospace's Stevenage facility.

(Below) Sisters under the skin. An extremely rare view of the Intercosmos 24 science satellite mounted atop its Soviet Tsyklon (Cyclone) booster. The small Magion 2 'sister satellite' also is clearly visible at the top of the stack.

(Above) **Intelsat 6-F2 semi-encased in the Ariane V34 vehicle's payload shroud/nosecone.**

Olympus 1: vital statistics

Launch mass:	2,595 kilograms
Payload mass:	359 kilograms
Mass in orbit:	1,450 kilograms
Power output:	3.2 to 3.6 kilowatts
Bus dimensions:	2.9x2.71x5.58 meters
Solar-cell array span:	25.67 meters
Orbital position:	19 degrees west
Operational lifespan:	5-7 years
Operating frequencies:	Ka-band, Ku-band

FltSatCom F8/Atlas-Centaur
25 September 1989

The last U.S. Navy FltSatCom fleet communications satellite, built by TRW, was launched on the last government-owned General Dynamics Atlas-Centaur from Pad 36B at a dark Cape Canaveral. The satellite should have been launched in June 1987, but was delayed when the previous spacecraft, FltSatCom F6, was lost when its Atlas-Centaur booster was struck by lightning and exploded after being committed to launch in extremely inclement weather.

Later, a freak launch pad accident involving its own Atlas-Centaur further delayed F8's departure for geosynchronous orbit. The last governmental Atlas-Centaur launch, this was the 58th success out of 69 launches since 1962, which included eight research and development missions. The first FltSatCom was launched in 1978, and in 1992 the fleet will be replaced by new Hughes UHF fleet communications satellites.

Navstar 2-4/Delta 188
21 October 1989

The fifth of the planned nine Block 2A Navstar GPS satellites routinely departed from Cape Canaveral's Complex 17 on 21 October. The U.S. Air Force plans to launch one every 60 to 90 days until a full 'constellation' of 21 satellites (three of them spares) are in their interweaving circular orbits, to fully replace the old fleet of seven Block 1 Navstar 1s.

Intelsat 6-F2/Ariane V34
27 October 1989

Weighing 4,240 kilograms at launch, with a telescoping 'drop skirt' solar-cell array producing 2.4 kilowatts, Intelsat 6 is a formidable beast. It measures 12 meters in height and is 3.6 meters in diameter, carrying 38 C-band transponders and ten Ku-band transponders capable of handling 24,000 simultaneous telephone calls and three TV channels.

Ariane V32

LIFT-OFF of Ariane mission V32 took place from the ELA-1 launch complex at the Guiana Space Center, Kourou at 19:14pm on Tuesday 11 July local time (12:14am, Wednesday 12 July, GMT). This was the final use of an Ariane 3 variant, and the final use of the ELA-1 launch pad after ten years of service. All future Ariane missions will employ the six versions of the Ariane 4 model and will be launched from the ELA-2 complex, which became operational in March 1986.

V32's launch was delayed over a week by a mechanical failure during the first countdown attempt on Friday 30 June. Four seconds before first-stage ignition that day, the count stopped automatically because one of the two cryogenic umbilical arms (which feed the third stage with liquid hydrogen and oxygen) did not detach properly.

Aboard Ariane V32 was a single payload; ESA's huge Olympus experimental comsat, which is the precursor of a new class of powerful communications platforms that will be launched over the next few years. The program that created it is also intended to stimulate users and promote new market applications for comsats using advanced payload technologies.

When you telephone Paris, telex Tokyo, or send computer data to New York, chances are you're employing an orbiting communications satellite. Most international tele-traffic is transmitted via comsats in geosynchronous orbit, 36,000 kilometers above the equator; only about one-third of it is carried along ocean-floor cables.

In these days of 'instant communications', we take for granted live TV coverage relayed across the world, yet it was only as recently as April 1965 that the world's first commercial communications satellite, Early Bird, was launched. This pioneering, Hughes-built comsat had 240 voice circuits, and relayed the first black-and-white trans-Atlantic TV broadcasts.

It started a revolution in communications, for today there are over 100 comsats dotted around the geosynchronous orbit like pearls on a string.

Europe was slow to develop its own satellite-based communications system. ESA had its first comsat — the Orbital Test Satellite, or OTS — carried aloft by an American Delta expendable launch vehicle on 11 May 1978. OTS was diminutive by modern standards. At launch it weighed just 444 kilograms, including on-board propellant.

Over the course of the 1980s, ESA has operated five larger — and considerably more sophisticated — ECS comsats, each capable of relaying two TV channels and

at least 12,000 telephone calls simultaneously. The latest European venture in this field, Olympus is the largest and most powerful civilian three-axis-stabilized comsat ever developed. From its operational location at 19 degrees West, it is following Early Bird's example by setting exciting new trends.

The Olympus program was originally known as L-Sat (Large Satellite), and it came into being in 1979, when ESA studies indicated that there was going to be a sore need for a new class of multi-purpose satellite capable of dealing with the higher volumes of communications traffic anticipated for the 1990s and beyond. Forecasts indicated there'd be a demand for comsats that could provide higher electrical power levels and tote heavier payloads than the current generation ECS/MARECS class of satellite.

Project-definition studies began in 1980, and full-scale development got under way in 1982. The name-change from L-Sat to Olympus came in 1983.

British Aerospace was appointed Olympus prime contractor, leading an unusual pan-European/Canadian mix of subcontractors; Aeritalia and Selenia Spazio of Italy, Fokker of the Netherlands, and Spar Aerospace of Ontario. Launch of Olympus 1 was originally scheduled for 1987, but was delayed when shortcomings in the design of the Ariane launch vehicle's third-stage motor caused the V18 accident in May 1986, and led to the entire Ariane fleet being grounded for 18 months.

The prototype Olympus carries four experimental payloads, and user demand for the services they provide is high, so their operation is being coordinated by an Olympus Utilization Program.

Distance learning

Direct-broadcasting of TV programs from space, such as those seen on the Sky and BSB channels available in Britain, is seen by many as the system of the future. Olympus 1 carries a Direct Broadcast System (DBS) payload, too, but it is intended to encourage educational use — particularly by companies establishing and operating internal training programs relayed by satellite — rather than to provide entertainment.

Europe still lags behind the USA and Japan in the use of satellite-borne in-company training schemes. Consequently, ESA is interested in developing so-called 'open-learning' and 'distance-learning' via satellite, in a manner not dissimilar to the UK's Open University. About 40 percent of Olympus 1's DBS channel time has been allocated to distance-learning activities, and more than 300 organizations from 20 countries have applied for time

(Left) Last-minute checks on Olympus 1 at Stevenage before shipment to the French Guiana launch site.

(Right) The V32 vehicle on the ELA-1 launch pad at Kourou. This was the final use of ELA-1, ending ten years of service.

on these channels — mainly educational establishments involved in adult education and language training.

The majority of applicants have been offered two years' free access, with live transmissions fitted into time slots between 09:00-14:00 and 16:00-17:00 GMT (the rest of the day is taken up with other experiments).

The Olympus DBS payload comprises two channels; one to serve Italy, the other to serve north-western Europe (the BBC is to operate the latter). These channels have such high outputs that antennas with diameters of 45 centimeters or less will be able to pick up the signal.

Another exciting application being fostered by the Olympus program is the creation of higher-quality, high-resolution TV images. At present, high-definition broadcasting by satellite is still not available in Europe. Improved TV picture resolution will only come when TV pictures are composed of 1,000 horizontal lines, instead of the current standard 625 lines.

Hand-in-hand with this, television broadcasters wish to introduce stereo sound comparable in quality to compact-disc reproduction, and several sound channels for different languages.

In order to achieve these goals, comsats will in future need to relay four to five times the current information-rate, and generate a much wider channel bandwidth (the latter increases the capacity of the DBS system).

Lower frequencies are already fully utilized by existing braodcasting services, so the transmission bandwidths needed to produce high-definition television (HDTV) will probably have to be at, or above, a frequency of 20GHz. There's a catch, however, because higher-frequency transmissions are more likely to be adversely affected by atmospheric conditions such as rain, cloud and ice crystals.

Use of a wider channel bandwidth helps sidestep this problem.

Many beams

Another payload aboard Olympus 1, the so-called Specialized Services payload, operates at low frequencies and has four wide-band channels operating through five spot-beams. The spot-beams

are steerable: pointing them independently at different users enables a wide geographical area to be covered, linking people all over Europe (eventually, the intention is to build satellites that have tens of beams, instead of just a single beam).

Two of the channels can be switched to double the bandwidth, when it becomes necessary to counteract atmospheric interference.

Instead of the large antennas that normally receive such signals, dishes only a meter across should be sufficient, and ESA is experimenting with small, mobile antennas called TDS-4s which can be placed in remote locations to serve them with instant telecommunications.

Use of higher frequencies with greater bandwidth but smaller spot-beams will be tested by the Advanced Communications payload on Olympus 1. This payload provides two wide-band (40MHz) channels with two spot-beams, which should be picked up by small-diameter Earth stations. Experiments with these channels have been set up in Canada and Europe to investigate the possibilities offered by trans-Atlantic data transfer, voice interaction, and a 'simultaneous presence' teleconferencing facility for company use.

Another Olympus 1 experiment involves high-speed data transfer between computer networks in different countries. Transmissions to ships and aircraft are also planned. Olympus 1 will also act as the forerunner of ESA's planned data-relay satellite (DRS, the European equivalent of NASA's TDRS). The Advanced Communications payload will serve as a data-relay for experiments conducted aboard the Eureca free-flying scientific platform, which is scheduled for launch in 1991.

A fourth payload on Olympus 1 bears three unusual horn-shaped antennas which transmit signals at three different frequencies. This experiment is intended solely to furnish more information on ways to improve the quality of satellite broadcasts at high frequencies. Comparisons between the reception of two high-frequency signals and a low-frequency signal beamed from Olympus 1 will provide new data on the effects of Earth's atmosphere on radio-waves, and on the ways of overcoming atmospheric signal loss and interference.

In addition to its communications payloads, Olympus 1 carries a highly-sensitive vibration monitor. This is collecting information on spacecraft disturbances of the type that would affect the pointing of laser beams. Laser beams may be used in future optical space communications systems, as they are capable of carrying more data than microwaves (high-frequency radio waves having

wavelengths between 1 and 300 millimeters), and are less prone to interference.

The second Olympus satellite is already partially assembled and will remain in the condition until ESA takes up the contract option for completion. Future satellites in the Olympus class will be even larger and more powerful than the prototype, with a launch mass of up to 4,200 kilograms (compared to Olympus 1's 2,600 kilograms), a payload of up to 600 kilograms (compared to 360 kilograms), and an operational lifetime of ten years (compared to 5-7 years).

These future-generation satellites will tote solar-cell arrays up to 56 meters long, and will have a power output of nearly eight kilowatts (corresponding figures for Olympus 1 are 25.6 meters and 3.6 kilowatts). Such a generous power output should be sufficient to carry 40 direct broadcast television channels, or relaying of up to 250,000 simultaneous telephone calls.

P.B./N.M.

(Above) In the unmanned mode, too, the venerable A-2 Soyuz booster continued to serve solidly throughout this *Space Year*.

(Left) Nocturnal scene at the Xichang site in the People's Republic of China. Asiasat 1 (formerly Westar 6) was relaunched atop this Long March 3.

Intelsat 6-F2 was the largest and most powerful commercial communications satellite ever launched. It also required the most powerful Ariane booster, the four-liquid-strap-on 44L model — this making its second launch.

Five Intelsat 6 satellites were planned; two more to fly aboard Arianes and two on the new Martin Marietta Commercial Titan, which — along with the McDonnell Douglas Delta and General Dynamics Atlas — was at last making forays into the international commercial launch market, almost an Arianespace monopoly.

COBE/Delta 190
18 November 1989

Delta launches are quite a rare event from SLC-4W at Vandenberg Air Force Base. The first occurred in 1966 and the 30th (two failed) on 18 November 1989 — carrying NASA's Cosmic Background Explorer satellite (COBE).

This is a rather rare satellite itself; the first dedicated to studying cosmic radiation — the vast uniform background glow of radiation that was seemingly emitted during the 'Big Bang'; the theoretical beginning of the Universe perhaps 15 billion years ago.

Acting like a fossil, this radiation could reveal the processes that have shaped the expansion of the Universe. Cosmic radiation has been difficult to observe before now, because it is so faint that it becomes absorbed easily by the Earth's atmosphere. But COBE is equipped with some extremely sensitive infrared instruments, which have to be cooled by 600 liters of liquid helium, reducing the lifetime of the spacecraft to about a year.

COBE was designed in 1974 and should have flown aboard the Space Shuttle from Vandenberg before plans to launch the vehicle from there were shelved in 1986. It carries a sunshade-like array of solar-cells providing 1.6 kilowatts and measures six meters high by nine meters in diameter.

Navstar 2-5/Delta 189
11 December 1989

Another of what had by now become routine launchings of McDonnell Douglas Delta 2s carrying a single Block 2A Navstar GPS satellite, took place on 11 December.

Skynet 4A+JC-Sat 2/
Commercial Titan 01
31 December 1989

The last satellite launch of 1989 — the first of 1990 if one goes by GMT — this mission marked the debut of the Martin Marietta Commercial Titan. The night launch from Pad 40 was a great success and inaugurated the career of a booster which had, at the time, only two other firm con-

(*Left*) **The first Commercial Titan departs Complex 40 at Cape Canaveral.**

(*Below*) **COBE's 600-liter cryogenic dewar being loaded into a transporter.**

tracts to its credit (Mars Observer was only officially signed-up in January 1990).

The second and third launches were to carry Intelsat 6s.

Britain's Nigel Wood — an RAF Squadron Leader — must have taken a philosophical approach to the harsh fact of Skynet's 4A launch. He was to have flown with it on Shuttle *Discovery* in June 1986, to become his country's first spacefarer. He and several other potential Shuttle passengers were grounded after the *Challenger* disaster.

SPOT-2 + microsats/Ariane V35
21 January 1990

Sounding like a pop group, 'SPOT 2 and the microsats' were lofted on 21 January — after a two-week delay due to technical problems. This flight marked the debut of the Ariane 40. The least powerful Ariane 4 variant, it has no thrust augmentation.

MUSES-A/M3S2
24 January 1990

Launched from Kagoshima Space Center on an all-solid-propellant 'Mu' booster, the MUSES-A spacecraft carried the tiny Hiten probe, which entered lunar orbit in March. The lunar flight was Japan's first, making it only the third nation to launch a spacecraft to the Moon. The last lunar mission had been the Soviet Union's Luna 24, launched in 1976.

For further details, see *Planetary Missions*.

(Above) **Japan became the third nation to shoot for the Moon when the MUSES-A mission launched from Kagoshima.**

(Right) **Italy's Lake Garda and the surrounding region, imaged by SPOT-2.**

(Below-right) **SPOT-2 at Kourou prior to integration with the V35 vehicle. The two HRV imaging instruments are prominent.**

Navstar 2-6/Delta 191
24 January 1990

Another routine Interim Delta 2 launch of a Block 2A Navstar GPS satellite from Cape Canaveral's Complex 17.

China 26/Long March 3
4 February 1990

The People's Republic of China did not make any satellite launches in 1988. China 26, on the sixth launch of a Long March 3 from Xichang, was the country's fourth operational communications satellite. Its launch was watched by Premier Li Peng.

China did not release very much new information about the satellite. The first Chinese communications satellite was STW-1, launched in 1984 on the second Long March 3 and placed at 125 degrees east. STW2 followed in '86, and was placed at 103 degrees east.

The third satellite, launched in 1988, operated from 87 degrees east, while another launched the same year went into a 111-degree-east position.

The 1988 launches were of uprated operational national communications satellites, sometimes referred to as Chinasat 1 and 2. At the time, the Chinese authorities said that Chinasat 3 would be placed at 98 degrees east.

Momo 1b + Orizuru + Fuji 2/H-1
7 February 1990

The second Marine Observation Satellite, dubbed Momo, was put into space with two sub-satellites — DEBUT and JAS-1B — which were then renamed Orizuru and Fuji, in the Japanese tradition. Launch from Tanegashima was by an H-1.

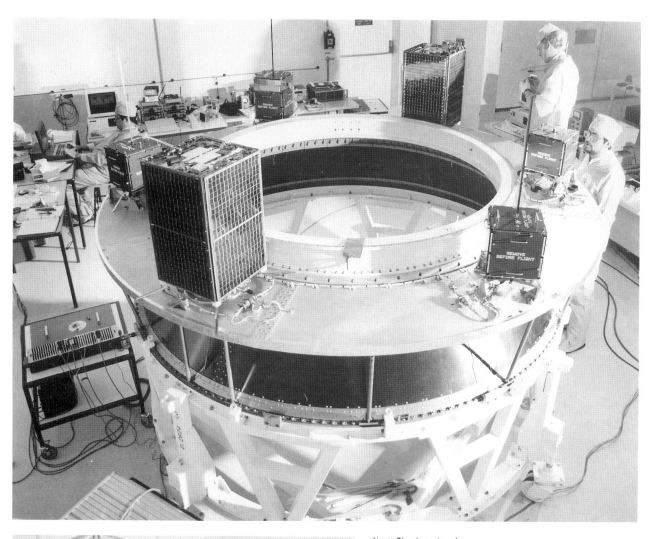

(Above) **Six microsats rode 'piggyback' on Ariane V35.**

(Left) **Orizuru.**

(Below) **Launch of the H-1 from Tanegashima on 7 February 1990.**

(Above) **LACE/RME insignia.**

(Right) **LACE satellite with its sensor-arrays deployed.**

(Below-right) **RME satellite prior to a thermal-vacuum chamber test.**

(Below) **Japan's JAS-1b.**

(Far-right) **The ill-fated Ariane V36 launch vehicle.**

LACE+RME/Delta 192
14 February 1990

This launch of a two-stage Interim Delta 2/6920 from Cape Canaveral was the third for the Strategic Defence Organization (SDIO). It was also the first Pentagon launch conducted on a commercial basis. McDonnell Douglas despatched its Delta 2 and delivered its customer's charges into a unique orbit. The Low Power Atmosphere Compensation Experiment, LACE, is studying the effects of low-power lasers directed through the atmosphere. The satellite carries an ultraviolet plume instrument which tests ways of detecting missile exhaust plumes, and an instrument to measure neutron emissions from the Earth into space.

The Relay Mirror Experiment, (RME) is being used to demonstrate that the beam from a ground-based laser can be redirected to another target in space.

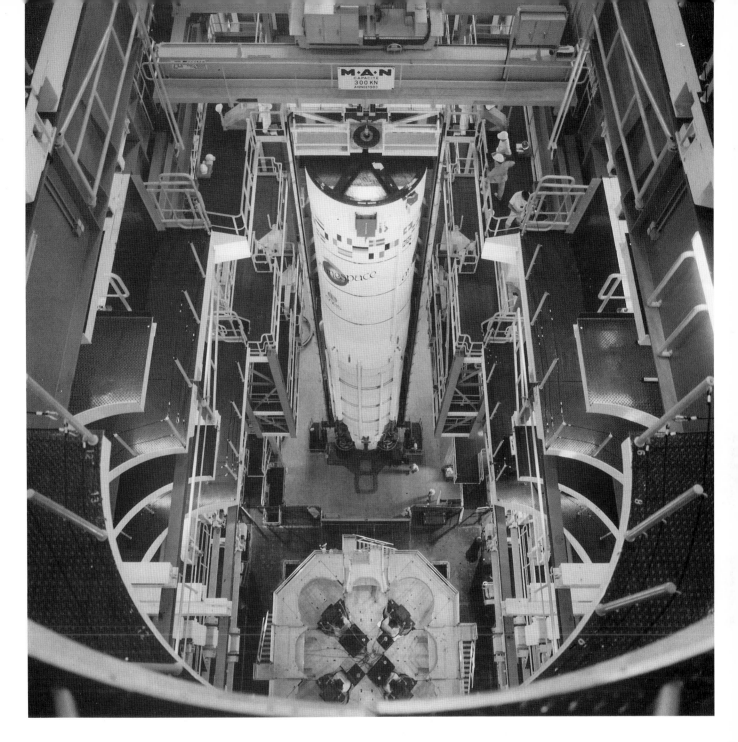

Superbird B+BS-2x/Ariane V36
26 February 1990

The 36th Ariane mission ended with an explosion 100 seconds after launch, with the loss of two Japanese satellites. It was the fifth Ariane failure, and the third during commercial Arianespace operations — but only after 17 consecutive flawless launches since September 1987.

Intelsat 6-F3/Commercial Titan 02
14 March 1990

The first Commercial Titan launch had been the only dual-satellite commercial effort planned by Martin Marietta, which decided to concentrate on single-launch contracts. The vehicle designated to carry Intelsat 6-F3 on the second commercial mission was accidentally wired-up to carry *two* satellites. Engineers reconfiguring the wire harnesses when installing Intelsat 6-F3 aboard the booster at the Cape made a 'crossed wire' error and the result was only to become apparent soon after the flawless launch from Pad 40 on 14 March.

Jubilation turned to horror as the comsat failed to separate from the Titan second stage in low-Earth orbit. Eventually, Intelsat 6-F3 was persuaded to separate — but at the cost of losing its Star solid-propellant perigee kick motor (PKM), and was thus left stranded in a useless 145 x 350-kilometer orbit.

Intelsat officials got talking with NASA. Was this a job for the Shuttle? The answer was affirmative, and a rescue mission to fix a new PKM to Intelsat 6-F3 to propel it to a proper orbit was provisionally placed on the Shuttle schedule for 1992 provided that comsat remained in good shape. One suc-

cess/one failure was bad news for Martin Marietta, but they had a chance to make amends later in the year with another Intelsat 6.

Navstar 2-7/Delta 193
25 March 1990

Another routine McDonnell Douglas launch of an Interim Delta 2/6925 from Cape Canaveral's Complex 17, carrying the seventh Block 2A Navstar GPS satellite.

Offeq 2/Shavit
3 April 1990

A two-stage eleven-meter-high Shavit solid-propellant booster soared away from Palmachin Air Force Base, south of Tel Aviv, on 13 April and flew straight across the Mediterranean Sea. It carried Offeq 2, Israel's second satellite, which duly entered

its highly-characteristic 140-degree-inclination orbit with the parameters of 210 x 1,500 kilometers.

The "improved test satellite" was almost identical to the first Offeq, which was launched by the 'protoflight' Jericho 2 missile-based Shavit in September 1988. It measured 2.3 meters high and weighed 160 kilograms, four kilograms heavier than Offeq 1. The launch was made chiefly to verify the capability for a two-way data link between a ground station and a satellite, with the uplinking of commands and the downlink of telemetry.

Offeq was by no means the 'spy satellite' that over-the-top (uninformed) media sources suggested it was, launched in response to Iraqi chemical weapons testing. The Israeli Space Agency says that two more Offeq science satellites are to be launched next, as technology demonstrators for the Amos communications satellite program.

Pegsat + GLOMR-2/Pegasus 01 5 April 1990

The first air-launched satellite delivery was conducted by the commercial OSC/Hercules Pegasus vehicle, dropped from a NASA/Boeing NB-52 'mother-ship' over the Pacific Ocean. Pegsat is the product of a joint NASA/DARPA teaming.

Asiasat 1/Long March 3 7 April 1990

This launch was characterized by a number of significant 'firsts', for besides being the 27th satellite-launch conducted by China and the seventh use of a Long March 3, it was the first commercial satellite launch by China and the first time a 'second-hand' communications satellite sent into space. The first second-hand spacecraft was the Gemini 2 capsule, which flew in an unmanned mode in 1965, and a year later was launched on an unmanned test for the military Manned Orbital Laboratory (MOL) program.

Asiasat 1 began life as one of a series of Westar communications satellites, deployed routinely by the Space Shuttle *Challenger* in February 1984. Unfortunately, in an episode that was at the time rather unfairly blamed on the Shuttle, the perigee kick motor (PKM) on Westar 6 — and its sister satellite, Palapa B2 — ignited and promptly cut out, leaving both comsats stranded in a useless in low-Earth orbit. Plans were almost immediately laid for the great Shuttle rescue mission, 51A/*Discovery*, which duly returned both satellites to Earth after heroic spacewalks by Dale

Gardner and Joe Allen.

The rescue mission had been funded by underwriters hoping to re-sell the satellites to recover some of their losses. Buyers for Westar 6 were hard to find, however, and several 'red herring' purchasers were reported before the satellite — refurbished by Hughes — became Asiasat, named for a Hong Kong-based consortium who planned to provide commercial communications services to China, Thailand, Pakistan and other Asian nations.

A commercial launch by China cost the consortium just $30 million, considerably less than some other launch vehicles, but the launch could only proceed with the approval of President Bush, who allowed the U.S.-built satellite to be shipped to communist China.

P87-2/Stacksat/Atlas-E 11 April 1990

Three tactical military communications satellites were orbited by an Atlas-E vehicle fitted with an Altair-based orbital insertion motor. Launch was from the SLC3 complex at Vandenberg Air Force Base, on 11 April. The Atlas-E launcher was the third of the final eleven converted-ICBMs to fly. Later in the 1990s, these will be superceded by the Titan 2.

(Bottom) **Pegasus and the NB-52 — an electrifying combination.**

(Below-left) **First-stage boost phase.**

(Below-right) **Pegsat and tiny GLOMR-2 mounted on the Pegasus third stage.**

(Right) **Palapa B-2R is relaunched atop Delta 194.**

(Below) **Two Palapa B-2R insignia.**

(Above-left) **Stacking the Long March 3 booster assigned to the Westar 6/Asiasat 1 relaunch.**

(Left) **The launch control center at Xichang, pictured during the Asiasat 1 campaign.**

Palapa B-2R/Delta 194
13 April 1990

The frenetic pace of satellite launches in April 1990 continued with the first commercial launch of an Interim Delta 2 carrying a non-government satellite; Palapa B-2R — the second refurbished communications satellite deployed from Shuttle *Challenger* in 1984 and 'lost' when its perigee kick motor (PKM) misfired. It was rescued (with Westar 6) and brought back to Earth by the crew of Shuttle mission 51A/*Discovery* in November 1984.

Palapa B-2R was refurbished by Hughes and eventually sold back to Indonesia.

(Left) **The twin-spacecraft Macsat (Multiple Access Communications Satellites) payload. Each satellite weighed 150 pounds at launch.**

(Below) **Launch of the Macsats atop a Vought Scout from Vandenberg, California.**

(Left) **A Hughes technician makes final adjustments to Palapa B-2R.**

Macsats 1 + 2/Scout
9 May 1990

This pair of tactical mobile communications satellites were launched on an all-solid-propellant, four-stage Vought Scout booster from SLC-5 at Vandenberg Air Force Base. Only once they reached orbit was a full program of communications tests mapped out for them.

137

Rosat/Delta 195
1 June 1990

This West German-built X-ray satellite, developed with NASA, was launched on an Interim Delta 2 from Complex 17 at Cape Canaveral by McDonnell Douglas. The launcher carried the first new 2.89-meter -diameter payload fairing, based on the original Delta but 0.34-meter wider, it was a two stage version of the Interim Delta, designated 6920.

Like COBE, launched some months earlier, one of Rosat's tasks during its 30 month-mission is to study cosmic background radiation, particularly in the X-ray and far-ultraviolet bands.

USA-59/Titan 4-2
8 June 1990

Further up 'gantry row' at Cape Canaveral — on Complex 41, the most northerly pad at the Cape and the closest to the Shuttle Pads 39A and B at the adjacent Kennedy Space Center — the second Titan 4 rode majestically and loudly into the sky carrying an electronic-intelligence satellite into a 52-degree-inclination orbit. To reach it, the Titan 4 flew close to the eastern seaboard of the USA.

The interval between the first Titan 4 launch — on 24 June 1989 — and this one, suggested that the US Air Force had experienced technical problems with the new booster. The Titan 4 was originally titled the Complementary Expendable Launch Vehicle (CELV), of which ten were ordered rather sheepishly in 1985 "just in case" the Shuttle couldn't manage to launch as many military payloads as NASA said it could.

As that fact became more glaringly obvious orders for the Titan 4 increased to a level where by the second launch, a further 39 were on order with an option for another eight!

Insat-1D/Delta 186
12 June 1990

The action moved down 'gantry row' again on 12 June, to Complex 17, where McDonnell Douglas conducted another commercial launch. India's INSAT-1D was launched by the very last 'Delta 1'. The launch should have taken place in the summer of 1989, but in an embarrassing launch pad accident, the satellite was damaged by a swinging crane hook and had to be returned to the manufacturers, Ford Aerospace, for repairs.

McDonnell Douglas was certainly demonstrating its rapid launch-rate capability, having launched ROSAT just eleven days earlier.

INSAT-1D was ordered by the Indian government after the failure of INSAT-1A in 1983, and was to have flown on the

(Right) **Installation of the nine strap-on solid rocket boosters gets under way on Delta 186 in the summer of '89. In the event, the launch was long-delayed after a crane hook struck the Insat-1D payload during integration.**

Shuttle accompanied by the first Indian citizen to fly aboard an American spacecraft (along with the first space journalist) in September 1986. It is a multipurpose communications and meteorological satellite providing TV, telephony, meteorology, radio and private network services to the Indian subcontinent.

Intelsat 6-F4/Commercial Titan 03 24 June 1990

Martin Marietta breathed a sigh of relief when its third Commercial Titan did its job and safely placed Intelsat 6-F4 into low-Earth orbit after launch from Complex 40 at Cape Canaveral. The satellite's Star solid-propellant motor ignited and placed it in geosynchronous transfer orbit, and an apogee kick motor (AKM) circularized the orbit.

With that, Martin Marietta went out of the 'sharp end' of the commercial launch business until 1992, when it lofts NASA's Mars Observer. In the meantime, it will concentrate on gaining further government business for 1993 and onwards, and refurbish Complex 40 to accommodate both the Commercial Titan and the Titan 4, providing the U.S. Air Force with two Titan 4 pads.

T.F.

SOVIET

We have adopted a different format for this section. As the Soviet 'public relations' system is not geared for it, it is not possible to provide detailed descriptions of the launch campaigns for in-dividual missions, and the volume of information on other aspects of the various missions is sub-stantially less than the pool we were able to draw on for the *International* section. Generally, the satellite and launch vehicle are integrated a few days before the mission, in an assembly area some distance away from the launch pad. The whole stack is then transported by rail to the launch complex, where it is lifted from the horizontal to the vertical position in preparation for propellant-loading and lift-off.

With Soyuz and Proton, there is a fair proportion of manual involvement in these processes, but with Tsyklon and Zenit, a large degree of automation has been introduced into both pad-installation and fuelling. Typically, a Zenit launch campaign runs for about 80 hours from rollout to lift-off and, after arrival at the pad, the whole process is totally automatic.

What follows is a review of orbital-launch activities at each of the three Soviet cosmodromes, classified by rocket-type and providing brief details of the outcome of each mission.

KAPUSTIN YAR

Although Kapustin Yar had the honor of launching the first three Cosmos satellites back in 1962, it has not seen a departure for orbit since January 1987, when Cosmos 1815 lifted-off aboard a C-1/Cosmos-2 vehicle. Kapustin Yar, opened in the 1940s was not originally intended to be an orbital launch site. Its purpose was to support high-altitude rocket launches, and tests of some of the Soviet Union's smaller ballistic missiles. Its entry into the space-launch stakes came when a second rocket-stage was added to the SS-4/Sandal missile to produce the silo-launched B-1/Cosmos-1 orbital vehicle.

BAIKONUR

Once the world's busiest spaceport, Baikonur has played second-fiddle to Plesetsk for several years. In this particular *Space Year*, an American site, Cape Canaveral/Kennedy Space Center, put more rockets into space — the first time this has happened since 1966. Baikonur is still the Soviet Union's main center for rocket and satellite research and development, but it now supports a variety of routine launches and missions, using the more powerful rockets in the Soviet inventory.

During 1989/90, in addition to seven missions in support of Mir, it saw 17 launches of rockets carrying a total of nineteen satellites into space. There were no reported failures to reach orbit.

Soyuz

One of the world's oldest rocket designs, the A-2/Soyuz accounted for five missions in support of Mir, and five applications-program launches. All of the non-Mir launches were six-and-a-half-tonne recoverable satellites going into relatively low (200-300-kilometer) orbits. Apart from Cosmos 2031, all successfully performed retrofire maneuvers for their Vostok-based cabin modules to make parachute-assisted landings on Soviet territory at mission's-end.

Satellite	Launch date	Orbit	Mission
Cosmos 2031	18 July 1989	51 degrees	photo-recon — 44 days (exploded on 31 August)
Cosmos 2045	22 September 1989	70 degrees	photo-recon — 10 days
Cosmos 2049	17 November 1989	65 degrees	photo-recon — 214 days
Cosmos 2072	13 April 1990	65 degrees	photo-recon — still in orbit on 30 June 1990 (anticipated as 200+ days)
Cosmos 2078	15 May 1990	70 degrees	photo-recon — 44 days

Proton

Unique to Baikonur, two versions of Proton are presently in use; one with three and the other with four rocket-stages. The three-stage version flew twice during the *Space Year* — both times in support of Mir. In the course of eight launch campaigns, the four-stage version lofted six two-tonne communications satellites, a triplet of 1,400-kilogram GLONASS navigation satellites, and the five-tonne Granat high-energy astrophysics observatory into space. The comsat and GLONASS missions involved a single restart of the Proton fourth stage, following initial injection into a 200-kilometer low-Earth orbit. In the case of the geosynchronous satellites, the low orbit was inclined at 51.6 degrees to the equator, and the initial fourth-stage burn produced a 47-degree elliptical transfer orbit. The second firing circularized the orbit at geosynchronous altitude, and reduced the inclination to near-zero.

Satellite	Launch date	Orbit	Mission
Gorizont (18)	05 July 1989	geosynchronous — 140 degrees east	international communications
Gorizont (19)	28 September 1989	geosynchronous — 96.5 degrees east	international communications
Granat	01 December 1989	52 degrees, 200 x 200,000 kilometers	high-energy astrophysics studies
Raduga (25)	15 December 1989	geosynchronous — 45 degrees east	domestic communications
Cosmos 2054	27 December 1989	geosynchronous — 16 degrees west	SDRN — satellite communications
Raduga (26)	15 February 1990	geosynchronous — 70 degrees east	domestic communications
Cosmos 2079-2081	19 May 1990	65 degrees, 20,000 kilometers	GLONASS, high-precision navigation
Gorizont (20)	20 June 1990	geosynchronous — 90 degrees east	international communications

Tsyklon

Strictly speaking, the two-stage F-1 vehicle, which regularly flies out of Baikonur, should probably not be referred to as 'Tsyklon'. The Soviet Union has always reserved this name for the three-stage version of the vehicle, which operates out of Plesetsk. The F-1 flew four missions during the *Space Year,* each carrying an ocean-survey/electronic-intelligence-gathering satellite, widely known as an EORSAT (electronic ocean-reconnaissance satellite). All missions were successes, placing their four-tonne payloads into 65-degree-inclination, 200-kilometer orbits, from which the satellites maneuvered themselves into their near-400-kilometer operational orbits.

Satellite	Launch date	Orbit	Mission
Cosmos 2033	23 July 1989	65 degrees, low	EORSAT
Cosmos 2046	27 September 1989	65 degrees, low	EORSAT
Cosmos 2051	24 November 1989	65 degrees, low	EORSAT
Cosmos 2060	14 March 1990	65 degrees, low	EORSAT

Zenit

Zenit exists as a two-stage rocket, with a three-stage version on the drawing-board. It flew once during 1989/90, following a direct ascent trajectory to place a 1,600 kilogram satellite into orbit.

Satellite	Launch date	Orbit	Mission
Cosmos 2082	23 May 1990	71 degrees 850 kilometers	ELINT

PLESETSK

The Northern Cosmodrome, as it used to be called by the Soviets, hosted 44 successful launches during the *Space Year,* plus one failure in which a satellite got into space but failed to reach its intended orbit. All of the regular Plesetsk stable of rockets were used during the course of the year.

Soyuz

The Soyuz/A-2 was the only vehicle to see action at both Plesetsk and Baikonur. Launching the same basic spacecraft designs as their Baikonur brothers, the Plesetsk-launched vehicles supported a wider range of programs. As with the equivalent Baikonur missions, there were no publicly-reported launch failures, and all the satellites — except Cosmos 2030 — re-entered successfully for recovery.

Satellite	Launch date	Orbit	Mission
Cosmos 2029	05 July 1989	82 degrees	photo-recon — 14 days
Cosmos 2030	12 July 1989	67 degrees	photo-recon — 16 days (exploded in orbit)
Resurs-F3	18 July 1989	83 degrees	Earth-resources photography — 21 days; also carried Pion 3 and Pion 4 sub-satellites
Cosmos 2032	20 July 1989	82 degrees	photo-recon — 14 days
Cosmos 2035	02 August 1989	83 degrees	photo-recon — 14 days
Resurs-F4	15 August 1989	82 degrees	Earth-resources photography — 30 days
Cosmos 2036	23 August 1989	63 degrees	photo-recon — 14 days
Resurs-F5	06 September 1989	82 degrees	Earth-resources photography — 16 days
Cosmos 2044	15 September 1989	82 degrees	microgravity/biological research — 14 days
Cosmos 2047	03 October 1989	67 degrees	photo-recon — 49 days
Cosmos 2048	17 October 1989	63 degrees	photo-recon — 9 days
Cosmos 2052	30 November 1989	67 degrees	photo-recon — 55 days
Cosmos 2055	17 January 1990	63 degrees	photo-recon — 12 days
Cosmos 2057	25 January 1990	63 degrees	photo-recon — 53 days
Cosmos 2062	22 March 1990	82 degrees	photo-recon — 14 days
Foton 3	11 April 1990	53 degrees	microgravity/materials-processing — 16 days
Cosmos 2073	17 April 1990	82 degrees	photo-recon — 11 days
Cosmos 2077	07 May 1990	63 degrees	photo-recon — 58 days
Resurs-F6	29 May 1990	82 degrees	Earth-resources photography — 16 days
Cosmos 2083	19 June 1990	83 degrees	photo-recon — 14 days

Molniya

Two comsat programs — Molniya-1 and Molniya-3 — regularly use the A-2-e/Molniya vehicle to reach highly-elliptical orbits. A similar orbit is used by a series of early-warning satellites which keep a watch for 'enemy' missile launches, and maybe monitor nuclear explosions. The launch technique involves injection into low-orbit of the fourth-stage plus its payload, and then a single burn of the rocket-stage after a half-hour coast period. A final 'trimming' maneuver' by the satellite gets it on-station and moving in-phase with satellites already in space. Both the Molniya comsats and the early-warning craft are in the one-and-a-half to two-tonne class.

The Molniya launcher sustained one failure during the year, when Cosmos 2084's fourth stage shut down immediately after ignition. The mission's event sequencer then released the satellite into a uselessly-low 580-kilometer orbit.

Satellite	Launch date	Orbit	Mission
Molniya-1 (76)	27 September 1989	63 degrees, 600 x 39,000 kilometers	domestic communications
Cosmos 2050	23 November 1989	63 degrees, 600 x 39,000 kilometers	early warning
Molniya-3 (36)	28 November 1989	63 degrees, 600 x 39,000 kilometers	international communications
Molniya-3 (37)	23 January 1990	63 degrees, 600 x 39,000 kilometers	international communications
Cosmos 2063	27 March 1990	63 degrees, 600 x 39,000 kilometers	early warning
Molniya-1 (77)	26 April 1990	63 degrees, 600 x 39,000 kilometers	domestic communications
Cosmos 2076	28 April 1990	63 degrees, 600 x 39,000 kilometers	early warning
Molniya-3 (38)	13 June 1990	63 degrees, 600 x 39,000 kilometers	international communications
Cosmos 2084	21 June 1990	63 degrees, 580 kilometers	early-warning — launch failure

Cosmos-2

The second rocket to carry the name 'Cosmos' is the only launch vehicle to have flown out of all three Soviet cosmodromes. It is now exclusive to Plesetsk, carrying a series of routine payloads all weighing around 800 kilograms, and most of them representing programs which have run for over many years.

Satellite	Launch date	Orbit	Mission
Nadezhda 1	04 July 1989	83 degrees, 1,000 kilometers	navigation/search and rescue
Cosmos 2034	27 July 1989	83 degrees, 1,000 kilometers	navigation
Cosmos 2056	18 January 1990	74 degrees, 800 kilometers	store/dump communications
Cosmos 2059	04 February 1990	66 degrees, 200 x 2,300 kilometers	military
Nadezhda 2	27 February 1990	83 degrees, 1,000 kilometers	navigation/search and rescue
Cosmos 2061	20 March 1990	83 degrees, 1,000 kilometers	navigation
Cosmos 2064-2071	06 April 1990	74 degrees, 1,450 kilometers	multiple payload/tactical communications
Cosmos 2074	20 April 1990	83 degrees, 1,000 kilometers	navigation
Cosmos 2075	25 April 1990	74 degrees, 550 kilometers	ELINT

Tsyklon

As a three-stage rocket, this version of the SS-9/Scarp missile-derived space launcher has only ever flown out of Plesetsk. It supports a number of programs, providing a high degree of accuracy at orbital insertion for satellites in the one-and-a-half tonne class. There have been no reports of launch failures during this _Space Year,_ but the four-month gap between February and June 1990 may indicate that a rocket was lost.

Satellite	Launch date	Orbit	Mission
Cosmos 2037	28 August 1989	74 degrees, 1,500 kilometers	geodesy
Cosmos 2038-2043	14 September 1989	83 degrees, 1,400 kilometers	multiple payload, possibly tactical communications
Intercosmos 24	28 September 1989	83 degrees, 500 x 2,500 kilometers	magnetospheric studies; released Magion 2 sub-satellite
Meteor 3 (3)	24 October 1989	83 degrees, 1,200 kilometers	meteorology
Cosmos 2053	26 December 1989	74 degrees, 520 kilometers	military/test target for ground-based radars
Cosmos 2058	30 January 1990	83 degrees, 650 kilometers	ELINT
Okean 2	28 February 1990	83 degrees, 650 kilometers	oceanographic studies
Meteor 2 (19)	27 June 1990	83 degrees, 950 kilometers	meteorology

R.D.C.

ORBITAL REVIEW

Not only are many new spacecraft launched each year, but many programs already have hardware in-orbit around the Earth, and travelling elsewhere in the Solar System. The planetary explorers are covered in detail in their own section of *Space Year,* but here is the first of our annual reviews of what has been going on in near-Earth space. The list is as complete as possible, but there can be great difficulty in discovering whether a satellite is fully- or partially-active, dormant or dead.

REMOTE-SENSING: EARTH-RESOURCES

Almaz

Cosmos 1870, the first of the Soviet Union's 18,500-kilogram Salyut-based Almaz platforms (equipped with a 30-meter-resolution, synthetic-aperture imaging-radar), was nearing the end of its two-year operational life in the summer of 1989. Although the orbit was still being adjusted periodically, it was running low on propellant and the mission came to an end with retrofire and a destructive re-entry on 29 July 1989. The next Almaz craft (*Almaz* is Russian for *diamond*), with improved 15-meter resolution, is due in the fall of 1990.

IRS

India's Soviet-launched remote-sensing satellite in sun-synchronous orbit continued to function throughout the year. Its imaging system provides pictures in four bands of the visible and infrared spectra, primarily for studying crop-growth.

Landsat

Two of America's Landsat-series satellites are currently operational. Landsat 5 is the prime vehicle, storing and transmitting multi-spectral, 30-meter-resolution images for use in studying vegetation growth and geological features. Landsat 4, carrying similar imaging equipment, is still functioning but has been suffering from a power-system problem since mid-1983. Like the Shuttle, the Landsats use NASA's TDRSS network to communicate with the ground.

MOS

Japan's indigenous, home-launched Marine Observation Satellite family received a new addition in February 1990 when the three-year-old Momo 1a satellite was joined by its twin, Momo 1b (Momo is Japanese for *peach blossom*). Both satellites are currently operational, but Momo 1a is nearing the end of its design-life, and has been operating on some of its backup systems since soon after launch. Both satellites are equipped with multispectral scanners to provide images of vegetation, geological features, sea clarity and ice formations.

Okean

The Soviet Union's maritime complement to the land-surveying Resurs-O program continues to operate. The lone Okean 1 satellite was only partially serviceable as of summer 1989, but the system was back in full operation early in 1990 with the arrival of Okean 2. The three-axis-stabilized platforms carry visible and infrared imaging scanners, a microwave scanner for surface-temperature measurements, and a 1.5-kilometer-resolution sideways-looking radar for ocean-surface imaging. The radar can probe to several meters depth in water, and in sand-covered desert areas. Okean's 'Condor' data-collection system interrogates remotely-located buoys and small weather-stations in Arctic areas, stores the data and plays it back on command.

Resurs-F

The Soviet Union's ongoing program of film-based Earth photography kept up its pace during late-1989, with five launches of the Vostok-style Resurs-F satellites. Resurs-F 2 was already operating in space at the start of the *Space Year,* with its camera-module returning to Earth on 11 July. The pace had slackened-off after a flurry in 1988-89, with only one mission in early-1990. Resurs-F satellites are equipped with multispectral cameras capable of six-meter resolution and operate in low, 200-300-kilometer orbits inclined at 82-83 degrees to the equator. There are two variants of the satellite, one battery-powered (Type 1) and one equipped with solar panels to supplement the power supply (Type 2).

Resurs-O

The only Soviet satellite currently operating in sun-synchronous orbit is Cosmos 1939/Resurs-O, a follow-on to the 1980 Meteor-Priroda satellite which was retired at the time of Cosmos 1939's launch. It complements the Resurs-F series satellite by returning 30-meter-resolution visible-light and infrared images of land areas, both in real-time and by means of stored-playback. A second Resurs-O is due for launch in 1991.

SPOT

France's commercial SPOT (*Satellite Probatoire d'Observation del la Terre*) system continued to operate throughout 1989 and 1990, returning 20-meter-resolution, visible-waveband Earth-surface cimages. SPOT 2 joined its compatriot early in 1990, even though SPOT 1 was functioning at full capability. On 23 March 1990, SPOT 2 assumed the role of prime satellite, with SPOT 1 being held as a backup.

Satellite	Launch date	Orbit/mission
Landsat 4	16 July 1982	sun-synchronous, 700 kilometers with daylight passes around 10:00 am local time; still operational and providing backup to Landsat 5
Landsat 5	01 March 1984	sun-synchronous, 700 kilometers with daylight passes around 10:00 am local time, in the same plane as Landsat 4, and acting as the prime Landsat satellite
SPOT 1	22 February 1986	sun-synchronous, 820 kilometers with daylight passes around 10:00 am local time; still operational
Momo 1a	19 February 1987	sun-synchronous, 900 kilometers with daylight passes around 10:00 am local time; still operational
Cosmos 1870	25 July 1987	72 degrees, 250 kilometers; mission completed — retrofire and destructive re-entry 29 July 1989
IRS 1A	17 March 1988	sun-synchronous, 900 kilometers with daylight passes at 10:00 am local time; still operational
Cosmos 1939	20 April 1988	sun-synchronous, 660 kilometers — Resurs-O satellite, still operational
Okean 1	05 July 1988	83 degrees, 650 kilometers; probably no longer operational
Resurs-F2	27 June 1989	83 degrees, 260 kilometers — Type 1 satellite; recovered after 14 days
Resurs-F3	18 July 1989	83 degrees, 200 kilometers — Type 1 satellite; recovered after 21 days, released the Pion (3) and Pion (4) atmospheric-studies satellites
Resurs-F4	15 August 1989	82 degrees, 260 kilometers — Type 2 satellite; recovered after 30 days
Resurs-F5	06 September 1989	82 degrees, 260 kilometers — Type 1 satellite; recovered after 15 days (also carried West German Cosima-2 microgravity experiments package)
SPOT 2	22 January 1990	sun-synchronous, 820 kilometers; in the same plane as SPOT 1, but acting as the primary operational satellite
Momo 1b	07 February 1990	sun-synchronous, 900 kilometers with daylight passes around 10:00 am local time; still operational
Okean 2	28 February 1990	83 degrees, 650 kilometers; still operational
Resurs-F6	29 May 1990	82 degrees, 260 kilometers — Type 1 satellite; recovered after 16 days (also carried West German Cosima-3 microgravity experiments package)

REMOTE-SENSING: METEOROLOGY

DMSP

America's Department of Defense operates its own Defense Meteorological Satellite Program (DMSP) to gather tactical and strategic worldwide weather information. Cloud-cover images can be stored and dumped directly to strategic command centers, and military units operating anywhere in the world can gather local weather data on-demand if necessary. The current generation of DMSP satellites is the eighth, known as Block 5D-2, and is similar in design to the civilian NOAA series. Six have been manufactured, and four have been put into orbit to date. Of these, two are operational.

GMS

Japan's Geostationary Meteorological Satellite System provides meteorological data for the Western Pacific, the Far East and Australasia. The Himawari satellites operate from a single location at 140 degrees west. Himawari 3 was joined by Himawari 4 in September 1989. Himawari 4 on 5 September 1989.

GOES

NOAA's Geosynchronous Orbit Environmental Satellite series complements the work of America's polar-orbiting metsats. There are two designated GOES locations; 75 degrees west (GOES-East) and 135 degrees east (GOES-West). During the *Space Year,* services were provided by a single satellite, GOES 7 at around 100 degrees west, while it awaited GOES 8's launch mid/late-1990. For a while, GOES-East's duties were undertaken by Europe's Meteosat 3.

Meteor 2

In June 1989, three polar-orbiting Meteor 2 satellites, numbers 16, 17 and 18, were operational in orbits separated by 60 degrees in longitude. Between them, they were providing near-overhead passes over any point on the Earth's surface every four hours, returning cloud-cover images in real-time, furnishing either visible-light or infrared views. The satellites also monitor radiation in near-Earth space. Meteor 2 (19) joined the group right at the end of June 1990, as a replacement/backup for Meteor 2 (16) which was delivering low picture-quality, possibly due to aperture-control problems with the imaging system.

Meteor 3

Two Meteor 3 satellites operated during 1989/90, returning visible-light and infrared images. Meteor 3 (2) was already in orbit on 1 July 1989, but by spring 1990, although it was still returning good-quality cloud-cover pictures, its power system was showing signs of weakness. Meteor 3 joined it in the fall of 1989. Like the Meteor 2 system, orbits are separated by 60 degrees in longitude, so a third satellite is needed to make up a complete system. Meteor 3 (4) is expected in the fall of 1990, carrying some French- and U.S.-supplied instrumentation.

Meteosat

Europe's Meteosat series operates from a geosynchronous location on the Greenwich meridian. Meteosat 3 was the primary operational satellite until 19 June 1989 when Meteosat 4, the first operational Meteosat, took over. Meteosat 3 was then placed on stand-by at 3 degrees west. It was 'loaned' to NOAA and moved mid-October to 'plug' the GOES gap, arriving on 4 November. it was moved back to the Greenwich meridian almost immediately after Meteosat 4 developed radio-noise problems, and took over while 4 was checked out. Meteosat 4 was back on-line by March 1990, and Meteosat 3 was once more "in-storage". An older satellite, Meteosat 2 was on station throughout the Year at 10 degrees west, but running out of propellant, and was due to be moved away from geosynchronous orbit during 1990.

NOAA

Three satellites in the U.S. National Oceanographic and Atmospheric Administration (NOAA) — operated fleet gave service throughout the _Space Year,_ providing constant transmission of visible-light and infrared cloud-cover images. Other sensors monitor sea-surface temperature and polar ice formations. NOAA's 'Argos' data-collection system interrogates remotely-located buoys and small weather-stations in Arctic areas, stores the data and plays it back on command. Starting with NOAA 8, satellites have carried SARSAT (Search and Rescue Satellite-Aided Tracking) receivers to monitor internationally-recognised radio-frequencies of 121.5 MHz and 406 MHz for emergency distress signals.

Satellite	Launch date	Orbit/mission
Meteosat 2	19 June 1981	10 degrees west, geosynchronous — in orbital storage; still party-operational, but in standby mode
Himawari 3	02 August 1984	geosynchronous, 140 degrees west — Japanese metsat, backup to Himawari 4 since the fall of 1989; still operational
NOAA 9	12 December 1984	sun-synchronous, 850 kilometers with daylight passes around 5:30 pm local time, also carrying the SARSAT-2 package and an Earth-radiation-budget experiment; still operational
NOAA 10	17 September 1986	sun-synchronous, 850 kilometers with daylight passes around 7:30 am local time, also carrying the SARSAT-3 package and an Earth-radiation-budget experiment; still operational
GOES 7	26 February 1987	geosynchronous, moved around between 98 degrees west and 108 degrees west according to need, providing complete-hemisphere meteorological data covering the U.S. and South America; still operational
USA-26	20 June 1987	sun-synchronous, 850 kilometers with daylight passes around 6:00 am/pm local time, third Block 5D-2 U.S. military metsat; still operational
Meteor 2 (16)	18 August 1987	83 degrees, 950 kilometers; still operational, but with degraded imaging capability
Meteor 2 (17)	30 January 1988	83 degrees, 950 kilometers; still operational
USA-29	03 February 1988	sun-synchronous, 850 kilometers with daylight passes around 9:00 am local time, fourth Block 5D-2 U.S. military metsat; still operational
Meteosat 3	15 June 1988	5 degrees west, geosynchronous, loaned to NOAA at 50 degrees west late-1989, now in orbital storage as backup to Meteosat 4; still operational
Meteor 3 (2)	26 July 1988	83 degrees, 1,200 kilometers; still operational
NOAA 11	24 September 1988	sun-synchronous, 850 kilometers with daylight passes around 2:00 pm local time, also carrying the SARSAT-4 package, and an ozone-mapping instrument; still operational
Meteor 2 (18)	28 February 1 89	83 degrees, 950 kilometers; still operational
Meteosat 4	06 March 1989	geosynchronous on the Greenwich meridian — primary satellite; still operational
Meteor 2 (19)	27 June 1989	83 degrees, 950 kilometers, launched as replacement for Meteor 2 (16); still operational
Himawari 4	05 September 1989	geosynchronous, 140 degrees west, primary Japanese metsat; still operational
Meteor 3 (3)	24 October 1989	83 degrees, 1,200 kilometers; still operational

RECONNAISSANCE: IMAGING

Cosmos

The USSR maintained its strategic photo-reconnaissance program with 21 satellites operating during the _Space Year._ Three satellites were already in orbit as the year opened, but all had been brought back by the end of September. Broadly speaking, they flew three types of mission. Eleven satellites each spent about two weeks in space. Nine were sent on longer-duration (up to two-month) missions, and two of them failed. One exploded after 44 days, possibly when retrorocket ignition was initiated, and the other exploded after only 16 days. Two half-year missions were mounted, and one mission of this type, from the previous _Space Year,_ came to a close in September 1989.

The two-week-duration satellites are probably battery-powered, like their Type-1 Resurs-F brothers, and are recovered at the end of the mission. The longer-endurance satellites rely on solar batteries. The two-month missions may send back film in small containers at regular intervals during the flight, with the main spacecraft being recovered at mission's-end. The half-year missions probably involve differently-designed satellites with the ability to send back digitized images over a radio-link.

Missions are launched from Baikonur (51, 65 and 70 degrees inclination) and Plesetsk (63, 67 and 82-83 degrees).

U.S. reconsats

Two CIA-owned, 13-tonne KH-11 reconsats are in space, launched from Vandenberg AFB by Titan 34Ds in 1984 and 1987. They have a digital-imaging system capable of returning images via a radio system from sun-synchronous orbit. Another 1987 launch placed a smaller satellite into (possibly sun-synchronous) orbit, though the actual mission is not confirmed.

June 1990 saw a Titan 4 vehicle place a multipurpose strategic reconsat into space (possibly a KH-12), where it joined USA-34/Lacrosse and USA-40 (KH-12). An AFP-731 orbited by the Shuttle _Atlantis_ early in 1990 failed when the satellite broke-up after a few days.

Satellite	Launch date	Orbit/mission
USA-6	04 December 1984	sun-synchronous, 300 kilometers, KH-11 digital-imaging; probably still operational
USA-21	12 February 1987	sun-synchronous, 250 kilometers digital-imaging; probably still operational
USA-27	26 October 1987	sun-synchronous, 300 kilometers, KH-11 digital-imaging; still operational
USA-34	02 December 1988	57 degrees, 670 kilometers, radar-imaging; still operational
Cosmos 2007	23 March 1989	65 degrees, 230 x 285 kilometers, digital-imaging; re-entered after 183 days
Cosmos 2020	17 May 1989	65 degrees, 173 x 344 kilometers, multiple film-capsules; recovered after 59 days
Cosmos 2021	24 May 1989	70 degrees, 218 x 284 kilometers, multiple film-capsules; recovered after 43 days

Cosmos 2028	16 June 1989	70 degrees, 209 x 291 kilometers, already in orbit at 01 July 1989; recovered after 20 days
Cosmos 2029	05 July 1989	82 degrees, 350 kilometers; recovered after 14 days
Cosmos 2030	12 July 1989	67 degrees, 164 x 351 kilometers, multiple film-capsules; exploded 28 July after 16 days
Cosmos 2031	18 July 1989	51 degrees, 231 x 354 kilometers, multiple film-capsules; exploded 31 August after 44 days
Cosmos 2032	20 July 1989	82 degrees, 250 kilometers; recovered after 14 days
Cosmos 2035	02 August 1989	83 degrees, 230 kilometers; recovered after 14 days
USA-40	08 August 1989	57 degrees, 300 kilometers, imaging reconsat, possibly KH-12; still operational
Cosmos 2036	23 August 1989	63 degrees, 230 x 297 kilometers; recovered after 14 days
Cosmos 2045	22 September 1989	70 degrees, 240 kilometers; recovered after 10 days
Cosmos 2047	03 October 1989	67 degrees, 165 x 276 kilometers, multiple film-capsules; recovered after 49 days
Cosmos 2048	17 October 1989	63 degrees, 238 x 359 kilometers, recovered after 9 days
Cosmos 2049	17 November 1989	65 degrees, 223 x 270 kilometers, digital-imaging; re-entered after 214 days
Cosmos 2052	30 November 1989	67 degrees,165 x 341 kilometers, multiple film-capsules; recovered after 55 days
Cosmos 2055	17 January 1990	63 degrees, 250 kilometers; recovered after 12 days
Cosmos 2057	25 January 1990	63 degrees, 185 x 332 kilometers, multiple film-capsules; recovered after 53 days
USA-53	01 March 1990	62 degrees, 250 kilometers, multipurpose reconsat; broke-up within one week of launch
Cosmos 2062	22 March 1990	82 degrees, 241 x 375 kilometers, recovered after 14 days
Cosmos 2072	13 April 1990	65 degrees, 241 x 288 kilometers, digital-imaging; still operational
Cosmos 2073	17 April 1990	82 degrees, 232 x 297 kilometers; recovered after 11 days
Cosmos 2077	07 May 1990	63 degrees, 184 x 329 kilometers, multiple film-capsules; recovered after 58 days
Cosmos 2078	15 May 1990	70 degrees, 213 x 278 kilometers, multiple film-capsules; recovered after 44 days
USA-59	08 June 1990	52 degrees, 275 kilometers, imaging reconsat, possibly KH-12; still operational
Cosmos 2083	19 June 1990	82 degrees, 298 x 412 kilometers, still in operation at the end of the *Space Year*. Recovered after 14 days

RECONNAISSANCE: MISSILE EARLY-WARNING

Cosmos: missile early-warning

One class of satellite stares at the Earth, looking for telltale rocket-exhaust plumes. They may also have the task of monitoring nuclear tests on the ground. The Soviet Union maintains a 'constellation' of nine such satellites in operational condition at any one time, moving in Molniya-type orbits and taking it in turns to 'hang' in space above the continental U.S. Four satellites in the series were launched during the *Space Year* to replace older vehicles, although one failed to reach its operational orbit due to a booster malfunction.

Defense Support Program

The U.S. early-warning system revolves around DSP satellites in geosynchronous orbit. They are located at 60 degrees east, 70 degrees west and 134 degrees west to watch for missile launches from the Soviet Union, or submarine-launched missiles off the east and west coast of the United States respectively. Five second-generation satellites are reportedly operational; three prime satellites and two on standby. Additionally, a third-generation vehicle was launched in June 1989 by a Titan 4.

Satellite	Launch date	Orbit/mission
DSP-2 (3)	10 June 1979	geosynchronous, second-generation DSP; probably still operational
DSP-2 (4)	16 March 1981	geosynchronous, fourth second-generation DSP; probably still operational
DSP-2 (5)	06 March 1982	geosynchronous, fifth second-generation DSP; probably still operational
DSP-2 (7)	15 April 1984	geosynchronous seventh second-generation DSP; probably still operational
Cosmos 1785	15 October 1986	63 degrees, Molniya-type orbit, missile early-warning; possibly still operational
Cosmos 1793	20 November 1986	63 degrees, Molniya-type orbit; ceased to operate early-1990
Cosmos 1849	04 June 1987	63 degrees, Molniya-type orbit; ceased to operate early-1990
USA-28	29 November 1987	geosynchronous, eighth second-generation DSP; still operational
Cosmos 1903	21 December 1987	63 degrees, Molniya-type orbit; ceased to operate late-1989
Cosmos 1922	26 February 1988	63 degrees, Molniya-type orbit, missile early-warning; still operational
Cosmos 1966	30 August 1988	63 degrees, Molniya-type orbit, missile early-warning; still operational
Cosmos 1974	3 October 1988	63 degrees, Molniya-type orbit, missile early-warning; still operational
Cosmos 1977	25 October 1988	63 degrees, Molniya-type orbit, ceased to operate early-1990
Cosmos 2001	14 February 1989	63 degrees, Molniya-type orbit; missile early-warning; still operational
USA-39	14 June 1989	geosynchronous, first third-generation DSP; still operational
Cosmos 2050	23 November 1989	63 degrees, Molniya-type orbit, missile early-warning, replaced Cosmos 1903; still operational
Cosmos 2063	27 March 1990	63 degrees, Molniya-type orbit, missile early-warning, replaced Cosmos 1793; still operational
Cosmos 2076	28 April 1990	63 degrees, Molniya-type orbit, missile early-warning, replaced Cosmos 1849; still operational
Cosmos 2084	21 June 1990	63 degrees, 600 kilometers, intended to replace Cosmos 1977 — missile early warning satellite, but launcher failed

RECONNAISSANCE: ELECTRONIC

Cosmos: ELINT/SIGINT

Two major Soviet general-purpose electronic-intelligence-gathering programs are in operation. Both satellite types appear to use the Okean oceanographic satellite design as a basic platform, and one program uses similar (83-degree, 650-kilometer) orbits to Okean and uses the same three-stage F-2/Tsyklon rocket. The other works from an 850-kilometer orbit at 71 degrees inclination after a launch by J-1/Zenit-2.

At any one time, six or more of the 83-degree-program satellites are in operation, and other — older — satellites may be available as backups. There are probably three of the Zenit-launched satellites currently in operation, and the system is being built-up, possibly to a total of four satellites. Some smaller, C-1/Cosmos-2-launched satellites may also carry special-purpose or developmental ELINT/SIGINT sensors.

Specialised satellites monitor electronic emissions from ships. Operating in groups of two or more satellites, they monitor naval radio-frequencies and maintain a watch on shipping movements . They are known as EORSATs (Electronic Ocean-Reconnaissance Satellites).

NOSS/White Cloud

The United States has its equivalent of the Soviet Union's EORSAT system, in the form of the White Cloud program, known more formally as the Navy Ocean Surveillance System (NOSS). NOSS payloads consist of a 'parent' satellite, plus a 'family' of three sub-satellites joined to it by several kilometers of wire. The cluster flies in formation, listening-in on maritime radio transmissions. It uses the slight variations in Doppler Effect, as detected by the individual satellites, to pinpoint the source. There were no White Cloud launches during the _Space Year_, but some of the earlier clusters are probably still active.

U.S. ELINT/SIGINT

U.S. intelligence 'cover-up' abilities are such that it is often impossible to distinguish between individual ELINT/SIGINT programs. Two main classes of program are identifiable, involving satellites in geosynchronous orbit, and some in polar orbit. Another specialized type of satellite is known by the codename 'Jumpseat'. It has the task of eavesdropping on the uplinks to the Soviet Molniya-1 comsats. Two satellites were working at the beginning of the _Space Year_.

Satellite	Launch date	Orbit/mission
Jumpseat 5	13 December 1980	63 degrees, Molniya-type; possibly still operational
U.S. (no name)	31 October 1981	geosynchronous; possibly still operational
Jumpseat 6	31 July 1983	63 degrees, Molniya-type; possibly still operational
Cosmos 1707	12 December 1985	83 degrees, 650 kilometers; possibly still operational
USA 15-18	09 February 1986	63 degrees, 1,100 kilometers, parent and sub-satellite NOSS/White Cloud cluster; probably still operational
Cosmos 1805	10 December 1986	83 degrees, 650 kilometers; possibly still operational
Cosmos 1812	14 January 1987	83 degrees, 650 kilometers; replaced by Cosmos 2058
USA 22-25	15 May 1987	63 degrees, 1,100 kilometers, parent and sub-satellite NOSS/White Cloud cluster; probably still operational
Cosmos 1892	20 October 1987	83 degrees, 650 kilometers; still operational
Cosmos 1908	06 January 1988	83 degrees, 650 kilometers; still operational
Cosmos 1933	15 March 1988	83 degrees, 650 kilometers; still operational
Cosmos 1943	15 May 1988	71 degrees, 850 kilometers; still operational
Cosmos 1949	27 May 1988	65 degrees, 400 kilometers, EORSAT, taken out of service November 1989;
Cosmos 1953	14 June 1988	83 degrees, 650 kilometers; still operational
Cosmos 1975	11 October 1988	83 degrees, 650 kilometers; still operational
Cosmos 1979	18 November 1988	65 degrees, 400 kilometers, EORSAT; taken out of service November 1989, re-entered 25 December 1989
Cosmos 1980	23 November 1988	71 degrees, 850 kilometers; still operational
USA-37	10 May 1989	geosynchronous; still operational
Cosmos 2027	14 June 1989	74 degrees, 500 kilometers; still operational
Cosmos 2033	23 July 1989	65 degrees, 400 kilometers, EORSAT; still operational
Cosmos 2046	27 September 1989	65 degrees, 400 kilometers, EORSAT; still operational
USA-48	23 November 1989	geosynchronous over Indian Ocean; still operational
Cosmos 2051	24 November 1989	65 degrees, 400 kilometers, EORSAT; still operational
Cosmos 2058	30 January 1990	83 degrees, 650 kilometers, replaced Cosmos 1812; still operational
Cosmos 2060	14 March 1990	65 degrees, 400 kilometers, EORSAT; still operational
Cosmos 2075	25 April 1990	74 degrees, 550 kilometers; still operational
Cosmos 2082	23 May 1990	71 degrees, 850 kilometers; still operational

COMMUNICATIONS

Communications is the largest single space-application, accounting for the vast majority of all operating satellites. Individual applications range from short-range, battlefield use to one satellite employing another as the means of 'talking' to its mission controllers. The sheer quantity of communications satellite programs makes it difficult to provide fine detail on each one, so this category is split into three sections; low-orbit, eccentric-orbit, and geosynchronous-orbit satellites.

COMSATS: LOW-ORBIT

Communications satellites in low-orbit are used in two ways; one is as a means of transmitting signals over relatively short distances — up to about 2,000 kilometers, as in a tactical battlefield scenario; and the other is as a store/dump device — usually for clandestine purposes. In this case, messages can be beamed-up to a satellite, and as the spacecraft passes over a suitable ground-station, the data can be beamed back to Earth.

The Soviet Union has been operating both systems for many years, and the U.S. has recently been experimenting with GLOMR (Global Message Relay) and Macsat (Multiple Access Communications Satellite) spacecraft. The Soviet satellites are launched eight at a time by C-1/Cosmos, and around 30 satellites are operational at any one time. A similar six-up satellite cluster appears from time-to-time, lofted by the F-2/three-stage-Tsyklon rocket. These satellites may have a similar mission, but this is by no means certain at the moment.

Satellite	Launch date	Orbit/mission
Cosmos 1827-32	11 March 1987	83 degrees, 1,400 kilometers, possibly tactical communications; some satellites probably still operating
Cosmos 1852-59	16 June 1987	74 degrees, 1,450 kilometers, tactical communications; some satellites probably still operating
Cosmos 1874-80	03 September 1987	83 degrees, 1,400 kilometers, possibly tactical communications; some satellites probably still operating
Cosmos 1909-14	15 January 1988	83 degrees, 1,400 kilometers, possibly tactical communications; some satellites probably still operating
Cosmos 1924-31	11 March 1988	74 degrees, 1,450 kilometers, tactical communications; some satellites probably still operating
Cosmos 1937	05 April 1988	74 degrees, 800 kilometers, store/dump; still operational
Cosmos 1954	21 June 1988	74 degrees, 800 kilometers, store/dump; still operational
Cosmos 1992	26 January 1989	74 degrees, 800 kilometers, store/dump; still operational
Cosmos 1994-99	10 February 1989	83 degrees, 1,400 kilometers, possibly tactical communications; some satellites probably still operating
Cosmos 2008-15	24 March 1989	74 degrees, 1,450 kilometers, tactical communications; some satellites probably still operating
Cosmos 2038-43	14 September 1989	83 degrees, 1,400 kilometers, possibly tactical communications; some satellites probably still operating
Cosmos 2056	18 January 1990	74 degrees, 800 kilometers, store/dump, replaced Cosmos 1937; still operational
USA-55	05 April 1990	near-sun-synchronous, 570 x 680 kilometers, GLOMR-2 message relay; still operational
Cosmos 2064-71	06 April 1990	74 degrees, 1,450 kilometers, tactical communications; some satellites probably still operating
USA-58	11 April 1990	90 degrees, 770 kilometers, U.S. Department of Defense Selective Communications Experiment using store/dump; still operational
Macsat 1&2	09 May 1990	90 degrees 610 x 770 kilometers, a pair of store/dump satellites; still operational

COMSATS: ECCENTRIC ORBIT

The Soviet Union's original long-range satellite communications system required some novel thinking because of the difficulty of getting satellites to geosynchronous orbit from Soviet territory. The Molniya orbit (63 degrees, 600 x 39,000 kilometers) was the answer; satellites following such a path appear to 'hang' in the sky above the northern hemisphere for about eight hours before moving rapidly around the southern hemisphere and reappearing once more above the north pole. The Molniya-1 and Molniya-3 series are current; Molniya-2 was a stop-gap prior to the Raduga geosynchronous satellites being available. Continuity of communications is ensured by having several satellites with orbits spaced at intervals around the equator. So, as one satellite 'sets' as seen by a ground-station, the next one is 'rising'.

The U.S. military Satellite Data System comsats use the Molniya-type orbit for communications between the U.S. mainland and military units operating in north-polar regions. The satellites also double as a space-to-ground link for military reconsats, relaying digitalized images direct to the Pentagon.

Satellite	Launch date	Orbit/mission
USA-4	28 August 1984	Satellite Data System; possibly still operational
Molniya-3 (24)	29 May 1985	Soviet domestic and international communications; taken out of service summer 1990
Molniya-3 (25)	17 July 1985	Soviet domestic and international communications; still operational
Molniya-3 (26)	03 October 1985	Soviet domestic and international communications; taken out of service winter 1989/90
USA-9	08 February 1986	Satellite Data System; possibly still operational
Molniya-1 (68)	05 September 1986	Soviet domestic communications and television distribution; still operational
Molniya-1 (69)	15 November 1986	Soviet domestic communications and television distribution; taken out of service fall 1989
Molniya-1 (70)	26 December 1986	Soviet domestic communications and television distribution; still operational
Molniya-3 (31)	27 January 1987	Soviet domestic and international communications; taken out of service fall 1989
USA-21	12 February 1987	Satellite Data System; possibly still operational
Molniya-1 (71)	11 March 1988	Soviet domestic communications and television distribution; still operational
Molniya-1 (72)	17 March 1988	Soviet domestic communications and television distribution; still operational
Molniya-3 (32)	26 May 1988	Soviet domestic and international communications; still operational
Molniya-1 (73)	12 August 1988	Soviet domestic communications and television distribution; still operational
Molniya-3 (33)	29 September 1988	Soviet domestic and international communications; still operational
Molniya-3 (34)	22 December 1988	Soviet domestic and international communications; still operational
Molniya-1 (74)	28 December 1988	Soviet domestic communications and television distribution; still operational
Molniya-1(75)	15 February 1989	Soviet domestic communications and television distribution; taken out of service spring 1990
Molniya-3 (35)	08 June 1989	Soviet domestic and international communications; still operational
Molniya-1 (76)	27 September 1989	Soviet domestic communications and television distribution, replaced Molniya-1 (69); still operational
Molniya-3 (36)	28 November 1989	Soviet domestic and international communications, replaced Molniya-3 (31); still operational
Molniya-3 (37)	23 January 1990	Soviet domestic and international communications, replaced Molniya-3 (26); still operational
Molniya-1 (77)	26 April 1990	Soviet domestic communications and television distribution, replaced Molniya-1 (75); still operational
Molniya-3 (38)	13 June 1990	Soviet domestic and international communications, replaced Molniya-2 (24); still operational

COMSATS: GEOSYNCHRONOUS ORBIT

The largest single class of satellite in use today consists of geosynchronous orbit comsats. They constitute the space segments of numerous communications networks, both public and private. Some offer specific point-to-point links, others distribute or broadcast television signals, and others provide spacecraft-to-ground links for satellites in low orbit. Some provide multiple services — like Inida's Insat-1 series, combining communications with meteorology — and Intelsat and Gorizont satellites offer 1.6 GHz maritime, ship-to-shore, communications channels.

Satellite	Launch date	Orbit/mission
ATS-1	07 December 1966	near-synchronous, experimental communications; still operational — weak signals only
ATS-3	05 November 1967	near-synchronous, 105 degrees west, experimental communications; transponder still usable
Marisat F-1	19 February 1976	106 degrees west, international maritime communications; still operational as backup to Marecs-B2
LES 9	15 March 1976	105 degrees west, experimental military communications; still operational
Marisat F-3	09 June 1976	72 degrees east, international maritime communications; still operational as backup to Intelsat 5 F-8 maritime comms package
Comstar 2	22 July 1976	76 degrees west, U.S. commercial communications; still operational
Marisat F-2	14 October 1976	176 degrees east, international maritime communications; still operational as backup to Intelsat 5 F-5 maritime communications package
Intelsat 4A F-4	26 May 1977	21.5 degrees west, international communications; taken out of service fall 1989
FltSatCom 1	09 February 1978	177 degrees west, U.S. Navy communications, still operational
OTS 2	11 May 1978	5 degrees east, European experimental communications; still operational
NATO 3C	19 November 1978	18 degrees west, international military communications; still operational
DSCS 2-11	14 December 1978	drifting slowly, U.S. Department of Defense strategic communications; possibly still operational
DSCS 2-12	14 December 1978	177 degrees east, U.S. Department of Defense strategic communications; still operational
FltSatCom 2	04 May 1979	73 degrees east, U.S. Navy communications; still operational
Westar 3	10 August 1979	91 degrees west, U.S. commercial communications; taken out of service spring 1990
DSCS 2-13	21 November 1979	179 degrees west, U.S. Department of Defense strategic communications; still operational
DSCS 2-14	21 November 1979	179 degrees west, U.S. Department of Defense strategic communications; still operational
FltSatCom 3	18 January 1980	25 degrees west, U.S. Navy communications; still operational
FltSatCom 4	31 October 1980	172 degrees east, U.S. Navy communications; still operational
SBS F-3	15 November 1980	99 degrees west, then moved to 117 degrees west spring 1990, U.S. commercial communications; still operational
Intelsat 5 F-2	06 December 1980	initially in storage at 12 degrees west, then moved to 21.5 degrees west fall 1989, international communications; still operational
Comstar 4	21 February 1981	76 degrees west, U.S. commercial communications; still operational
Intelsat 5 F-1	23 May 1981	177 degrees east, international communications; still operational
SBS F-1	24 September 1981	99 degrees west, U.S. commercial communications; still operational
RCA Satcom 3R	20 November 1981	131 degrees west, U.S. commercial communications; still operational
Intelsat 5 F-3	15 December 1981	174 degrees east, international communications; still operational
Marecs A	20 December 1981	177.5 degrees west, European-built maritime comsat, leased by Inmarsat for international use, still operational as backup to Intelsat 5 F-5 maritime communications package
RCA Satcom 4	16 January 1982	82 degrees west, U.S. commercial communications; still operational
Westar 4	26 February 1982	99 degrees west, U.S. commercial communications; still operational
Intelsat 5 F-4	05 March 1982	34.5 degrees west, international communications; still operational
Westar 5	09 June 1982	123 degrees west, U.S. commercial communications; still operational
Anik D1	26 August 1982	105 degrees west, Canadian domestic communications; still operational
Intelsat 5 F-5	28 September 1982	63 degrees east, international communications; still operational
RCA Satcom 5	28 October 1982	143 degrees west, U.S. commercial communications; still operational
DSCS 2-15	30 October 1982	60 degrees east, U.S. Department of Defense strategic communications; still operational
DSCS 3-1	30 October 1982	130 degrees west, U.S. Department of Defense strategic communications; still operational
SBS F-2	11 November 1982	95 degrees west, U.S. commercial communications; still operational
Anik C3	12 November 1982	115 degrees west, Canadian domestic communications; still operational
Sakura 2A	04 February 1983	128 degrees east, Japanese domestic communications; still operational
TDRS 1	04 April 1983	79 degrees west, then moved to 171 degrees west spring 1990, satellite-to-ground communications via NASA's Tracking and Data Relay Satellite System (TDRSS); partially operational
RCA Satcom 1R	11 April 1983	139 degrees west, U.S. commercial communications; still operational
Intelsat 5 F-6	19 May 1983	18.5 degrees west, international communications; still operational
Eutelsat 1 F-1	16 June 1983	16 degrees east, European communications; still operational
Anik C2	18 June 1983	110 degrees west, Canadian domestic communications; still operational
Palapa B1	19 June 1983	108 degrees east, Indonesian domestic communications; still operational
Galaxy 1	28 June 1983	134 degrees west, U.S. commercial communications; still operational
Telstar 3A	28 July 1983	96 degrees west, U.S. commercial communications; still operational
Sakura 2B	05 August 1983	127 degrees east, Japanese domestic communications; out of service early 1990
Insat-1B	31 August 1983	74 degrees east, Indian combined metsat, domestic communications and data-collection; still operational
RCA Satcom 2R	08 September 1983	72 degrees west, U.S. commercial communications; still operational
Galaxy 2	22 September 1983	74 degrees west, U.S. commercial communications; still operational
Intelsat 5 F-7	19 October 1983	66 degrees east, international communications; still operational
Intelsat 5 F-8	05 March 1984	180 degrees longitude, international communications; still operational
Spacenet 1	23 May 1984	120 degrees longitude, international communications; still operational
Gorizont 10	01 August 1984	170 degrees west, Soviet domestic and international communications; still operational
Eutelsat 1 F-2	04 August 1984	7 degrees east, European communications; still operational
Telecom 1A	04 August 1984	8 degrees west, French combined civil and military communications; still operational
SBS F-4	30 August 1984	91 degrees west, U.S. commercial communications; still operational

Syncom 4 F-2	31 August 1984	73 degrees west, U.S. commercial comsat, leased to the U.S. Navy; out of service early-1990
Telstar 3C	01 September 1984	85 degrees west, Canadian domestic communications; still operational
Galaxy 3	21 September 1984	94 degrees west, U.S. commercial communications; still operational
Anik D2	09 November 1984	111 degrees west, Canadian domestic communications; still operational
Syncom 4 F-1	10 November 1984	16 degrees west, U.S. commercial comsat, leased to the U.S. Navy; out of service early-1990
Marecs B-2	10 November 1984	26 degrees west, European built maritime comsat, leased by Inmarsat for international use; still operational
Spacenet 2	10 November 1984	69 degrees west, U.S. commercial communications; still operational
NATO 3D	14 November 1984	22 degrees west, international military communications; still operational
Gorizont 11	18 January 1985	12 degrees west, Soviet domestic and international communications; still operational
Arabsat 1A	08 February 1985	19 degrees east, Arab nations' communications; still operational
Brasilsat 1	08 February 1985	65 degrees west, Brazilian domestic communications; still operational
Intelsat 5 F-10	23 March 1985	24.5 degrees west, international communications; still operational
Anik C1	12 April 1985	107 degrees west, Canadian domestic communications; still operational
Syncom 4 F-3	13 April 1985	105 degrees west, U.S. commercial comsat leased by the U.S. Navy; still operational
GStar 1	08 May 1985	103 degrees west, U.S. commercial communications; still operational
Morelos 1	17 June 1985	113 degrees west, Mexican domestic communications; still operational
Arabsat 1B	18 June 1985	26 degrees east, Arab nations' communications; still operational
Telstar 3D	19 June 1985	125 degrees west, U.S. commercial communications; still operational
Intelsat 5 F-11	30 June 1985	27.5 degrees west, international communications; still operational
Aussat 1	27 August 1985	160 degrees east, Australian domestic communications; still operational
ASC 1	27 August 1985	128 degrees west, U.S. commercial communications; still operational
Intelsat 5 F-12	28 September 1985	1 degree west, international communications; still operational
DSCS 3-3	03 October 1985	U.S. Department of Defense strategic communications; still operational
DSCS 3-4	03 October 1985	U.S. Department of Defense strategic communications; still operational
Raduga 17	15 November 1985	70 degrees east, then moved to 85 degrees east early-1990, Soviet domestic communications; still operational
Morelos 2	27 November 1985	117 degrees west, Mexican domestic communications; still operational
Aussat 2	28 November 1985	156 degrees east, Australian domestic communications; still operational
RCA Satcom K2	28 November 1985	81 degrees west, U.S. commercial communications; still operational
RCA Satcom K1	12 January 1986	85 degrees west, U.S. commercial communications; still operational
Raduga 18	17 January 1986	171 degrees west, Soviet domestic communications; still operational
STTW-1 (1)	01 February 1986	103 degrees east, Chinese domestic communications; still operational
Yuri 2B	12 February 1986	110 degrees east, Japanese television distribution; still operational
GStar 2	28 March 1986	105 degrees west, U.S. commercial communications; still operational
Brasilsat 2	28 March 1986	70 degrees west, Brazilian domestic communications; still operational
Cosmos 1738	04 April 1986	14 degrees west, satellite-to-ground communications via Satellite and Data Relay Network (SDRN-West); taken out of service summer 1989
Gorizont 12	10 June 1986	40 degrees east, Soviet domestic and international communications; still operational
Raduga 19	25 October 1986	45 degrees east, Soviet domestic communications; still operational
Gorizont 13	18 November 1986	90 degrees east, Soviet domestic and international communications; still operational
Raduga 20	19 March 1987	85 degrees east, Soviet domestic communications; still operational
Palapa B-2P	20 March 1987	113 degrees east, Indonesian domestic communications; still operational
Gorizont 14	11 May 1987	103 degrees east, Soviet domestic and international communications; still operational
Kiku 5	.27 August 1987	150 degrees east, Japanese experimental communications; still operational
Ekran (16)	03 September 1987	99 degrees east, Soviet television distribution; operational until fall 1989
Aussat K3	16 September 1987	164 degrees east, Australian domestic communications; still operational
Eutelsat 1 F-4	16 September 1987	13 degrees east, European communications; still operational
Cosmos 1888	01 October 1987	80 degrees east, Soviet government communications; still operational
Cosmos 1894	28 October 1987	24 degrees west, Soviet government communications; still operational
Cosmos 1897	26 November 1987	95 degrees east, satellite-to-ground communications via Satellite and Data Relay Network (SDRN-Central); still operational
Raduga 21	10 December 1987	128 degrees east, Soviet domestic communications; still operational
Ekran (17)	27 December 1987	99 degrees east, Soviet television distribution; still operational
Sakura 3A	19 February 1988	132 degrees east, Japanese domestic communications; still operational
STTW-1 (2)	07 March 1988	87 degrees east, Chinese domestic communications; still operational
Spacenet 3R	11 March 1988	87 degrees west, U.S. commercial communications; still operational
Telecom 1C	11 March 1988	5 degrees west, French combined civil and military communications; still operational
Gorizont 15	31 March 1988	14 degrees west, Soviet domestic communications; still operational
Ekran 18	06 May 1988	99 degrees east, Soviet television distribution, still operational
Intelsat 5A F-13	18 May 1988	53 degrees west, international communications; still operational
Panamsat 1	15 June 1988	45 degrees west, U.S. commercial communications; still operational
Insat 1C	21 July 1988	94 degrees east, Indian combined metsat, communications and data-collection; still operational
Eutelsat 1 F-5	21 July 1988	10 degrees east, European communications; still operational
Cosmos 1961	01 August 1988	14 degrees west, Soviet government communications; still operational
Gorizont 16	18 August 1988	80 degrees east, Soviet domestic and international communications; still operational
GStar 3	08 September 1988	93 degrees west, U.S. commercial communications; never fully-operational
SBS 5	08 September 1988	123 degrees west, U.S. commercial communications; still operational
Sakura 3B	16 September 1988	135 degrees east, Japanese domestic communications; still operational
TDRS 3	29 September 1988	171 degrees west, then moved to 174 degrees west spring 1990, satellite-to-ground communications via NASA's tracking and Data Relay Satellite System (TDRSS); partially operational
Raduga 22	20 October 1988	35 degrees east, Soviet domestic communications; still operational
TDF 1	28 October 1988	19 degrees west, French television distribution; still operational
Ekran (19)	10 December 1988	99 degrees east, Soviet television distribution; still operational
Astra 1A	11 December 1988	19 degrees east, European television distribution; still operational

Skynet 4B	11 December 1988	1 degree west, British strategic communications; still operational
STTW-1 (3)	22 December 1988	110 degrees east, Chinese domestic communications; still operational
Gorizont 17	26 January 1989	53 degrees east, Soviet domestic and international communications; still operational
Intelsat 5A F-15	27 January 1989	60 degrees east, international communications; still operational
JCSat 1	06 March 1989	150 degrees east, Japanese commercial communications; still operational
TDRS 4	13 March 1989	41 degrees west, satellite-to-ground communications via Tracking and Data Relay Satellite System (TDRSS); still operational
Tele-X	02 April 1989	5 degrees east, Swedish television distribution; still operational
Raduga 23	14 April 1989	25 degrees west, Soviet domestic communications; still operational
Superbird 1	05 June 1989	158 degrees east, Japanese commercial communications; still operational
DFS 1	05 June 1989	24 degrees east, German domestic communications; still operational
Raduga 24	21 June 1989	45 degrees east, Soviet domestic communications; still operational
Gorizont 18	5 July 1989	140 degrees, Soviet domestic and international communications; still operational
Olympus	12 July 1989	19 degrees west, European experimental communications; still operational
TV-Sat 2	8 August 1989	19 degrees west, German television distribution; still operational
Marcopolo 1	27 August 1989	31 degrees west, British television distribution; still operational
DSCS 2-16	04 September 1989	position unknown, U.S. Department of Defense strategic communications; still operational
DSCS 3-5	04 September 1989	position unknown, U.S. Department of Defense strategic communications; still operational
FltSatCom 8	25 September 1989	23 degrees west, U.S. Navy communications; still operational
Gorizont 19	28 September 1989	97 degrees east, Soviet domestic and international communications; still operational
Intelsat 6 F-2	27 October 1989	24.5 degrees west, international communications; still operational
Raduga 25	15 December 1989	45 degrees east, Soviet domestic communications; still operational
Cosmos 2054	27 December 1989	16 degrees west, satellite-to-ground communications via Satellite and Data Relay Network (SDRN-West); still operational
Skynet 4A	01 January 1990	8 degrees east, British strategic military communications; still operational
JCSat 2	01 January 1990	154 degrees east, Japanese television distribution and commercial communications; still operational
Syncom 4 F-5	10 January 1990	178 degrees east, U.S. commercial comsat, leased by the U.S. Navy; still operational
STTW-2 (1)	04 February 1990	98 degrees east, Chinese domestic communications; still operational
Raduga 26	15 February 1990	70 degrees east, Soviet domestic communications; still operational
Asiasat 1	07 April 1990	105.5 degrees east, Far East commercial communications; still operational
Palapa B-2R	13 April 1990	118 degrees east, Indonesian domestic communications; still operational
Intelsat 6 F-3	14 March 1990	29 degrees inclination, 400 kilometers low-orbit, awaiting Shuttle rescue mission
Insat-1D	12 June 1990	83 degrees east, Indian combined metsat, communications and data-collection; still operational
Gorizont 20	20 June 1990	90 degrees east, Soviet domestic and international communications; still operational
Intelsat 6 F-4	23 June 1990	60 degrees east, international communications; still operational

AMATEUR RADIO

Oscar

Transmission and reception of radio signals has been an amateur activity for many years. Way back in 1961, OSCAR 1 (Orbiting Satellite Carrying Amateur Radio), the first satellite for use by amateur radio operators, hitched a lift into orbit. This is still the method by which amateur satellites reach space — getting a piggyback with their larger, 'professional' brothers. In one case, two amateur-band transponders were built into an operational satellite, when the RS-10 and RS-11 payloads were integrated into the Cosmos 1861 navsat (RS stands for _Radio-Sport_ — in Russian of course). Just as with full-blown space agency satellites, a guaranteed list of working satellites is not possible, as apparently non-working satellites occasionally come back to life.

Satellite	Launch date	Orbit/mission
OSCAR 9	06 October 1981	97.5 degrees, 540 kilometers, British Uosat 1; operational, but then re-entered 13 October 1989
OSCAR 10	16 June 1983	26 degrees, 4,000 x 35,500 kilometers, West German Amsat 3B; still operational, but not fully
OSCAR 12	12 August 1986	50 degrees, 1,500 kilometers, Japanese Fuji-1; still operational
RS10/11	23 June 1987	83 degrees, 1,000 kilometers, pair of amateur-radio transponders built into Cosmos 1861 navsat; still operational
OSCAR 13	15 June 1988	56 degrees, 2,400 x 36,000 kilometers, West German Amsat 3C; still operational
OSCAR 14	22 January 1990	99 degrees, 800 kilometers, British UoSat 3; still operational
OSCAR 15	22 January 1990	99 degrees, 800 kilometers, British UoSat 4; not yet properly operational
OSCAR 16	22 January 1990	99 degrees, 800 kilometers, U.S. Pacsat for packet-radio experiments; still operational
OSCAR 17	22 January 1990	99 degrees, 800 kilometers, Brazilian DOVE, synthesised-voice telemetry; still operational
OSCAR 18	22 January 1990	99 degrees, 800 kilometers, U.S. amateur imaging satellite; still operational
OSCAR 19	22 January 1990	99 degrees, 800 kilometers, Argentinian LUsat for packet-radio experiments; still operational
OSCAR 20	07 February 1990	99 degrees, 900 x 1,750 kilometers, Japanese Fuji 2; still operational

NAVIGATION
GLONASS

A series of satellites with the Cosmos name fl, in 20,000-kilometer orbits to provide high-precision navigation for ships and aircraft. System operation is still experimental, so there are fewer operating satellites than with GPS. GLONASS satellites also carry laser reflectors for geodetic studies.

GPS

The Navstar (Navigation System using Timing and Ranging) satellites support the joint civil/military Global Positioning System. Moving in similar orbits to GLONASS spacecraft, in excess of 20 satellites will be needed to operate a complete system, and with the steady build-up of Block-2 satellites appearing in space, system completion will be well in advance of the Soviet system.

Nadezhda

The Nadezhda (Hope) satellites support the Tsikada (Cricket) network, named for the sound of the satellites' signals. There are normally four operating Tsikada (System-1) satellites, in orbits spaced at 45-degree intervals around the equator. Until recently, the satellites have received 'Cosmos' names, but the last two satellites also carry COSPAS search-and-rescue-beacon receivers, hence the new name.

USSR System 2

Satellites in the second Soviet system have orbits spaced at 45-degree intervals around the equator, and six are normally operational — though older satellites may be sitting 'in-reserve'. They transmit similar signals to Tsikada, but satellites are replaced more frequently, often before their performance is noticeably degraded. This suggests that it is a primarily military system.

U.S. Navy Navigation Satellite System

America's low-orbit system was set up in the 1960s to guide missile-toting submarines. It is some times known as 'Program Oscar' from the international phonetic alphabet — not to be confused with the OSCAR amateur-radio satellites. Several satellites are operating at any one time, though the orbit-plane spacings are less precise than for their Soviet counterparts. During the late 1980s, several spare satellites were transferred from ground storage to storage in orbit to save costs! Some NNSS spacecraft have carried supplementary science payloads (Hilat and Polar BEAR), and the Nova satellites represent experimental technology being put to practical use.

Satellite	Launch date	Orbit/mission
Oscar (Nav) 20	30 October 1973	90 degrees, 900 x 1,150 kilometers, U.S. NNSS; still operational
Navstar 1-4	11 December 1978	63 degrees, 20,000 kilometers, fourth Block-1 Navstar; still operational
Navstar 1-6	26 April 1980	63 degrees, 20,000 kilometers, sixth Block-1 Navstar and the first to carry nuclear explosion-detection sensors; still operational
Nova 1	15 May 1981	90 degrees, 1,180 kilometers, improved design, U.S. NNSS; still operational
Hilat	27 June 1983	82 degrees, 770 x 840 kilometers, ionospheric studies experiments plus normal U.S. NNSS operation; switched-off 21 July 1989 because of battery problems
Navstar 1-8	14 July 1983	63 degrees, 20,000 kilometers, eighth Block-1 Navstar including nuclear explosion-detectors; still operational
USA-1	13 June 1984	63 degrees, 20,000 kilometers, ninth Block-1 Navstar including nuclear explosion-detectors; still operational
USA-5	08 September 1984	63 degrees, 20,000 kilometers, tenth Block-1 Navstar including nuclear explosion-detectors; still operational
Nova 3	12 October 1984	90 degrees, 1,180 kilometers, improved design, U.S. NNSS; still operational
Cosmos 1655	30 May 1985	83 degrees, 1,000 kilometers, Soviet System 1 navsat; still operational
Oscar (Nav) 24	03 August 1985	90 degrees, 1,000 x 1,260 kilometers, U.S. NNSS; still operational
Oscar (Nav) 30	03 August 1985	90 degrees, 1,000 x 1,260 kilometers, U.S. NNSS; still operational, but stored in orbit
USA-10	09 October 1985	63 degrees, 20,000 kilometers, eleventh Block-1 Navstar including nuclear explosion-detectors; still operational
Cosmos 1791	13 November 1986	83 degrees, 1,000 kilometers, Soviet System 1 navsat; out of service July 1989
Polar BEAR	14 November 1986	90 degrees, 990 kilometers, Beacon Experiments and Auroral studies, plus normal U.S. NNSS operation; still operational
Cosmos 1816	29 January 1987	83 degrees, 1,000 kilometers, Soviet System 1 navsat; out of service early-1990
Cosmos 1861	23 June 1987	83 degrees, 1,000 kilometers, Soviet System 1 navsat, also carrying RS-10/11 amateur-radio transponders; still operational
Oscar (Nav) 27	16 September 1987	90 degrees, 1,020 x 1,180 kilometers, U.S. NNSS; still operational
Oscar (Nav) 29	16 September 1987	90 degrees, 1,020 x 1,180 kilometers, U.S. NNSS; operational, but stored in orbit
Cosmos 1864	06 July 1987	83 degrees, 1,000 kilometers, Soviet System 2 navsat; out of service July 1989
Cosmos 1904	23 December 1987	83 degrees, 1,000 kilometers, Soviet System 2 navsat; out of service April 1990
Oscar (Nav) 23	26 April 1988	90 degrees 1,020 x 1,300 kilometers, U.S. NNSS; still operational
Oscar (Nav) 32	26 April 1988	90 degrees, 1,020 x 1,300 kilometers, U.S. NNSS; operational, but stored in orbit
Cosmos 1946	21 May 1988	65 degrees, 19,000 kilometers, GLONASS; still operational
Cosmos 1947	21 May 1988	65 degrees, 19,000 kilometers, GLONASS; still operational
Cosmos 1948	21 May 1988	65 degrees, 19,000 kilometers, GLONASS; still operational
Nova 2	16 June 1988	90 degrees, 1,180 kilometers, improved design, U.S. NNSS; still operational
Cosmos 1959	18 July 1988	83 degrees, 1,000 kilometers, Soviet System 2 navsat; out of service March 1990
Oscar (Nav) 31	25 August 1988	90 degrees, 1,040 x 1,180 kilometers, U.S. NNSS; operational, but stored in orbit
Oscar (Nav) 25	25 August 1988	90 degrees, 1,040 x 1,180 kilometers, U.S. NNSS; operational, but stored in orbit
USA-35	14 February 1989	55 degrees, 20,000 kilometers, first Block-2 Navstar including nuclear explosion-detectors; still operational
Cosmos 2004	22 February 1989	83 degrees, 1,000 kilometers, Soviet System 2 navsat; still operational
Cosmos 2016	04 April 1989	83 degrees, 1,000 kilometers, Soviet System 2 navsat; still operational
Cosmos 2022	31 May 1989	65 degrees, 19,000 kilometers, GLONASS; still operational

Cosmos 2023	31 May 1989	65 degrees, 19,000 kilometers, GLONASS; still operational
Cosmos 2026	07 June 1989	83 degrees, 1,000 kilometers, Soviet System 2 navsat; still operational
USA-38	10 June 1989	55 degrees, 20,000 kilometers, second Block-2 Navstar including nuclear explosion-detectors; still operational
Nadezhda 1	04 July 1989	83 degrees, 1,000 kilometers, Soviet System 2 navsat, replacement for Cosmos 1791, including COSPAS-4 search-and-rescue-beacon locator; still operational
Cosmos 2034	27 July 1989	83 degrees, 1,000 kilometers, Soviet System 2 navsat; replacement for Cosmos 1864; still operational
USA-42	18 August 1989	55 degrees, 20,0000 kilometers, third Block-2 Navstar including nuclear explosion-detectors; still operational
USA-47	21 October 1989	55 degrees, 20,000 kilometers, fourth Block-2 Navstar including nuclear explosion-detectors; still operational
USA-49	11 December 1989	55 degrees, 20,000 kilometers, fifth Block-2 Navstar including nuclear explosion-detectors; still operational
USA-50	24 January 1990	55 degrees, 20,000 kilometers, sixth Block-2 Navstar; still operational
Nadezhda 2	27 February 1990	83 degrees, 1,000 kilometers, Soviet System 1 navsat, replacement for Cosmos 1816, including COSPAS-5 search-and-rescue-beacon locator; still operational
Cosmos 2061	20 March 1990	83 degrees, 1,000 kilometers, Soviet System 2 navsat, replacement for Cosmos 1959; still operational
USA-54	26 March 1990	55 degrees, 20,000 kilometers, seventh Block-2 Navstar including nuclear explosion-detectors; still operational
Cosmos 2074	20 April 1990	83 degrees, 1,000 kilometers, Soviet System 2 navsat, replacement for Cosmos 1904; still operational
Cosmos 2079	19 May 1990	65 degrees, 19,000 kilometers, GLONASS; still operational
Cosmos 2080	19 May 1990	65 degrees, 19,000 kilometers, GLONASS; still operational
Cosmos 2081	19 May 1990	65 degrees, 19,000 kilometers, GLONASS; still operational

GEODESY

Several countries operate geodetic satellite programs, and satellites not originally launched for geodetic studies are sometimes used for geodetic measurement. Often, satellites in non-geodetic programs have built-in laser-reflectors for accurate distance-measurement. Some of the Meteor weather satellites are examples, as are all of the GLONASS satellites — showing how geodesy and satellite navigation are closely linked. Both are related to positional measurement on the Earth's surface.

Because of the variety of ways in which satellite-based geodesy can be performed, individual program descriptions have been omitted, but there follows a list of examples of geodetic satellites which are still in use. Identifying currently-operational geodetic programs is difficult because so many payloads are passive in nature, having no electronics on-board and merely serving to reflect light projected from the ground. They can be used for many years without that fact being obvious.

Satellite	Launch date	Orbit/mission
Starlette	06 February 1975	50 degrees, 800 x 1,100 kilometers, French laser-reflector
LAGEOS	04 May 1976	110 degrees, 5,900 kilometers, Laser Geodynamics Satellite, passive laser-reflector
Ajisai	12 August 1986	50 degrees, 1,500 kilometers, Japan's Experimental Geodetic Satellite, light/laser-reflecting satellite; still operational
Cosmos 1950	30 May 1988	74 degrees, 1,500 kilometers, GEO-IKI satellite, fitted with laser-reflectors; still operational
Cosmos 1989	10 January 1989	65 degrees, 19,000 kilometers, Etalon 1 passive laser-reflection satellite; still operational
Cosmos 2024	31 May 1989	65 degrees, 19,000 kilometers, Etalon 2 passive laser-reflection satellite; still operational
Cosmos 2037	28 August 1989	74 degrees, 1,500 kilometers, GEO-IK2 satellite, fitted with laser-reflectors; still operational

SPACE RESEARCH: SCIENCE

Satellite programs exist which are purely exploratory in nature; studying the upper-atmosphere, space itself, or taking advantage of the availability of an orbital platform to undertake research which would be impractical from the Earth's surface.

Satellite	Launch date	Orbit/mission
IUE	26 January 1978	29 degrees, geosynchronous, International Ultraviolet Explorer astronomy satellite; still operational
Ariel 6	02 June 1979	55 degrees, 600 kilometers, British X-ray astronomy satellite; no longer operational, but still transmitting
Bhaskara 2	20 November 1981	51 degrees, 550 kilometers, Indian remote-sensing test satellite; no longer operational, but still transmitting
Charge Coupled Explorer	16 August 1984	5 degrees, 1,100 x 50,000 kilometers, part of the Active Magnetic Particles Tracing Experiment (AMPTE) magnetospheric-studies program; still operational
ERBS	05 October 1984	57 degrees, 610 kilometers, Earth Radiation Budget Satellite studying the Earth's solar-radiation/heat balance; still operational
Ginga	05 February 1987	31 degrees, 510 x 700 kilometers, Japan's ASTRO-C astronomy satellite; still operational
Akebono	21 February 1989	75 degrees, 280 x 10,500 kilometers, Japan's EXOS-D auroral-studies satellite; still operational
Pion 1/2	08 June 1989	83 degrees, 260 kilometers, a pair of small satellites released from Resurs-F1 for upper-air density studies; re-entered 23 July and 24 July 1989 respectively

Pion 3/4	07 August 1989	83 degrees, 260 kilometers, a pair of small satellites released from Soviet Resurs-F3 for upper-air density studies; both re-entered on 19 September 1989
Hipparcos	08 August 1989	7 degrees, 550 x 36,000 kilometers, European astrometric satellite, not in planned synchronous orbit because of rocket-motor failure; still operational
Intercosmos 24	28 September 1989	83 degrees, 500 x 2,500 kilometers, Soviet/international magnetospheric studies, working with its Magion sub-satellite (released 3 October); still operational
COBE	18 November 1989	sun-synchronous, 900 kilometers, NASA's Cosmic Background Explorer studying radiation in the galaxy; still operational
Granat	01 December 1989	52 degrees, 2,000 x 200,000 kilometers, Soviet/French high-energy (gamma-radiation) astronomical observatory; still operational
Hubble Space Telescope	25 April 1990	29 degrees, 620 kilometers, NASA's orbiting astronomical telescope; operational but at a reduced level of effectiveness due to a manufacturing error
ROSAT	01 June 1990	53 degrees, 570 kilometers, U.S./German high-energy (ultraviolet and X-ray) astronomical observatory; still operational

SPACE RESEARCH: MICROGRAVITY AND SPACE-ENVIRONMENT

Some missions are launched to study the effects of space itself has on satellites, or on experiments carried aboard satellites. Some missions are related to satellite design, checking-out the effects of the outer-space vacuum, radiation and air-density. Others test space sensors, and new equipment for use in future satellite designs. The series of U.S. missions conducted under the auspices of the Strategic Defense Initiative (SDI) are examples of these. The microgravity environment of near-Earth orbit is also of interest, in terms of its effects on living organisms and the way in which materials behave under its influence.

Again, as mission types are so diverse, there is no individual breakdown of programs under this category. What follows is a straightforward list of satellites which have operated during the _Space Year_.

Satellite	Launch date	Orbit/mission
Salyut 7 & Cosmos 1686	19 April 1982 & 27 September 1985	52 degrees, 470 kilometers, defunct space station plus add-on module, used to test systems' longevity; may still be operational, but radio-transmissions ceased early-1990
LDEF	06 April 1984	28.5 degrees, 475 kilometers, NASA's Long Duration Exposure Facility; retrieved 12 January 1990 and returned to Earth 20 January 1990
USA-36	24 March 1989	48 degrees, 1,570 kilometers, U.S. SDI Delta Star rocket-plume detection tests; mission completed early-1990
Cosmos 2044	15 September 1989	82 degrees, 200 x 260 kilometers, Biocosmos 9 microgravity biosat; recovered after 14 days
Cosmos 2053	26 December 1989	74 degrees, 530 kilometers, possible calibration target for ground-based radars; no longer operational
Orizuru	07 February 1990	99 degrees, 910 x 1750 kilometers, Japanese technology experiment to test an extending/retracting boom, and an unfurlable 'umbrella' antenna
USA-51	14 February 1990	43 degrees, 540 kilometers, U.S. SDI Laser Composition Experiment; still operational
USA-52	14 February 1990	43 degrees, 470 kilometers, U.S. SDI Relay Mirror Experiment; still operational
Offeq 2	03 April 1990	143 degrees, 200 x 1,600 kilometers, Israeli satellite-systems test satellite; ceased to operate summer 1990
Pegsat	05 April 1990	94 degrees, 570 x 680 kilometers, U.S. Pegasus vehicle performance-monitoring, plus ionospheric studies; still operational
Foton 3	11 April 1990	63 degrees, 220 x 380 kilometers, microgravity materials-processing; recovered after 16 days
Cosmos 2059	04 February 1990	66 degrees, 600 x 2,300 kilometers, possible space-technology experimentation; possibly still operational
USA-56	11 April 1990	90 degrees, 770 kilometers, U.S. Department of Defense Polar Orbit Geomagnetic Survey and Solid State Recorder; still operational
USA-57	11 April 1990	90 degrees, 770 kilometers, U.S. Department of Defense Transceiver Experiment; still operational

SUBORBITAL
MISSIONS

SUBORBITAL MISSIONS

(Overleaf) Space Data's High Performance Booster (HPB) at the start of its first flight.

For completeness, we felt that *any* category of mission bound for space should be eligible for inclusion, rather than restricting the 'lower limit' to orbital flights alone. Sounding rockets and other types of suborbital boosters enter space briefly, then perform a standard re-entry. In the process, they cross the magical 100-kilometer mark defined by the FAI as the begining of space. We have insufficient details to record Soviet suborbital activities.

Sounding rocket launch vehicles carry research payloads with scientific instruments to altitudes ranging from 30 miles up to 600 miles. Experiment time above the Earth's surface in microgravity conditions ranges to around 15 minutes and scientific data are collected and usually returned to Earth via telemetry links.

Sounding rockets provide the only means of making *in-situ* measurements in those regions between the maximum altitude for balloons and the minimum altitude for satellites, the latter being about 100 miles. They are routinely launched from established ranges all over the world, including; Wallops Island, Virginia; Poker Flat Research Range, Alaska; White Sands Missile Range, New Mexico; Churchill Range, Canada; Andoya, Norway; Esrange, Sweden; Woomera, Australia; and sites in the Soviet Union and Japan.

When there is a special need, rockets can also be launched from temporary ranges, and such missions have taken place from such locations as; Puntas Lobos, Peru; Rio Grande, Brazil; Keweenaw, Michigan, Red Lake and Cape Parry, Canada; Puerto Rico; Alaska; Greenland; Antarctica; and Alice Springs, Australia.

The NASA sounding rocket program, managed by the Goddard Space Flight Center and based at Wallops Island Flight Facility, is one of the world's largest and supports some 35-45 launches per year.

It serves not only NASA, but other government agencies, universities, industry and foreign countries as well. Sounding rocket programs are in general a low-cost, quick-response activity when compared to orbital missions.

On 23 October 1989, NASA successfully conducted a rocketborne experiment from Wallops Island to study physical changes in the ionosphere caused by small amounts of chemical released from the payload. NASA officials described it as the first Nickel Carbonyl Release Experiment (NICARE) to be conducted in space. It was designed to study the effects on optical sensors and radio instruments from clouds that may be generated by future material-sciences experiments on the *Freedom* Space Station.

Launched by a two-stage Terrier-Black Brant rocket, the 'daughter' section of the separated payload vented small amounts of halon and nickel-carbonyl at an altitude of 170 miles.

A new four-stage solid-propellant sounding rocket combination, the Black Brant 12, was launched from Wallops on 5 December. The purpose of the launch was to flight-test and qualify a redesigned fourth-stage rocket motor, the Nihka, which had experienced a premature loss of thrust during its first test flight on 30 September 1988.

A secondary purpose was to conduct an experiment for the University of California to measure ultraviolet spectral emissions of hydrogen, helium and oxygen atoms and their ions in the Earth's atmosphere. The experiment was lofted to a peak altitude of 907 miles.

The new configuration has been developed to provide a low-cost, high-altitude platform capable of carrying payloads to altitudes greater than 870 miles. It consists of off-the-shelf motors currently used in various other sounding rockets.

Low cost is realised by using two surplus military rocket motors — a Talos for the first stage and a Taurus for the second. The third and fourth stages are a Black Brant 5C motor and the redesigned Nihka motor, also used as the upper two stages of the Black Brant 10 and purchased from Canada's Bristol Aerospace.

Addition of the Black Brant 12 to the sounding rocket family provides the capability to carry lightweight payloads of 300 pounds to an altitude some 310 miles higher than with the Black Brant 10.

On 5 April 1990, NASA conducted a rocketborne experiment from Wallops to study physical changes in the ionosphere caused by radiowaves transmitted from the rocket's payload during the suborbital flight. Referred to as WISP (Waves in Space Plasmas), the experiment used radio transmitters, receivers and antenna systems to study wave particle interactions.

A Black Brant 10 lofted the two sections — a 547-pound primary payload and a small subsatellite — to a peak altitude of 364 miles.

The capability of responding quickly to new scientific discoveries or events was demonstrated on 21 and 28 April 1990, when two NASA sounding rockets were launched from the White Sands Missile Range, New Mexico, carrying scientific instruments to observe Comet Austin. Both rockets were two-stage Black Brant 11s. The first carried Johns Hopkins University's faint object telescope and a spectrograph to observe the comet in the far-ultraviolet spectral range. The second vehicle carried a far-ultraviolet spectrometer for the University of Colorado.

The U.S. military maintains an active sounding rocket program, recording a number of launches during the *Space Year*.

On 27 April 1990, an experiment on a suborbital rocket launched from White Sands simulated the effects of nuclear weapons exploding high in the atmosphere. The aim was to gauge the threat to a future U.S. strategic defense system.

The experiment used an Aries booster to place the 5,000-pound payload on a path that climbed to a height of 72 miles before returning to Earth some six and a half minutes after launch.

A two-stage Terrier-Malemute sounding rocket launched into a ballistic trajectory from NASA's Wallops Island, Virginia facility on 29 March carried an experiment payload called Firefly, built by Sandia Laboratories. The Firefly mission was part of a program to demonstrate the ability of a high-resolution imaging radar to discriminate between an inflatable decoy and a genuine re-entry warhead.

The Firefly flight lasted 700 seconds and ended with an impact in the Atlantic Ocean some 400 kilometers east of Wallops Island. An inflatable decoy was launched near the peak of the booster's trajectory, at an altitude of 480 kilometers. A coherent carbon-dioxide laser radar and auxiliary Argon ion laser located near Westford, Massachusetts, tracked the conical decoy, which measured six feet long when fully-inflated.

A follow-on Firefly mission, dubbed Firebird, will take place in 1991. As well as refining the radar tracking procedures employed on this first test, the Firebird flight will have the decoy 'pinged' by laser pulses to see how accurately computers can ascertain its nature: i.e., it is a decoy or is it a real warhead?

Two small Terrier-Malemutes launched from the Kauai facility in Hawaii on 4 and 11 September 1989 carried a pair of small 'Star Wars'-related Starmate space vehicles on ten-minute suborbital flights to provide data on 'stealth' spacecraft technology.

Starmate, a $6-million project, was the first use by the SDIO 'Star Wars' organization of a space test to validate laboratory findings on 'stealth' techniques. Radar, and infrared, visible-light and ultraviolet sensors located on Kauai, Maui and Oahu observed the Starmate payloads as they ascended to their 450-mile maximum altitudes above the Pacific Ocean. The sensors were mimicing Soviet defenses, which would employ the same techniques to detect SDI spacecraft in Earth orbit.

The Consort program scored an important success on 16 May 1990, when a Starfire sounding rocket provided seven minutes of near-weightlessness for twelve experiments. A problem similar to that which caused the loss of the Consort 2 vehicle on 15 November 1989 was averted just minutes before lift-off, when technicians discovered and solved a fault in a gyroscope in the guidance system.

Space Services Incorporated (SSI) has supplied the Starfire rockets for all three Consort missions to date. Starfire 1 is a two-stage vehicle employing a Morton Thiokol booster derived from the U.S. Navy's SM-2 missile and a Black Brant 5C sustainer motor for the second stage.

The rocket is 52 feet tall and weights 6,000-pounds at lift-off; the twelve-foot-tall Consort payload weighed 1,004 pounds.

The Consort program is sponsored by the Consortium for Materials Development in Space at the University of Alabama in Huntsville. Costs of $1.9 million for launch and payload integration are met by NASA and the consortium's industrial partners.

Efforts to launch the first commercial hybrid rocket received a serious setback on 5 October, when an engine failure resulted in the total loss of the prototype Amroc IRR booster at Vandenberg, California. The countdown proceeded smoothly until the moment of engine ignition, when the vehicle remained on the pad.

Hybrid motors burn a combination of solid rubber-like fuel and a liquid oxidizer. It was revealed that an insufficient amount of liquid oxygen was injected into the motor (probably due to a malfunctioning valve), resulting in delivery of less than full power. The ignition sequence was automatically terminated at this point. An attempt to re-secure the vehicle on the pad was made by commanding the hold-down clamps to re-engage, but the rocket had moved upward slightly during the aborted ignition and the clamps would not seat. The vehicle then toppled off the launch stand, its liquid oxygen tank ruptured, and a fire ensued.

It was an added blow to Amroc, whose president and co-founder George Koopman, was killed in an automobile accident near Edwards Air Force Base, California on 19 July.

During the summer of 1989, the SDIO program sired a number of missions, Black Brant vehicles being fired from Poker Flat, Alaska, and Wallops Island, in support of the Delta 183 experiment. An Aries vehicle (the first stage of a Minuteman missile) was also launched from White Sands as part of the SDIO's Bear experiment.

An improved version of the Aries made its first flight on 30 January 1990, from Wallops. Developed by the Chandler, Arizona-based Space Data Division of Orbital Sciences, the so-called High Performance Booster (HPB) features a modified Minuteman 1 second-stage motor atop the Aries vehicle's standard Talos first-stage motor, considerably uprating capability.

HPB-1 reached a maximum altitude of 250 nautical miles, and impacted the Atlantic Ocean 103 nautical miles features a modified Minuteman 1 second-stage motor atop the Aries vehicle's standard Talos first-stage motor, considerably uprating capability.

HPB-1 reached a maximum altitude of 250 nautical miles, and impacted the Atlantic Ocean 103 nautical miles downrange. The booster carried extensive diagnostic instrumentation, and a number of secondary payloads for both the U.S. Air Force's Ballistic Systems Division and the Massachusetts Institute of Technology's Lincoln Laboratories.

The vehicle's gross lift-off weight was 19,470 pounds, which included 3,035 pounds of payload.

On 20 February, the first Minuteman CFE module was successfully launched from Vandenberg Air Force Base, California, atop a three-stage Minuteman 1 ballistic missile. The CFE (Consolidated Front End) is an avionics, power and payload support module for the Minuteman 1. It was designed, developed and built by Space Data to replace the vehicle's current, outdated 'front-end' unit.

During 1990, the Space Data Division was also awarded a contract to develop, produce and launch 20 suborbital vehicles for the SDIO's test programs. The first of the launches, from either White Sands or Cape Canaveral Air Force Station, was due at the end of the year.

A year earlier, Space Data received a contract from the Consortium for Materials Development in Space to launch the Joust 1 and Joust 2 payloads. Joust 1 was planned for November 1990, with Joust 2 to follow a year later. Space Data's 27,000-pound Prospector will launch the experiments from the U.S. Air Force's Eastern Test Range to a height of 600 miles, providing between 12 and 15 minutes of microgravity.

Meanwhile, the Spaceport Florida authority — created in 1989 to provide commercial launch services in the State — announced plans in mid-1990 to buy six small sounding rockets that will be used to provide 'free' rides into space for university research payloads.

The launches will be from Cape San Blas and are part of a broader strategy to attract business, researchers and tourists to Florida.

On the opposite side of the Atlantic, Europe's suborbital microgravity program has been flourishing, too. During 1990 the Swedish Space Corporation and MBB-ERNO of West Germany announced a joint venture to build the Maxus vehicle, which will offer around 15 minutes of microgravity. The first launch is scheduled for April 1991.

The launcher will be based on a modified version of Delta 2's strap-on boosters — the Castor 4B engine — which MBB purchased in 1990 from Morton Thiokol.

Maxus launches will reach an altitude of 620 miles above Sweden's Esrange launch

(Left) TR-1/3, the last in the series of sub-scale test rockets launched to support development of Japan's H-2 heavy-lift booster, streaks away from Tanegashima on 20 August 1989.

(Bottom-left) A technician at Poker Flat Research Range, Alaska inspects a sounding rocket's payload module.

(Bottom-right) Helicopter recovery of the payload module from Sweden's Maser 4 mission in March 1990.

site, carrying payloads of up to 1,100 pounds. This will be far higher than Europe's other two sounding rockets — Texus and Maser — which rarely exceed 155 miles.

ESA's Maser 4 mission was launched from Esrange on 29 March 1990. It used a Black Brant 9 two-stage motor and the payload carried five experiment modules — funded by ESA and the Society of Japanese Aerospace Companies.

The flight achieved microgravity conditions for seven minutes and 19 seconds, with the payload landing back on Earth after approximately 15 minutes. Experiment boxes that required early recovery were returned to the laboratories in the launch area by helicopters, which were guided by radar and a beacon transmitter in the payload to its touchdown location.

On 13 May 1990, Texus 25 was launched from Esrange. It carried an ESA density relaxation experiment. Two days later, on the 15th, Texus 26 was successfully launched, carrying a further two ESA experiments on materials-composition.

The Japanese national space agency, NASDA, has made three suborbital flights as part of the development program for its H-2 heavy-lift vehicle. The final flight in the series took place on 20 August 1989, when the TR-1/3 test rocket was launched from the Tanegashima Space Center.

TR-1s were quarter-scale versions of the H-2 vehicle. The final test came to an end when a data recorder in a dummy solid rocket booster was successfully recovered the same day.

The main objectives of the mission were to obtain flight data — pertaining to aerodynamic heating pressure, acoustic, atmospheric interface, and thermal radiation from the exhaust plume — and confirm the SRB separation mechanism performed properly.

Iraq is preparing to launch two science/technology satellite missions following the suborbital test of its Abid (Worshipper) three-stage rocket on 5 December 1989. Both rocket and satellite designs were entirely 'homegrown' according to Amir Hammudi al Sa'di, an under-secretary in the Ministry of Industry and Military Industrialization.

C.S.

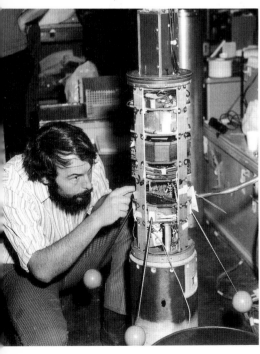

INTO
ORBIT

What follows is a complete, unique listing of every spacecraft launch to orbit between 1 July 1989 and 30 June 1990. Details are given of the launch itself, the orbit attained by the satellite — with all significant maneuvers being listed, and the purpose of its mission. Where they are available, precise lift-off times are listed. However, the Soviet Union does not normally announce launch times for routine missions, so they have been calculated by 'back-tracking' round the orbit to the launch site. In a worst-case, the time listed is within three minutes of the actual lift-off, but in many instances, it is precise to the actual minute. Orbit details themselves are derived from data orginating within the U.S. North American Defense Command (NORAD), and distributed by NASA's Goddard Space Flight Center.

NAME, INT'I DESIG'N (CATALOG NO.)	LAUNCH TIME & DATE (GMT)	LAUNCH SITE & VEHICLE	PERIGEE (KM)	APOGEE (KM)	PERIOD (MINS)	INCLINATION (DEGREES)
Nadezhda 1 1989-50A (20103)	3:22 pm 4 July	Plesetsk, USSR C-1 (Cosmos 2)	960	1014	104.9	83.0

Polar-orbiting navigation satellite in the 'Tsikada' system, equipped with radio beacons operating at 150 and 400 MHz. It also carries a COSPAS SARSAT search and rescue system package to monitor international distress frequencies.

Cosmos 2029 1989-51A (20105)	8:00 am 5 July	Plesetsk, USSR A-2 (Soyuz)	181 338	242 362	88.8 91.6	82.4 82.4

Recoverable, maneuverable satellite based on the Vostok design, carrying out strategic photo-reconnaissance. The cabin section containing film and cameras landed in Khazakstan on 19 July. Listed are the initial orbit, and the operational orbit reached after a two-phase maneuver on 6 July.

Gorizont (18) 1989-52A (20107)	10:45 pm 5 July	Baikonur, USSR D-1-e (four-stage Proton)	34970 35774	35233 35807	1401.2 1436.1	1.5 1.3
		geosynchronous — 140 degrees east				

Communications satellite at the Statsionar-7 location, serving the Orbita-2 system — both within the USSR and (through Intersputnik) abroad — with telecommunications links at C-band (6/4 GHz). A separate C-band transponder supplies Central Television programs to the Soviet Moskva TV-distribution network, and single transponders support both the K-band (14/11 GHz) Luch system and the L-band (1.6 GHz) Volna maritime and aeronautical communications system. Listed are the drift orbit and the operational orbit.

Olympus 1 1989-53A (20122)	12:14 am 12 July	Kourou, French Guiana Ariane 3 (V32)	235 33303 35766	36208 36113 35808	639.3 1381.2 1436.1	6.1 0.2 0.1
		geosynchronous — 19 degrees west				

European Space Agency's experimental communications satellite, demonstrating the concept of a large, multi-purpose platform. It is equipped with transponders operating at Ka-band (30/20 GHz) and Ku-band (14/12 GHz). Listed are the transfer orbit, the drift orbit achieved 36 hours after launch, and the geosynchronous orbit reached on 4 August.

Cosmos 2030 1989-54A (20124)	3:00 pm 12 July	Plesetsk, USSR A-2 (Soyuz)	164	351	89.7	67.2

Strategic photo-reconnaissance satellite, possibly carrying several return-capsules for periodic recovery of film. It was destroyed, probably by deliberate explosion, on 28 July.

Resurs-F3 1989-55A (20134)	9:45 am 18 July	Plesetsk, USSR A-2 (Soyuz)	183	225	88.6	82.6

Recoverable, maneuverable satellite based on the Vostok design, carrying out Earth-resources photography. The cabin section containing film and cameras landed in Khazakstan on 8 August.

Cosmos 2031 1989-56A (20136)	12:10 pm 18 July	Baikonur, USSR A-2 (Soyuz)	194 231 229	265 354 233	89.0 90.3 89.1	50.6 50.6 50.6

Strategic photo-reconnaissance satellite carrying several return-capsules for periodic recovery of film. It re-entered the Earth's atmosphere on 15 September, and the camera module may have been recovered. Listed are the initial orbit, and the operational orbit reached after maneuvers on 25 July and 29 July.

NAME, INT'I DESIG'N (CATALOG NO.)	LAUNCH TIME & DATE (GMT)	LAUNCH SITE & VEHICLE	PERIGEE (KM)	APOGEE (KM)	PERIOD (MINS)	INCLINATION (DEGREES)
Cosmos 2032 1989-57A (20145)	9:00 am 20 July	Plesetsk, USSR A-2 (Soyuz)	180 232 232	246 363 245	88.8 90.5 89.3	82.3 82.3 82.3

Recoverable, maneuverable satellite based on the Vostok design, carrying out strategic photo-reconnaissance. The cabin section containing film and cameras landed in Khazakstan on 3 August. Listed are the initial orbit, and operational orbit reached after maneuvers on 25 July and 29 July.

| Cosmos 2033 1989-58A (20147) | 11:56 pm 23 July | Baikonur, USSR F-1 (Tsyklon) | 404 | 417 | 92.8 | 65.0 |

Electronic-intelligence-gathering satellite, particularly monitoring naval military radio traffic and shipping movements. The orbit is maintained against air-drag by frequent operation of a low-thrust motor.

| Cosmos 2034 1989-59A (20149) | 7:49 am 25 July | Plesetsk, USSR C-1 (Cosmos 2) | 968 | 1013 | 105.0 | 82.9 |

Polar-orbiting navigation satellite, with radio beacons operating at 150 and 400 MHz.

| Cosmos 2035 1989-60A (20151) | 11:30 am 2 August | Plesetsk, USSR A-2 (Soyuz) | 180 231 229 | 230 357 242 | 88.6 90.5 89.3 | 82.6 82.6 82.6 |

Recoverable, maneuverable satellite based on the Vostok design, carrying out strategic photo-reconnaissance. The cabin section containing film and cameras landed in Khazakstan on 16 August. Listed are the initial orbit, and orbit reached after maneuvers on 4 August and 11 August.

| Pion (3) 1989-55C (20160) | — 7 August | Resurs-F3 — | 255 | 272 | 89.8 | 82.6 |

Passive satellite for upper-air density studies, built by students at the Korolyov Aviation Institute and released from Resurs-F3. It re-entered the Earth's atmosphere on 18 September.

| Pion (4) 1989-55D (20161) | — 7 August | Resurs-F3 — | 255 | 272 | 89.8 | 82.6 |

Passive satellite for upper-air density studies, built by students at the Korolyov Aviation Institute and released from Resurs-F3. It re-entered the Earth's atmosphere on 19 September.

| STS-28 1989-61A (20164) | 12:37 pm 8 August | Kennedy SC, USA Shuttle Columbia | 296 | 308 | 90.5 | 57.0 |

Piloted space mission devoted to launching a military satellite and conducting military and Strategic Defense Initiative (SDI 'Star Wars') experiments. Mission Commander was USAF Colonel Brewster Shaw; Pilot, U.S. Navy Commander Richard Richards; and Mission Specialists, U.S. Navy Commander David Leestma, U.S. Army Lt-Col James Adamson and USAF Major Mark Brown, Columbia landed at Edwards Air Force Base at 10:37pm on 13 August.

| USA-40 1989-61B (20167) | 8:06 pm 8 August | Columbia payload bay | 296 | 303 | 90.5 | 57.0 |

Probably an AFP-731 (Air Force Program 731) maneuverable multi-purpose reconsat, equipped with a digital-imaging system and signals-intelligence (SIGINT) radio receivers.

| USA-41 1989-61C (20172) | — 8 August | Columbia payload bay | 296 | 307 | 90.5 | 57.0 |

Either an electronic-intelligence-gathering (ELINT) satellite, or part of a Strategic Defense Initiative (SDI 'Star Wars') experiment.

| TV-Sat 2 1989-62A (20168) | 11:26 pm 8 August | Kourou, French Guiana Ariane 44LP (V33) | 355 35541 35769 | 35961 35788 35806 | 636.9 1429.8 1436.1 | 7.2 0.2 0.0 |
| | | geosynchronous — 19 degrees west | | | | |

West German direct-broadcasting television satellite, launched to replace the failed TV-Sat 1 (1988-95A). Listed are the transfer orbit, the drift orbit and the operational orbit.

| Hipparcos 1989-62B (20169) | 11:26pm 8 August | Kourou, French Guiana Ariane 44LP (V33 | 222 547 | 35623 35875 | 627.7 639.0 | 7.0 6.9 |

High Precision Parallax Collecting Satellite, the European Space Agency's astrometry satellite for accurate measurement of the position of stars. Its apogee boost motor failed to operate, preventing it from reaching geosynchronous orbit and its station above 12 degrees west. Early September, after reaching the second of the orbits listed by using its on-board maneuvering thrusters, Hipparcos embarked on a modified version of its mission.

| Resurs-F4 1989-63A (20175) | 10:30 am 15 August | Plesetsk, USSR A-2 (Soyuz) | 181 259 | 228 268 | 88.7 89.8 | 82.3 82.3 |

Recoverable, maneuverable satellite based on the Vostok design, carrying out Earth-resources photography. The cabin section containing film and cameras landed in Khazakstan on 14 September.

NAME, INT'L DESIG'N (CATALOG NO.)	LAUNCH TIME & DATE (GMT)	LAUNCH SITE & VEHICLE	PERIGEE (KM)	APOGEE (KM)	PERIOD (MINS)	INCLINATION (DEGREES)
USA-42 (Navstar 2-3) 1989-64A (20185)	5:58 am 18 August	Cape Canaveral AFS, USA Delta 2 (6925)/PAM-D	156 19937 20113	20334 20130 20249	355.3 711.9 717.9	37.7 55.0 55.0

Uprated Block-2 navigation satellite in the joint civil military Global Positioning System (GPS). Additional equipment is fitted to monitor ground-based nuclear explosions. Listed are the transfer orbit, the drift orbit, and the operational orbit achieved at the end of August.

Cosmos 2036 1989-65A (20188)	1:00pm 22 August	Plesetsk, USSR A-2 (Soyuz)	246 230	261 29	89.6 89.8	62.8 62.8

Recoverable, maneuverable satellite based on the Vostok design, carrying out strategic photo-reconnaissance. The cabin section containing film and cameras landed in Khazakstan on 5 September. Listed are the initial orbit, and the operational orbit achieved after a maneuver on 24 August.

Progress M1 1989-66A (20191)	3:10 am 23 August	Baikonur, USSR A-2 (Soyuz)	187 273 382	217 400 397	88.5 91.2 92.3	51.6 51.6 51.6

Cargo vessel carrying two tonnes of equipment and supplies to the resident crew of the Mir complex. It docked with Mir's forward-facing axial port, the first Progress ever to use that port, at 5:19 am on 25 August. It undocked at 9:02 am on 1 December, and re-entered the Earth's atmosphere after a retrofiring and about three hours later. Listed are the initial orbit, the transfer orbit and the orbit after docking.

Marcopolo 1 1989-67A (20193)	10:59 pm 27 August	Cape Canaveral AFS, USA Delta 1 (4925)	204 35777 35777	36894 35787 35798	652.1 1435.8 1436.1	23.2 0.2 0.1
			geosynchronous — 31 degrees west			

Direct television-transmission satellite for the U.K. equipped with Ku-band (14/12 GHz) transponders, and owned by British Satellite Broadcasting (BSB). Listed are the initial orbit, the drift orbit and the operational orbit.

Cosmos 2037 1989-68A (20196)	12:16 am 28 August	Plesetsk, USSR F-2 (Tsyklon)	1484	1525	116.1	73.6

Geodetic satellite in near-polar orbit. Its onboard equipment includes corner-cube reflectors for laser range-finding.

USA-43 (DSCS-2) 1989-69A (20202)	5:30 am 4 September	Cape Canaveral AFS, USA Titan 34D/IUS	geosynchronous orbit			

Second-generation Defense Communications Satellite System, U.S. strategic communication satellite equipped with transponders operating at C-band (8/7 GHz)

USA-44 (DSCS-3) 1989-69B (20203)	5:30 am 4 September	Cape Canaveral AFS, USA Titan 34D/IUS	geosynchronous orbit			

Third-generation Defense Communications Satellite System, U.S. strategic communications satellite equipped with transponders operating at C-band (8/7 GHz).

Himawari 4 (GMS 4) 1989-70A (20217)	7:11 pm 5 September	Tanegashima SC, Japan H-1	214 35258 35720	38027 36057 35856	674.8 1429.4 1436.1	28.7 1.7 1.6
			geosynchronous — 104 degrees east			

Japanese meteorological satellite, providing cloud-cover imagery and other meteorological data. Listed are the transfer orbit, the drift orbit and the operational orbit.

Soyuz TM-8 1989-71A (20218)	9:38 pm 5 September	Baikonur, USSR A-2 (Soyuz)	197 321 381	200 369 395	88.4 91.4 92.3	51.6 51.6 51.6

Piloted space mission to transport a crew of two to the Mir complex, consisting of its Commander, Soviet Air Force Colonel Aleksandr Viktorenko, and flight engineer Aleksandr Serebrov. It docked with the aft-facing port of Kvant at 10:25 pm on 7 September, following a five-minute delay caused by an orientation problem with Mir. The crew transferred to the station 90 minutes later. At 8:23 am on 12 December, it undocked and was then re-docked with Mir's forward-facing axial port after about 20 minutes. Listed are the initial orbit, the transfer orbit and the orbit after docking.

USA-45 1989-72A (20220)	1:55 am 6 September	Vandenberg AFB, USA Titan 2	orbit details not available			

Military satellite of undisclosed purpose, probably in near-polar orbit.

Resurs-F5 1989-73A (20222)	10:50 am 6 September	Plesetsk, USSR A-2 (Soyuz)	179 262	233 273	88.7 89.9	82.3 82.3

Recoverable, maneuverable satellite based on the Vostok design, carrying out Earth-resources photography. A secondary payload was a West German Japanese package of microgravity experiments. The cabin section containing film, cameras and experiment results landed in Khazakstan at 7:10 am on 22 September. Listed are the initial orbit, and the operational orbit achieved after a maneuver on 7 September.

NAME, INT'I DESIG'N (CATALOG NO.)	LAUNCH TIME & DATE (GMT)	LAUNCH SITE & VEHICLE	PERIGEE (KM)	APOGEE (KM)	PERIOD (MINS)	INCLINATION (DEGREES)
Cosmos 2038 to 2043	9:54 am	Plesetsk, USSR	1386	1411	113.8	82.6
1989-74B, A, D, E, F, C	14 September	F-2 (Tsyklon)	1392	1412	113.9	82.6
(20233, 20232			1397	1412	113.9	82.6
20235-37, 20234)			1402	1412	114.0	82.6
			1408	1412	114.1	82.6
			1411	1416	114.1	82.6

Single launch of six small satellites, possibly to be used for short-range, tactical military communications. A scattering of satellites around the orbit, along with those from previous launches, guarantees almost 100-percent availability during the day. Orbit details are listed for each satellite.

Cosmos 2044	6:30 am	Plesetsk, USSR	207	267	89.3	82.3
1989-75A (20242)	15 September	A-2 (Soyuz)				

Biocosmos 9, an international biological satellite based on the Vostok design, carrying a payload consisting of two Rhesus monkeys, Zabiyaka and Zhakoni, rats, insects, and other specimens. The cabin section containing experimental results, landed in Khazakstan on 29 September.

Cosmos 2045	8:00 am	Baikonur, USSR	207	297	89.6	70.0
1989-76A (20244)	22 September	A-2 (Soyuz)	235	390	90.8	70.0

Recoverable, maneuverable satellite based on the Vostok design, carrying out strategic photo-reconnaissance. The cabin section containing film and cameras landed in Khazakstan on 2 October. Listed are the initial orbit and the operational orbit reached after a maneuver soon after launch.

USA-46 (FltSatCom 8)	8:41 am	Cape Canaveral AFS, USA	167	34861	612.0	28.6
1989-77A (20253)	25 September	Atlas/Centaur	34765	35924	1413.5	5.1
			35792	35793	1436.3	5.0
			geosynchronous — 23 degrees west			

U.S. Navy communications satellite equipped with transponders operating at UHF (around 250 MHz) frequencies. Listed are the transfer orbit, the drift orbit and the operational orbit.

Molniya-1 (76)	2:37 pm	Plesetsk, USSR	618	38961	702.1	62.8
1989-78A (20255)	27 September	A-2-e (Molniya)	636	39704	717.5	62.8

Soviet domestic communications satellite serving the more northerly ground-stations in the Orbita system. It carries transponders operating at C-band (6/4 GHz), and a transponder operating in the 800-1000 MHz band. Listed are the initial orbit and the operational orbit achieved after an engine-firing on 14 October.

Cosmos 2046	4:19 pm	Baikonur, USSR	406	417	92.8	65.0
1989-79A (20259)	27 September	F-1 (two-stage Tsykon)				

Electronic-intelligence-gathering satellite, particularly monitoring naval military radio traffic and shipping movements. The orbit is maintained against air-drag by a low-thrust motor.

Intercosmos 24	12:05 am	Plesetsk, USSR	507	2491	116.0	82.6
1989-80A (20261)	28 September	F-2 (three-stage Tsyklon)				

International scientific satellite launched under the Aktivny project to investigate the Earth's magnetosphere, by studying the propagation of low-frequency radio waves.

Gorizont (19)	5:05 pm	Baikonur, USSR	35647	35876	1434.7	1.4
1989-81A (20263)	28 September	D-1-e (four-stage Proton)	35784	35795	1436.1	1.3
			geosynchronous — 96.5 degrees east			

Communications satellite at the Statsionar-14 location, serving the Orbita-2 system — both within the USSR and (through Intersputnik) abroad — with telecommunications links at C-band (6/4 GHz). A separate C-band transponder supplies Central Television programs to the Soviet Moskva TV-distribution network, and single transponders support both the Ku-band (14/11 GHz) Luch system, and the L-band (1.6 GHz) Volna maritime and aeronautical communications system. Listed are the drift orbit and the operational orbit.

Magion 2	—	Intercosmos 24	500	2492	116.0	82.6
1989-80B (20281)	3 October	—				

Small satellite released from Intercosmos 24 and used as a source of low-frequency radio signals for Intercosmos 24's detectors. An onboard micro-thruster allows it to maintain station with the parent satellite.

Cosmos 2047	3:00 pm	Plesetsk, USSR	165	276	88.9	67.1
1989-82A (20279)	3 October	A-2 (Soyuz)				

Strategic photo-reconnaissance satellite, possibly carrying several return-capsules for periodic recovery of film. It re-entered the Earth's atmosphere on 21 November, and the camera module may have been recovered.

NAME, INT'I DESIG'N (CATALOG NO.)	LAUNCH TIME & DATE (GMT)	LAUNCH SITE & VEHICLE	PERIGEE (KM)	APOGEE (KM)	PERIOD (MINS)	INCLINATION (DEGREES)
Cosmos 2048	1:00 pm	Plesetsk, USSR	244	259	89.5	62.8
1989-83A (20292)	17 October	A-2 (Soyuz)	238	359	90.5	62.8

Recoverable, maneuverable satellite based on the Vostok design, carrying out strategic photo-reconnaissance. The cabin section containing film and cameras landed in Khazakstan on 26 October. Listed are the initial orbit and the operational orbit reached after a maneuver on 18 October.

STS-34	4:54 pm	Kennedy SC, USA	300	333	90.7	34.3
1989-84A (20297)	18 October	Shuttle _Atlantis_				

Piloted space mission devoted principally to launching the Galileo Jupiter-explorer. Mission Commander was U.S. Navy Captain Donald Williams; Pilot — U.S. Navy Commander Michael McCulley; and Mission Specialists Franklin Chang-Diaz, Shannon Lucid and Ellen Baker. Atlantis _landed at Edwards Air Force Base at 4:33 pm on 23 October._

Galileo	11:15 pm	_Atlantis_ payload bay	heliocentric orbit			
1989-84B (20298)	18 October	IUS				

Jupiter-explorer, due to arrive at the planet in December 1995. Its trajectory will use gravity-assist from Venus and Earth (twice), and en-route it will pass close to two asteroids — Gaspra and Ida.

USA-47 (Navstar 2-4)	9:31 am	Cape Canaveral AFS, USA	164	20307	355.0	37.7
1989-85A (20302)	21 October	Delta 2 (6925)/PAM-D	20162	20464	723.3	54.8
			20077	20285	717.9	54.7

Block-2 navigation satellite in the joint civil military Global Positioning System (GPS). Additional equipment is fitted to monitor ground nuclear explosions. Listed are the transfer orbit, the drift orbit, and the operational orbit achieved in November.

Meteor 3 (3)	9:37 pm	Plesetsk, USSR	1188	1213	109.5	82.6
1989-86A (20305)	24 October	F-2 (three-stage Tsyklon)				

Soviet third-generation meteorological and remote-sensing satellite providing visible and infrared imagery.

Intelsat 6 (F-2)	11:05	Kourou, French Guiana	304	35799	632.6	7.1
1989-87A (20315)	27 October	Ariane 44L (V34)	35714	35844	1435.6	0.1
			35727	35849	1436.1	0.1
			geosynchronous — 24.5 degrees west			

First launch of a new-generation commercial communications satellite equipped with transponders operating at C-band (6 4 GHz) and Ku-band (14 11 GHz). Listed are the transfer orbit, the drift orbit and the operational orbit.

Cosmos 2049	10:50 am	Baikonur, USSR	180	264	89.0	64.8
1989-88A (20320)	17 November	A-2 (Soyuz)	223	270	89.5	64.8

Strategic photo-reconnaissance satellite, possibly carrying several return-capsules for periodic recovery of film. It re-entered the Earth's atmosphere, possibly for recovery, on 19 June 1990. Listed are the initial orbit and the operational orbit.

COBE	2:34 pm	Vandenberg AFB, USA	887	898	102.9	99.0
1989-89A (20322)	18 November	Delta 2 (6920)				

Cosmic Background Explorer, a NASA science satellite studying infrared radiation remaining from the cosmic 'Big Bang'.

STS-33	12:23 am	Kennedy SC, USA	237	561	92.4	28.5
1989-90A (20329)	23 November	Shuttle _Discovery_				

Piloted space mission devoted to launching a military satellite, and probably conducting Strategic Defense Initiative (SDI 'Star Wars') experiments. Mission Commander was U.S. Air Force Colonel Frederick Gregory; Pilot, U.S. Air Force Colonel John Blaha; and Mission Specialists U.S. Navy Captain Manley Carter, Story Musgrave and Kathryn Thornton. Discovery _landed at Edwards Air Force Base at 12:31 am on 28 November, following a one-day delay forced by bad weather._

USA-48	10:15 am	_Discovery_ payload bay	geosynchronous orbit — Indian Ocean			
1989-90B (20355)	23 November	IUS				

Large signals-intelligence (SIGINT) satellite, eavesdropping on radio transmissions emanating from the USSR and China. The release time quoted is accurate to within one hour.

Cosmos 2050	8:35 pm	Plesetsk, USSR	592	39280	708.0	63.0
1989-91A (20330)	23 November	A-2-e (Molniya)	596	39762	717.8	63.0

Satellite in Molniya-type orbit, carrying rocket-launch detectors and acting as part of the Soviet Union's missile early-warning system. Listed are the initial orbit and the operational orbit achieved after an engine-firing on 30 November.

Cosmos 2051	11:20 pm	Baikonur, USSR	280	420	91.6	64.9
1989-92A (20334)	24 November	F-1 (two-stage Tsyklon)	400	415	92.7	65.0

Electronic-intelligence-gathering satellite, particularly monitoring naval military radio traffic and shipping movements. The orbit is maintained against air-drag by frequent operation of a low-thrust motor. Listed are the initial orbit and the operational orbit.

NAME, INT'L DESIG'N (CATALOG NO.)	LAUNCH TIME & DATE (GMT)	LAUNCH SITE & VEHICLE	PERIGEE (KM)	APOGEE (KM)	PERIOD (MINS)	INCLINATION (DEGREES)
Kvant-2 1989-93A (20335)	1:02 pm 26 November	Baikonur, USSR D-1 (three-stage Proton)	215 339 371 394	321 395 398 398	89.8 91.8 92.2 92.4	51.6 51.6 51.6 51.6

Twenty-tonne add-on module for Mir to provide additional working space for the crew as well as a large airlock for spacewalkers. An on-board cargo included supplies for the crew, two 'Orlan-DMA' spacesuits, and the 'Ikar' piloted maneuvering unit. An initial attempt at docking with Mir on 2 December failed because of a problem with Kvant 2's rendezvous computer. A successful link-up with Mir's forward-facing axial port was achieved at 12:22 pm on 6 December. On 8 December, Kvant-2 used the 'Ljappa' manipulator arm to transfer itself to Mir's forward, upper docking port. Listed are the initial orbit, the transfer orbit, the orbit immediately prior to the 2 December rendezvous attempt, and the orbit after docking with Mir.

NAME, INT'L DESIG'N (CATALOG NO.)	LAUNCH TIME & DATE (GMT)	LAUNCH SITE & VEHICLE	PERIGEE (KM)	APOGEE (KM)	PERIOD (MINS)	INCLINATION (DEGREES)
Molniya-3 (36) 1989-94A (20338)	10:02 am 28 November	Plesetsk, USSR A-2-e (Molniya)	636 636	40597 39674	735.7 716.9	62.9 62.9

Communications satellite serving the Orbita-2 system — both within the USSR and (through Intersputnik) abroad — carrying telecommunications links at C-band (6/4 GHz). Listed are the initial orbit, and the operational orbit achieved after an engine-firing on 3 December.

NAME, INT'L DESIG'N (CATALOG NO.)	LAUNCH TIME & DATE (GMT)	LAUNCH SITE & VEHICLE	PERIGEE (KM)	APOGEE (KM)	PERIOD (MINS)	INCLINATION (DEGREES)
Cosmos 2052 1989-95A (20350)	3:00 pm 30 November	Plesetsk, USSR A-2 (Soyuz)	165	341	89.6	67.2

Strategic photo-reconnaissance satellite, possibly carrying several return-capsules for periodic recovery of film. It re-entered the Earth's atmosphere on 22 January, and the camera module may have been recovered.

NAME, INT'L DESIG'N (CATALOG NO.)	LAUNCH TIME & DATE (GMT)	LAUNCH SITE & VEHICLE	PERIGEE (KM)	APOGEE (KM)	PERIOD (MINS)	INCLINATION (DEGREES)
Granat 1989-96A (20352)	8:21 pm 1 December	Baikonur, USSR D-1-e (four-stage Proton)	1675	202088	5908.3	52.5

Soviet-built, international science satellite observing gamma-radiation from sources outside the Solar System. The largest portion of the payload is a French-built gamma-ray telescope. Other instrumentation was provided by the USSR, Bulgaria and Denmark.

NAME, INT'L DESIG'N (CATALOG NO.)	LAUNCH TIME & DATE (GMT)	LAUNCH SITE & VEHICLE	PERIGEE (KM)	APOGEE (KM)	PERIOD (MINS)	INCLINATION (DEGREES)
USA-49 (Navstar 2-5) 1989-97A (20361)	6:10 pm 11 December	Cape Canaveral AFS, USA Delta 2 (6925)/PAM-D	157 20209 20010	20366 20561 20357	355.8 726.2 718.0	37.6 55.0 55.0

'Block-2' navigation satellite in the joint civil military Global Positioning System (GPS). Additional equipment is fitted to monitor ground nuclear explosions. Listed are the transfer orbit, the drift orbit, and the operational orbit reached in January 1990.

NAME, INT'L DESIG'N (CATALOG NO.)	LAUNCH TIME & DATE (GMT)	LAUNCH SITE & VEHICLE	PERIGEE (KM)	APOGEE (KM)	PERIOD (MINS)	INCLINATION (DEGREES)
Raduga (24) 1989-98A (20367)	11:30 am 15 December	Baikonur, USSR D-1-e (four-stage Proton)	36511 35765	36592 35810	1475.3 1436.0	1.5 1.4
		geosynchronous — 45 degrees east				

Communications satellite at the Statsionar-9 location, serving the Orbita-2 system within the USSR with telecommunications links at C-band (6/4 GHz). Single transponders support both the K-band (14/11 GHz) Luch system, and the L-band (1.6 GHz) Volna maritime and aeronautical communications system. Listed are the drift orbit and the operational orbit.

NAME, INT'L DESIG'N (CATALOG NO.)	LAUNCH TIME & DATE (GMT)	LAUNCH SITE & VEHICLE	PERIGEE (KM)	APOGEE (KM)	PERIOD (MINS)	INCLINATION (DEGREES)
Progress M2 1989-99A (20373)	3:31 am 20 December	Baikonur, USSR A-2 (Soyuz)	187 276 392	212 390 395	88.4 91.1 92.4	51.6 51.6 51.6

Cargo vessel carrying two tonnes of equipment, supplies and experiment material to the resident crew of the Mir complex. Part of the cargo was an American crystal-growth experiments package being flown under a commercial deal with Payload Systems Inc of the U.S. It docked with Kvant-1's rear port on 22 December. At 1:33 am on 9 February 1990, it undocked and re-entered the Earth's atmosphere soon after, following retrofire. While in free flight, it conducted radio-communications tests through Cosmos 2054 SDRN-West (1989-101A). Listed are the initial orbit, the transfer orbit and the orbit after docking.

NAME, INT'L DESIG'N (CATALOG NO.)	LAUNCH TIME & DATE (GMT)	LAUNCH SITE & VEHICLE	PERIGEE (KM)	APOGEE (KM)	PERIOD (MINS)	INCLINATION (DEGREES)
Cosmos 2053 1989-100A (20389)	11:59 pm 26 December	Plesetsk, USSR F-2 (three-stage Tsyklon)	518	536	95.2	73.6

Military satellite, possibly equipped with a battery of dummy warheads for use in testing and checking-out ground-based missile-detection radars.

NAME, INT'L DESIG'N (CATALOG NO.)	LAUNCH TIME & DATE (GMT)	LAUNCH SITE & VEHICLE	PERIGEE (KM)	APOGEE (KM)	PERIOD (MINS)	INCLINATION (DEGREES)
Cosmos 2054 1989-101A (20391)	11:10 am 27 December	Baikonur, USSR D-1-e (four-stage Proton)	36374 35708	36505 35859	1469.6 1435.8	1.5 1.4
		geosynchronous — 16 degrees west				

Satellite and Data Relay Network communications satellite at the SDRN-West location, operating in the Ku-band (14/11 GHz). It includes a satellite-to-ground communications link for Mir and other low-orbit satellites and spacecraft. Listed are the drift orbit and the operational orbit.

NAME, INT'L DESIG'N (CATALOG NO.)	LAUNCH TIME & DATE (GMT)	LAUNCH SITE & VEHICLE	PERIGEE (KM)	APOGEE (KM)	PERIOD (MINS)	INCLINATION (DEGREES)
Skynet 4A 1990-1A (20401)	12:07 am 01 January	Cape Canaveral AFS, USA Commercial Titan/PAM-D2	307 33676 35784	34814 35704 35792	613.8 1380.3 1436.1	21.7 3.4 3.3
		geosynchronous — 6 degrees east				

British strategic communications satellite equipped with transponders operating at C-band (8/7 GHz) and UHF (310/225 MHz), as well as experimental equipment relating to the design of future military comsats. Listed are the transfer orbit, the drift orbit and the operational orbit.

NAME, INT'L DESIG'N (CATALOG NO.)	LAUNCH TIME & DATE (GMT)	LAUNCH SITE & VEHICLE	PERIGEE (KM)	APOGEE (KM)	PERIOD (MINS)	INCLINATION (DEGREES)
JCSat-2 1990-1B (20402)	12:07 am 01 January	Cape Canaveral AFS, USA Commercial Titan/Orbus 7S	299 35669 35780	19294 35912 35795	340.0 1436.2 1436.1	26.8 0.4 0.1

geosynchronous — 154 degrees east

Communications satellite owned by the Japanese Communications Satellite Company. It is equipped with 32 transponders operating at Ku-band (14/12 GHz). Listed are the transfer orbit, the drift orbit and the operational orbit.

| **STS-32** 1990-2A (20409) | 12:35 pm 9 January | Kennedy SC, USA Shuttle _Columbia_ | 293 319 329 | 358 358 335 | 90.9 91.1 91.0 | 28.5 28.5 28.5 |

Piloted space mission devoted principally to launching a Syncom comsat and recovering NASA's Long Duration Exposure Facility (LDEF). Mission Commander was U.S. Navy Captain Daniel Brandenstein; Pilot, U.S. Navy Lt-Commander James Wetherbee; and Mission Specialists Marsha Ivins, Bonnie Dunbar and David Low. LDEF was captured by the remote manipulator arm at 3:16 pm GMT on 12 January and anchored in the payload bay at 8:49 pm. Columbia landed on the Edwards Air Force Base runway at 9:35 am on 20 January. Listed are the initial orbit, the orbit immediately after the Syncom deployment, and the orbit at the time the LDEF was retrieved.

| **Syncom 4-F5** 1990-2B (20410) | 1:18 pm 10 January | _Columbia_ payload bay — | 320 34858 35259 | 15076 36363 36163 | 276.7 1427.0 1436.0 | 27.2 1.4 3.3 |

geosynchronous — 178 degrees east

Strategic communications satellite, owned by Hughes Communications Inc. and leased to the U.S. Navy. It is equipped with transponders operating at UHF (around 250-300 MHz). Listed are the transfer orbit, the drift orbit and the operational orbit.

| **Cosmos 2055** 1990-3A (20426) | 2:45 pm 17 January | Plesetsk, USSR A-2 (Soyuz) | 249 249 | 262 321 | 89.6 90.2 | 62.8 62.8 |

Recoverable, maneuverable satellite based on the Vostok design, carrying out strategic photo-reconnaissance. The cabin section containing film and cameras landed in Khazakstan on 29 January. Listed are the initial orbit and the operational orbit achieved after a rocket-firing on 18 January.

| **Cosmos 2056** 1990-4A (20432) | 12:55 pm 18 January | Plesetsk, USSR C-1 (Cosmos 2) | 775 | 810 | 100.8 | 74.0 |

Communications satellite, receiving and storing military and clandestine radio messages, then re-transmitting them on command.

| **SPOT-2** 1990-5A (20436) | 1:35 am 22 January | Kourou, French Guiana Ariane 40 (V35) | 800 819 | 805 822 | 101.0 101.4 | 98.7 98.7 |

Satellite Probatoire d'Observation de la Terre, a French commercial remote-sensing satellite in sun-synchronous orbit, providing images with 10-20 meters resolution. Listed are the initial orbit and the operational orbit.

| **Oscar 14 (UoSat 3)** 1990-5B (20437) | 1:35 am 22 January | Kourou, French Guiana Ariane 40 (V35) | 789 | 804 | 100.9 | 98.7 |

British-built (University of Surrey) experimental satellite launched alongside SPOT-2. It is equipped with a packet-radio transponder and sensors to study cosmic-rays and radiation.

| **Oscar 15 (UoSat 4)** 1990-5C (20438) | 1:35 am 22 January | Kourou, French Guiana Ariane 40 (V35) | 790 | 805 | 100.9 | 98.7 |

British-built (University of Surrey) experimental satellite launched alongside SPOT-2. UoSat 4 is equipped with radiation sensors, an experimental transputer, experimental solar cells and an Earth-imaging camera.

| **Oscar 16 (Microsat 1)** 1990-5D (20439) | 1:35 am 22 January | Kourou, French Guiana Ariane 40 (V35) | 789 | 805 | 100.9 | 98.7 |

Technology satellite belonging to Amsat North America and launched alongside SPOT-2. It provides digital store/dump radio communications using packet radio, hence its alternative name of Pacsat.

| **Oscar 17 (Microsat 2)** 1990-5E (20440) | 1:35 am 22 January | Kourou, French Guiana Ariane 40 (V35) | 786 | 807 | 100.9 | 98.7 |

Technology satellite belonging to Amsat-Brazil (Bramsat) and launched alongside SPOT-2. It carries a voice encoder to tranmit information, and is alternatively known as DOVE (Digital Orbiting Voice Encoder).

| **Oscar 18 (Microsat 3)** 1990-5F (20441) | 1:35 am 22 January | Kourou, French Guiana Ariane 40 (V35) | 787 | 805 | 100.9 | 98.7 |

Technology satellite belonging to Amsat North America and launched alongside SPOT-2. it carries a magnetometer, an imaging system and a visible-light spectrometer, and was built by Weber State College of Ogden, Utah, hence its alternative name of Webersat.

| **Oscar 19 (Microsat 4)** 1990-5G (20442) | 1:35 am 22 January | Kourou, French Guiana Ariane 40 (V35) | 788 | 804 | 100.9 | 98.7 |

Technology satellite belonging to Amsat-Argentina and launched alongside SPOT-2. It provides digital store/dump radio communications using packet-radio.

NAME, INT'l DESIG'N (CATALOG NO.)	LAUNCH TIME & DATE (GMT)	LAUNCH SITE & VEHICLE	PERIGEE (KM)	APOGEE (KM)	PERIOD (MINS)	INCLINATION (DEGREES)
Molniya-3 (37) 1990-6A (20444)	2:52 am 23 January	Plesetsk, USSR A-2-e (Molniya)	606 599	38900 39692	700.6 716.5	62.8 62.8

Communications satellite serving the Orbita-2 system — both within the USSR and (through Intersputnik) abroad — carrying tele-communications links at C-band (6/4 GHz). Listed are the initial orbit and the operational orbit achieved after an engine-firing early on 28 January.

Hiten (MUSES-A) 1990-7A (20448)	11:46 am 24 January	Kagoshima SC, Japan M-3S-2	4893 86889	435037 767664	17861 47366	29.7 27.6

Japanese lunar-studies spacecraft in barycentric orbit. It passed 16,472 kilometers above the Moon on its first swing-by at 8:04 pm on 18 March. It carried Hagoromo, a small lunar satellite released on 18 March. Listed are the initial orbit and the orbit following the 18 March lunar swing-by.

USA-50 (Navstar 2-6) 1990-8A (20452)	10:55 pm 24 January	Cape Canaveral AFS, USA Delta 2 (6925)/PAM-D	171 19974 20088	20270 20173 20276	354.5 713.6 718.0	37.7 54.7 54.7

'Block-2' navigation satellite in the joint civil military Global Positioning System (GPS). Additional equipment is fitted to monitor ground nuclear explosions. Listed are the transfer orbit, the drift orbit and the operational orbit achieved after a rocket-firing on 1 February.

Cosmos 2057 1990-9A (20457)	5:15 pm 25 January	Plesetsk, USSR A-2 (Soyuz)	185	332	89.7	62.8

Strategic photographic-reconnaissance satellite, possibly carrying several return-capsules for periodic recovery of film. It re-entered the Earth's atmosphere, possibly for recovery, on 19 March.

Cosmos 2058 1990-10A (20457)	11:21 am 30 January	Plesetsk, USSR F-2 (three-stage Tsyklon)	633	665	97.8	82.5

Electronic-intelligence-gathering (ELINT) satellite in near-polar orbit, eavesdropping on foreign government and military communications.

STTW-2-1 1990-11A (20473)	12:27 pm 4 February,	Xichang, PRC CZ-3 (Long March 3)	215 35780 35780	35630 37199 35795	627.9 1472.1 1436.1	30.7 0.5 0.1
		geosynchronous - 98 degrees east				

Chinese domestic communications satellite equipped with transponders operating at C-band (6/4 GHz). Listed are the transfer orbit, the drift orbit it entered after a rocket firing at 1:34 on 6 February, and the operational orbit.

Cosmos 2059 1990-12A (20476)	6:20 pm 6 February	Plesetsk, USSR C-1 (Cosmos 2)	190	2281	110.2	65.8

Small satellite of military nature, possibly for space experiments.

Momo 1b (MOS 1b) 1990-13A (20478)	1:20 am 7 February	Tanegashima, Japan H-1	912	920	103.5	99.1

Japanese Marine Observation Satellite, a remote-sensing satellite studying particularly the world's oceans. Its orbit is sun-synchronous, providing overhead passes at 10:00 am local time.

Orizuru (Debut) 1990-13B (20479)	1:20 am 7 February	Tanegashima, Japan H-1	892	1611	110.6	99.1

Deployable Boom and Umbrella Test, a Japanese-built space-technology development satellite launched alongside Momo 1b.

Fuji 2 1990-13C (20480)	1:20 am 7 February	Tanegashima, Japan H-1	912	1746	112.,3	99.1

Small satellite carried into orbit alongside Momo 1b for use by amateur radio operators around the world.

Soyuz TM-9 1990-14A (20494)	6:16 am 11 February	Baikonur, USSR A-2 (Soyuz)	185 290 374	219 333 419	88.5 90.7 92.4	51.6 51.6 51.6

Piloted space mission to transport a replacement crew to the Mir complex, consisting of its Commander, Lt-Col Anatoly Solovyov, and flight engineer Aleksandr Balandin. It docked with the rear port of Kvant 1 on 13 February. On 20 February, with Solovyov and Balandin aboard, Soyuz TM-9 undocked from Kvant 1 and re-docked with Mir's extreme forward-facing port, then on 28 May it reversed the procedure, undocking at 11:48 am and re-docking with Kvant 1 after 24 minutes, and again, on 3 July it returned to Mir's forward port, undocking at 10:08 pm — re-docking after 26 minutes. Listed are the initial orbit, the transfer orbit and the orbit after the initial docking.

USA-51 (LACE) 1990-15A (20496)	4:15 pm 14 February	Cape Canaveral AFS, USA Delta 2 (6920)	531	550	95.3	43.1

Low-power Atmospheric Composition Experiment satellite, launched under the Strategic Defense Initiative (SDI 'Star Wars') program to study the way in which the atmosphere distorts laser beams directed from the ground into space. A second experiment studies ultraviolet radiation emitted from rocket exhaust-plumes during launch. LACE is intended to operate for about 30 months.

NAME, INT'I DESIG'N (CATALOG NO.)	LAUNCH TIME & DATE (GMT)	LAUNCH SITE & VEHICLE	PERIGEE (KM)	APOGEE (KM)	PERIOD (MINS)	INCLINATION (DEGREES)
USA-52 (RME) 1990-15B (20497)	4:15 pm 14 February	Cape Canaveral AFS, USA Delta 2 (6920)	457	478	93.9	43.1

Relay Mirror Experiment satellite launched under the Strategic Defense Initiative (SDI 'Star Wars') program, used to reflect laser beams from the ground onto a 'target', also on the ground. A second onboard experiment is studying the vibration characteristics of the satellite. RME is expected to operate for about seven months.

Raduga (25) 1990-16A (20499)	7:52 am 15 February	Baikonur, USSR D-1-e (four-stage Proton)	35798 35766	36090 35808,	1444.0 1436.1	1.6 1.5
			geosynchronous — 70 degrees east			

Communications satellite at the Statsionar-20 location, serving the Orbita-2 system within the USSR with telecommunications links at C-band (6/4 GHz). Single transponders support both the K-band (14/11 GHz) Luch system, and the L-band (1.6 GHz) Volna maritime and aeronautical communications system. Listed are the drift orbit and the operational orbit.

Nadezhda 2 1990-17A (20508)	9:00 pm 27 February	Plesetsk, USSR C-1 (Cosmos 2)	956	1021	104.9	83.0

Polar-orbiting navigation satellite in the 'Tsikada' system, equipped with radio beacons operating at 150 and 400 MHz. It also carries a COSPAS-SARSAT search and rescue system package to monitor international distress frequencies.

Okean 2 1990-18A (20510)	12:56 am 28 February	Plesetsk, USSR F-2 (Tsyklon)	639	666	97.9	82.5

Oceanographic remote-sensing satellite studying the sea surface and some land areas, using optical, radar and microwave imaging equipment.

STS-36 1990-19A (20512)	7:50 am 28 February	Kennedy SC, USA Shuttle *Atlantis*	200 241 238	209 253 242	88.6 89.4 89.3	62.0 62.0 62.0

Piloted space mission devoted principally to launching a strategic-reconnaissance satellite. Mission Commander was U.S. Navy Captain John Creighton; Pilot, USAF Colonel John Casper; and Mission Specialists USMC Lt-Col David Hilmers, USAF Colonel Michael Mullane and U.S. Navy Lt-Cdr Pierre Thuot. Atlantis landed at Edwards Air Force Base at 6:09 pm on 4 March. Listed are the initial orbit, and the orbit at the time of AFP-731's deployment.

USA-53 1990-19B (20515)	11:00 am 1 March	*Atlantis* payload bay	241	253	89.4	62.0

AFP-731 (Air Force Program-731), maneuverable reconnaissance satellite equipped with a digital imaging system and signals-intelligence (SIGINT) radio receivers. The time listed for deployment from Atlantis is accurate to within thirty minutes, and the orbit is an estmate. USA-53 reportedly broke-up on 7 March.

Progress M3 1990-20A (20513)	11:11 pm 28 February	Baikonur, USSR A-2 (Soyuz)	183 276 378	228 332 402	88.6 90.6 92.3	51.6 51.6 51.6

Cargo vessel carrying two tonnes of equipment and supplies to the resident crew of the Mir complex. It docked with Kvant-1's rear port at 1:05 am on 3 March. At around midnight on 26/27 April it undocked and, following a retrorocket firing, re-entered the Earth's atmosphere about 24 hours later. Listed are the initial orbit, the transfer orbit and the orbit after docking.

Intelsat 6 (F-3) 1990-21A (20523)	11:52 am 14 March	Cape Canaveral AFS, USA Commercial Titan	169 375	355 401	89.6 92.1	28.6 28.4

International telecommunications satellite, stranded in low orbit due to a software hardware problem in the separation mechanism between the satellite and the upper stage of the Titan. Listed are the initial orbit and the orbit achieved by 18 March after several firings of the satellite's station-keeping thrusters.

Cosmos 2060 1990-22A (20525)	3:25 pm 14 March	Baikonur, USSR F-1 (two-stage Tsyklon)	399 403	429 418	92.9 92.8	65.0 65.0

Electronic-intelligence-gathering satellite, particularly monitoring naval military radio traffic and shipping movements. The orbit is maintained against air-drag by frequent operation of a low-thrust motor. Listed are the initial orbit and the operational orbit.

Hagoromo 1990-7E	7:37 pm 18 March	Hiten/MUSES-A —	circumlunar orbit			

Small lunar-science satellite released from Hiten (1990-7A) and propelled into orbit around the Moon by an onboard motor. Hiten was launched from Kagoshima, Japan on 24 January 1990.

Cosmos 2061 1990-23A (20527)	12:25 am 20 March	Plesetsk, USSR C-1 (Cosmos 2)	973	1017	105.1	82.9

Polar-orbiting navigation satellite, with radio beacons operating at 150 and 400 MHz.

Cosmos 2062 1990-24A (20529)	7:20 am 22 March	Plesetsk, USSR A-2 (Soyuz)	182 241	224 375	88.6 90.7	82.3 82.3

Recoverable, maneuverable satellite based on the Vostok design, carrying out strategic photo-reconnaissance. The cabin section carrying film and cameras, landed in Khazakstan on 5 April. Listed are the initial orbit, and the operational orbit achieved by 26 March.

NAME, INT'L DESIG'N (CATALOG NO.)	LAUNCH TIME & DATE (GMT)	LAUNCH SITE & VEHICLE	PERIGEE (KM)	APOGEE (KM)	PERIOD (MINS)	INCLINATION (DEGREES)
USA-54 (Navstar 2-7) 1990-25A (20533)	2:45 am 26 March	Cape Canaveral AFS, USA Delta 2 (6925)/PAM-D	168 19769 20082	20243 20085 20260	354.0 707.6 717.5	37.5 55.0 55.0

'Block 2' navigation satellite in the joint civil military Global Navigation Satellite System (GPS). Additional equipment is fitted to monitor ground nuclear explosions. Listed are the transfer orbit, the drift orbit and the operational orbit.

Cosmos 2063 1990-26A (20537)	4:35 pm 27 March	Plesetsk, USSR A-2-e (Molniya)	606 608	39328 39739	709.3 717.6	62.8 62.8

Satellite in Molniya-type orbit, carrying rocket-launch detectors and acting as part of the Soviet Union's missile early-warning system. Listed are the initial orbit and the operational orbit.

Offeq 2 1990-27A (20540)	12:00 noon 3 April	Palmachim, Israel Shavit	207	1583	102.8	143.2

Israeli space-technology development satellite.

Pegsat 1990-28A (20546)	6:03 pm 5 April	Edwards AFB, USA Boeing NB-52/Pegasus	572	684	97.3	94.2

Instrumentation package attached to the final rocket stage, designed to measure the performance of Pegasus during ascent and injection into orbit. It also carried two barium-release experiments for ionospheric studies. Separation of Pegasus rocket from the NB-52 took place at 7:10 pm over the Pacific Ocean, when the aircraft/rocket combination was at a height of 14 kilometers, and 60 kilometers abeam the Morro bay area.

USA-55 (GLOMR 2) 1990-28B (20547)	6:03 pm 5 April	Edwards AFB, USA Boeing NB-52/Pegasus	495	680	96.5	94.2

Global Message Relay Satellite, a small U.S. Navy satellite used for controlling and interrogating land-based and sea-based sensors.

Cosmos 2064 to 2071 1990-29C-H, A&B (20551-6, 20550, 20549)	3:13 am 6 April 1415	Plesetsk, USSR C-1 (Cosmos 2) 1463	1387 1401 114.7 1430 1444 1460 1462 1463	1463 1463 74.0 1463 1463 1463 1476 1491	114.4 114.5 114.9 115.0 115.2 115.3 115.5	74.0 74.0 74.0 74.0 74.0 74.0 74.0

Single launch of eight small satellites to be used for short-range, tactical military communications. A scattering of satellites around the orbit, along with those from previous launches, guarantees almost 100-percent availability during the day. Orbit details are listed for each satellite.

Asiasat 1 1990-30A (20558)	1:30 pm 7 April	Xichang, PRC CZ-3 (Long March 3)	212 35791 35786	36696 36744 35788	648.6 1460.6 1436.6	31.2 0.3 0.2
			geosynchronous — 105.5 degrees east			

Commercial C-band (6 4 GHz) communications satellite owned by the Asia Satellite Telecommunications Company. It reached its operational geosynchronous location on 15 April. Asiasat 1 was originally launched February 1984 as Westar 6 (1984-11B) and, following a rocket-motor failure, retrieved during the 51-A/Discovery mission in November 1984 for refurbishment. Listed are the transfer orbit, the drift orbit and the operational orbit.

USA-56 (POGS/SSR) 1990-31A (20560)	4:00 pm 11 April	Vandenberg AFB, USA Atlas-E/Altair	760	780	100.0	90.0

Polar Orbit Geomagnetic Survey experiment for mapping the Earth's magnetic field, plus the experimental Solid-State Recorder for data storage — part of the P87-2 Stacksat triple-satellite space technology experiments payload. The Altair stage of the launching rocket was equipped with an experimental satellite release-latch. The orbit listed is approximate.

USA-57 (TEX) 1990-31B (20561)	4:00 pm 11 April	Vandenberg AFB, USA Atlas-E/Altair	760	780	100.0	90.0

Transceiver Experiment to study ionospheric irregularities which effect radio transmission; part of the P87-2 Stacksat technology experiments payload. The orbit listed is appropriate.

USA-58 (SCE) 1990-31C (20562)	4:00 pm 11 April	Vandenberg AFB, USA Atlas-E/Altair	760	780	100.0	90.0

Selective Communications Experiment, a store/dump communications package; part of the P87-2 Stacksat space technology experiments payload. The orbit listed is approximate.

Foton 3 1990-32A (20566)	5:00 pm 11 April	Plesetsk, USSR A-2 (Soyuz)	218	376	90.5	62.8

Recoverable satellite based on the Vostok design, carrying a microgravity experiments payload which included equipment provided by CNES, the French space agency. The cabin section containing experiment results landed in Khazakstan on 27 April.

NAME, INT'L DESIG'N (CATALOG NO.)	LAUNCH TIME & DATE (GMT)	LAUNCH SITE & VEHICLE	PERIGEE (KM)	APOGEE (KM)	PERIOD (MINS)	INCLINATION (DEGREES)
Cosmos 2072 1990-33A (20568)	6:53 pm 13 April	Baikonur, USSR A-2 (Soyuz)	183	253	88.9	64.8

Strategic photographic reconnaissance satellite carrying several return-capsules for periodic recovery of film.

| **Palapa B-2R** 1990-34A (20570) | 11:31 pm 13 April | Cape Canaveral AFS, USA Delta 2 (6925)/PAM-D | 203 35717 35680 | 37627 37785 35895 | 666.6 1485.5 1436.0 | 18.9 0.4 0.1 |

geosynchronous — 118 degrees east

Indonesian C-band (6 4GHz) communications satellite, originally launched in February 1984 as Palapa B-2 (1984-11D) and, following a rocket-motor failure, retrieved during the 51-A/Discovery mission. November 1984 for refurbishment. Listed are the transfer orbit, the drift orbit and the operational orbit.

| **Cosmos 2073** 1990-35A (20573) | 8:00 am 17 April | Plesetsk, USSR A-2(Soyuz) | 178 232 | 239 297 | 88.7 89.9 | 82.4 82.4 |

Recoverable, maneuverable satellite based on the Vostok design, carrying out strategic photo-reconnaissance. The cabin section containing film and cameras landed on 28 April. Listed are the initial orbit and the operational orbit reached on 18 April.

| **Cosmos 2074** 1990-36A (20577) | 6:41 pm 20 April | Plesetsk, USSR C-1 (Cosmos 2) | 967 | 1006 | 104.9 | 83.0 |

Polar-orbiting navigation satellite, with radio beacons operating at 150 and 400 MHz.

| **STS-31** 1990-37A (20579) | 12:34pm 24 April | Kennedy SC, USA Shuttle *Discovery* | 612 | 621 | 96.8 | 28.5 |

Piloted space mission devoted to launching the Hubble Space Telescope. Mission Commander was USAF Colonel Loren Shriver; Pilot, USMC Colonel Charles Bolden; and Mission Specialists, Bruce McCandless, Steven Hawley and Kathryn Sullivan. Discovery landed at Edwards Air Force Base at 2:49 pm on 29 April.

| **Hubble Space Telescope** 1990-37B (20580) | 6:59 pm 25 April | *Discovery* payload bay — | 613 | 620 | 96.8 | 28.5 |

Orbiting astronomical telescope, equipped with a 2.4-meter-diameter primary mirror, named after the 20th-century astronomer Edwin P. Hubble. A design flaw prevents it from operating to its full potential.

| **Cosmos 2075** 1990-38A (20581) | 1:02 pm 25 April | Plesetsk, USSR C-1 (Cosmos 2) | 515 | 584 | 94.7 | 74.0 |

Small satellite in near-polar orbit, possibly carrying an electronic-intelligence-gathering (ELINT) payload to eavesdrop on foreign government and military transmissions.

| **Molniya-1 (77)** 1990-39A (20583) | 1:37 am 26 April | Plesetsk, USSR A-2-e (Molniya) | 615 630 | 40657 39723 | 736.4 717.8 | 62.8 62.8 |

Soviet domestic communications satellite serving the more northerly ground-stations in the Orbita system. Listed are the initial orbit and the operational orbit achieved after an engine-firing on 2 May, followed by a minor trimming-maneuver on 9 May.

| **Cosmos 2076** 1990-40A (20596) | 11:37 am 28 April | Plesetsk, USSR A-2-e (Molniya) | 571 577 | 39319 39776 | 708.4 717.7 | 63.0 63.0 |

Satellite in Molniya-type orbit, carrying rocket-launch detectors and acting as part of the Soviet Union's missile early-warning system. Listed are the initial orbit and the operational orbit.

| **Progress 42** 1990-41A (20602) | 8:44 pm 5 May | Baikonur, USSR A-2 (Soyuz) | 188 221 324 384 | 243 327 398 398 | 88.8 89.9 91.7 92.3 | 51.6 51.6 51.6 51.6 |

Cargo vessel carrying two tonnes of equipment and supplies to the resident crew of the Mir complex. It docked with Kvant-1's rear port at 10:45 pm on 7 May. It undocked at 7:09 am on 27 May, and, following a retrorocket firing, made a destructive re-entry into the Earth's atmosphere a few hours later. Listed are the initial orbit, orbits achieved after engine-firings on the day of launch and 6 May respectively and the orbit after docking.

| **Cosmos 2077** 1990-42A (20604) | 6:40 pm 7 May | Plesetsk, USSR A-2 (Soyuz) | 184 | 329 | 89.6 | 62.8 |

Strategic photographic-reconnaissance satellite carrying several return-capsules for periodic recovery of film. It re-entered the Earth's atmosphere, possibly for recovery, on 4 July.

NAME, INT'l DESIG'N (CATALOG NO.)	LAUNCH TIME & DATE (GMT)	LAUNCH SITE & VEHICLE	PERIGEE (KM)	APOGEE (KM)	PERIOD (MINS)	INCLINATION (DEGREES)
Macsat 1 & 2 1990-43A&B (20607 & 20608)	5:50 pm 9 May	Vandenberg AFB, USA Scout	612 614	769 767	98.6 98.6	90.0 90.0

Multiple Access Communications Satellite, a pair of experimental, U.S. military comsats. An orbit is listed for each satellite.

Cosmos 2078 1990-44A (20615)	9:55 am 15 May	Baikonur, USSR A-2 (Soyuz)	198 213	283 278	89.4 89.4	70.0 70.0

Strategic photographic-reconnaissance satellite carrying several return-capsules for periodic recovery of film. It re-entered the Earth's atmosphere, possibly for recovery, on 28 June. Listed are the initial orbit and the operational orbit achieved after engine-firings on 16 May.

Cosmos 2079 1990-45A (20619)	8:40 am 19 May	Baikonur, USSR D-1-e (four-stage Proton)	18565 19075	19131 19183	664.6 675.7	64.9 64.9

One of a triplet of satellites in the Soviet Union's Global Navigation Satellite System (GLONASS). Listed are the initial orbit, and the operational orbit achieved after a maneuver in early-June.

Cosmos 2080 1990-45B (20620)	8:40 am 19 May	Baikonur, USSR D-1-e (four-stage Proton)	18910 19108	19127 19151	671.3 675.7	64.9 64.9

One of a triplet of satellites in the Soviet Union's Global Navigation Satellite System (GLONASS). Listed are the initial orbit, and the operational orbit achieved after a maneuver in early-June.

Cosmos 2081 1990-45C (20621)	8:40 am 19 May	Baikonur, USSR D-1-e (four-stage Proton)	18693 19099	19125 19160	667.0 675.7	64.8 64.9

One of a triplet of satellites in the Soviet Union's Global Navigation Satellite System (GLONASS). Listed are the initial orbit, and the operational orbit achieved after a maneuver in early-June.

Cosmos 2082 1990-46A (20624)	5:20 am 23 May	Baikonur, USSR J-1 (Zenit-2)	849	855	102.0	71.0

Large electronic-intelligence-gathering (ELINT) satellite, eavesdropping on foreign government and military radio transmissions.

Resurs-F 6 1990-47A (20632)	7:20 am 29 May	Plesetsk, USSR A-2 (Soyuz)	180 259	233 273	88.7 89.9	82.3 82.4

Recoverable, maneuverable satellite based on the Vostok design, carrying out Earth resources photography. It also carried Cosima-3, a West German microgravity experiments package being flown under a commercial agreement. The cabin section containing film, cameras and experiment results landed in Khazakstan on 14 June. Listed are the initial orbit and the operational orbit achieved after an engine-firing on 30 May.

Kristall 1990-48A (20635)	10:33 am 31 May	Baikonur, USSR D-1 (three-stage Proton)	215 278 292 376	326 368 366 391	89.9 90.9 91.1 92.2	51.6 51.6 51.6 51.6

Twenty-tonne add-on module for Mir, fitted-out with microgravity materials processing laboratory and a pair of new-type androgynous docking units, and carrying supplies and equipment for the crew. An initial docket attempt, intended for 11:30 am on 6 June, was called-off when an attitude-control thruster failed. A second attempt on 10 June was successful. It docked initially with the forward-facing port of Mir, and was transferred to the downward-facing port by its 'Ljappa' manipulator arm on 11 June. Listed are the initial orbit, the orbits after engine-firings on 3 June and 4 June respectively, and the orbit after docking with Mir.

ROSAT 1990-49A (20638)	10:48 pm 1 June	Cape Canaveral AFS, USA Delta 2 (6920)	565	584	96.1	53.0

Roentgen Satellite, a U.S. German joint venture for conducting an all-sky survey of ultraviolet and X-ray astronomical sources. Some of the onboard sensors were provided by the UK.

USA-59 1990-50A (20641)	5:22 am 8 June	Cape Canaveral AFS, USA Titan 4	275	275	90.0	52.0

Multi-purpose USAF reconnaissance satellite. The orbit listed is approximate.

Insat-1D 1990-51A (20643)	5:52 am 12 June	Cape Canaveral AFS, USA Delta 1 (4925)/PAM-D	32388 35768	39962 35811	1455.9 1436.1	0.4 0.2
		geosynchronous — 83 degrees east				

Indian combined communciations and meteorological satellite, offering transponders operating at C-band (6/4 GHz) and S-band (6 GHz uplink and 2.6 GHz downlink), and providing cloud-cover images as well as relaying weather information from remote data-collection platforms at sea and on the Earth's surface. It will eventually replace Insat-1B (1983-89B), which is nearing the end of its useful life. Listed are the drift orbit and the operational orbit achieved after about one week.

NAME, INT'L DESIG'N (CATALOG NO.)	LAUNCH TIME & DATE (GMT)	LAUNCH SITE & VEHICLE	PERIGEE (KM)	APOGEE (KM)	PERIOD (MINS)	INCLINATION (DEGREES)
Molniya-3 (38) 1990-52A (20646)	1:07 am 13 June	Plesetsk, USSR A-2-e (Molniya)	453 464	40846 39888	737.0 717.7	62.9 62.8

Communications satellite serving the Orbita-2 system — both within the USSR and (through Intersputnik) abroad — carrying telecommunications links at C-band (6/4 GHz). Orbits shown are the initial orbit, and the operational orbit achieved following a rocket-firing on 17 June.

Cosmos 2083 1990-53A (20657)	8:45 am 19 June	Plesetsk A-2 (Soyuz)	181 298	231 412	88.7 91.7	82.6 82.6

Recoverable, maneuverable satellite based on the Vostok design, carrying out strategic photo-reconnaissance. The cabin section containing film and cameras landed in Khazakstan on 3 July. Orbits shown are the initial orbit, and the operational orbit achieved following rocket-firings on 20 June.

Gorizont (20) 1990-54A (20659)	11:36 pm 20 June	Baikonur, USSR D-1-e (four-stage Proton)	35718	35863	1436.2	1.5
			geosynchronous — 90 degrees east			

Communications satellite at the Statsionar 6 location, serving the Orbita-2 system — both within the USSR and (through Intersputnik) abroad — with telecommunications links at C-band (6/4 GHz). A separate C-band transponder supplies Central Television programs to the Soviet Moskva TV-distribution network. Single transponders support the K-band (14/11 GHz) Luch system, and the L-band (1.6 GHz) Volna maritime/aeronautical communications system. An experimental transponder, Mayak (Beacon), operates at 20 GHz — It was developed jointly by the USSR, Bulgaria, Hungary, East Germany and Czechoslovakia, under the Intercosmos program.

Cosmos 2084 1990-55A (20663)	8:46 pm 21 June	Plesetsk, USSR A-2-e (Molniya)	586	757	98.2	62.8

Satellite carrying rocket-launch detectors, intended to reach a Molniya-type orbit and act as part of the Soviet Union's missile early-warning system. An early shut-down of the final rocket stage left the satellite in an unusable orbit.

Intelsat 6 (F-4) 1990-56A (20667)	11:19 am 23 June	Cape Canaveral AFS, USA Commercial Titan	35689	35886	1436.1	0.4
			geosynchronous — 38 degrees west			

Commercial communications satellite, equipped with transponders operating at C-band (6/4 GHz) and Ku-band (14/12 GHz). Listed is its checkout location, from where it will be moved before it becomes operational in September 1990.

Meteor 2 (19) 1990-57A (20670)	10:32 pm 27 June	Plesetsk, USSR F-2 (three-stage Tsyklon)	939	961	104.1	82.6

Meteorological and remote-sensing satellite working in the visible and infrared bands. It is equipped for both direct transmission and storage of images for later playback, and further sensors are carried to monitor radiation streams reaching the vicinity of the Earth.

R.D.C.

EARTHBOUND:

Some satellites already in orbit at the start of the *Space Year* re-entered the atmosphere by one means or another during the relevant timeframe. They are listed below.

Satellite	Launch date Re-entry date	Launch site	Orbit/mission
OSO 2	03 February 1965 09 August 1989	Cape Canaveral, USA	33 degrees, 550 x 634 kilometers, Orbiting Solar Observatory
Cosmos 58	26 February 1965 25 February 1990	Baikonur, USSR,	65 degrees, 563 x 647 kilometers, metsat development
DMSP 3-2	18 March 1965 31 December 1989	Vandenberg, USA	99 degrees, 525 x 764 kilometers, DoD metsat
Cosmos 103	27 December 1965 02 January 1990	Baikonur, USSR	56 degrees, 594 x 636 kilometers, ELINT prototype
Cosmos 122	25 June 1966 14 November 1989	Baikonur, USSR	65 degrees, 583 x 657 kilometers, experimental metsat
Cosmos 156	27 April 1967 23 October 1989	Plesetsk, USSR	81 degrees, 593 x 635 kilometers, prototype metsat
Cosmos 236	27 August 1968 04 March 1990	Baikonur, USSR	56 degrees, 588 x 630 kilometers, store/dump communications
Cosmos 358	20 August 1970 26 June 1990	Plesetsk, USSR	74 degrees, 515 x 539 kilometers, ELINT
Calsphere 5	17 February 1971 07 January 1990	Vandenberg, USA	99 degrees, 773 x 832 kilometers, radar calibration
Cosmos 851	27 August 1976 05 August 1989	Plesetsk, USSR	81 degrees, 565 x 638 kilometers, ELINT
Cosmos 1064	20 December 1978 12 November 1989	Plesetsk, USSR	83 degrees, 422 x 963 kilometers, navsat; failure
Molniya-1 (43)	12 April 1979 09 December 1989	Plesetsk, USSR	63 degrees, 636 x 39,716 kilometers, comsat
CAT-1	24 December 1979 27 November 1989	Kourou, French Guiana	18 degrees, 191 x 35,827 kilometers, Ariane test equipment
SMM	14 February 1980 22 December 1989	Cape Canaveral, USA	28.5 degrees, 563 x 570 kilometers, Solar Maximum Mission
Cosmos 1179	14 May 1980 18 July 1989	Plesetsk, USSR	73 degrees, 301 x 1,550 kilometers, space experiments
Iskra	10 July 1981 16 April 1990	Plesetsk, USSR	98 degrees, 632 x 666 kilometers, space technology experiments
OSCAR 9	06 October 1981 13 October 1989	Vandenberg, USA	98 degrees, 536 x 540 kilometers, UoSat 1, amateur radio
Cosmos 1345	31 March 1982 27 September 1989	Plesetsk, USSR	74 degrees, 504 x 545 kilometers, ELINT
Cosmos 1450	06 April 1983 30 May 1990	Plesetsk, USSR	66 degrees, 468 x 510 kilometers, ELINT
Rohini 3	17 April 1983 19 April 1990	Sriharikota, India	47 degrees, 389 x 852 kilometers, Earth-imaging
Ohzora	14 February 1984 19 July 1989	Kagoshima, Japan	75 degrees, 356 x 887 kilometers, upper-atmosphere studies
LDEF	06 April 1984 20 January 1990	Kennedy SC, USA	29 degrees, 477 x 479 kilometers, Long Duration Exposure Facility, deployed from 41-C/*Challenger* 7 April 1984
Cosmos 1601	27 September 1984 29 November 1989	Plesetsk, USSR	66 degrees, 475 x 515 kilometers, radar calibration
Cosmos 1662	19 June 1985 16 November 1989	Plesetsk, USSR	66 degrees, 476 x 513 kilometers, radar calibration
USA-13	13 December 1985 11 May 1989	Wallops Island, USA	37 degrees, 313 x 774 kilometers, ASAT target
Cosmos 1776	03 September 1986 15 December 1989	Plesetsk, USSR	74 degrees, 474 x 516 kilometers, ELINT
Cosmos 1870	25 July 1987 29 July 1989	Baikonur, USSR	72 degrees, 237 x 249 kilometers, radar-imaging
Cosmos 1949	27 May 1988 23 April 1990	Baikonur, USSR	65 degrees, 403 x 418 kilometers, EORSAT
Cosmos 1960	28 July 1988 9 April 1990	Plesetsk, USSR	66 degrees, 473 x 512 kilometers, radar calibration
Pion 1	25 May 1989 23 July 1989	Plesetsk, USSR	82 degrees, 256 x 268 kilometers, upper-air studies, released from Resurs-F1 8 June 1989
Pion 2	25 May 1989 24 July 1989	Plesetsk, USSR	82 degrees, 257 x 268 kilometers, upper-air studies, released from Resurs-F1 8 June 1989
Resurs-F2	27 June 1989 11 July 1989	Plesetsk, USSR	83 degrees, 253 x 282 kilometers, Earth-resources
Cosmos 2007	23 March 1990 22 September 1990	Baikonur, USSR	65 degrees, 230 x 285 kilometers, photo-reconnaissance
Cosmos 2020	17 May 1990 06 July 1990	Baikonur, USSR	65 degrees, 173 x 344 kilometers, photo-reconnaissance
Cosmos 2021	24 May 1990 06 July 1990	Baikonur, USSR	70 degrees, 218 x 284 kilometers, photo-reconnaissance
Cosmos 2028	16 June 1990 15 July 1990	Baikonur, USSR	70 degrees, 209 x 291 kilometers, photo-reconnaissance

R.D.C.

INDEX